T0305479

Lawyers and the Proceeds of Crime

The role played by legal professionals in the laundering of criminal proceeds generated by others has become a priority concern for authorities at national and international levels. This ground-breaking book presents an in-depth empirical analysis of the nature of lawyers' involvement in the facilitation of money laundering and its control through criminal justice and regulatory mechanisms. It is based on qualitative research combining analysis of cases of lawyers convicted of money laundering offences with interviews with criminal justice practitioners, members of professional and regulatory bodies and practising solicitors, and analysis of relevant national and international legislative and regulatory frameworks.

The book demonstrates the complex and diverse nature of lawyers' involvement in laundering activity, and shows that their actions and the decisions they take must be understood in relation to the specific situational contexts in which they occur. It provides significant new insights into the criminal justice and regulatory response to professional facilitation of money laundering in the UK, raising questions about the effectiveness and appropriateness of the response and the challenges involved. The book develops a framework for future research and analysis in this area, and proposes a range of potential strategies for controlling the facilitation of money laundering.

Lawyers and the Proceeds of Crime is essential reading for those researching money laundering, white-collar crime or organised crime, and for practitioners and policy makers concerned with preventing the facilitation of money laundering.

Katie Benson is Lecturer in Criminology at Lancaster University, where she teaches and researches in the fields of money laundering and organised, white-collar and financial crimes. Her current and recent research focuses on money laundering, anti-money laundering and the legal profession; (anti-)bribery and corruption in multinational businesses; the distribution of counterfeit alcohol; and the development of an alternative framework for the conceptualisation and analysis of money laundering. Dr Benson previously held roles within UK law enforcement and has worked with, or provided advisory/consultancy services to, various government bodies, law enforcement organisations, research institutions and investigations.

The Law of Financial Crime
Series Editor: Nicholas Ryder

Available titles in this series include:

Countering Economic Crime
A Comparative Analysis
Axel Palmer

The Global Anti-Corruption Regime
The Case of Papua New Guinea
Hannah Harris

Financial Crime and Corporate Misconduct
A Critical Evaluation of Fraud Legislation
Edited by Chris Monaghan and Nicola Monaghan

Corporate Liability for Insider Trading
Juliette Overland

Corruption in the Global Era
Causes, Sources and Forms of Manifestation
Lorenzo Pasculli and Nicholas Ryder

Counter-Terrorist Financing Law and Policy
An Analysis of Turkey
Burke Uğur Başaranel and Umut Turksen

Integrity and Corruption and The Law
Global Regulatory Challenges
Edited by Nicholas Ryder and Lorenzo Pasculli

For more information about this series, please visit: www.routledge.com/
The-Law-of-Financial-Crime/book-series/FINCRIME

Lawyers and the Proceeds of Crime

The Facilitation of Money Laundering and its Control

Katie Benson

Routledge
Taylor & Francis Group

LONDON AND NEW YORK

First published 2020
by Routledge
2 Park Square, Milton Park, Abingdon, Oxon OX14 4RN

and by Routledge
605 Third Avenue, New York, NY 10017

First issued in paperback 2021

Routledge is an imprint of the Taylor & Francis Group, an informa business

British Library Cataloguing-in-Publication Data
A catalogue record for this book is available from the British Library

Library of Congress Cataloging-in-Publication Data
Names: Benson, Katie, author.
Title: Lawyers and the proceeds of crime : the facilitation of money
    laundering and its control / Katie Benson.
Description: Abingdon, Oxon ; New York, NY : Routledge, 2020. |
    Series: The law of financial crime | Based on author's thesis
    (doctoral -University of Manchester, 2016) issued under title: The
    facilitation of money laundering by legal and financial professionals. |
    Includes bibliographical references and index.
Identifiers: LCCN 2019052690 (print) | LCCN 2019052691
    (ebook) | ISBN 9781138744868 (hardback) | ISBN
    9781315179735 (ebook)
Subjects: LCSH: Practice of law—Great Britain—Criminal provisions. |
    Money laundering—Law and legislation—Great Britain.
Classification: LCC KD479 .B465 2020 (print) | LCC KD479
    (ebook) | DDC 345.41/0268—dc23
LC record available at https://lccn.loc.gov/2019052690
LC ebook record available at https://lccn.loc.gov/2019052691

ISBN 13: 978-1-03-223713-8 (pbk)
ISBN 13: 978-1-138-74486-8 (hbk)

DOI: 10.4324/9781315179735

Typeset in Galliard
by Apex CoVantage, LLC

To Mum and Dad, for a lifetime of love and support, tolerance and encouragement, roots and wings.

To Jack, for keeping me company while I write.

Contents

Figures and tables

Figures

Tables

Abbreviations

ABS	Alternative Business Structure
ASP	Accountancy Service Provider
CJA	Criminal Justice Act
COPFS	Crown Office and Procurator Fiscal Service
CPS	Crown Prosecution Service
DNFBP	Designated Non-Financial Businesses and Professions
DTA	Drug Trafficking Act
ECFIU	Economic Crime and Financial Investigation Unit
EU	European Union
FATF	Financial Action Task Force
FCA	Financial Conduct Authority
FIU	Financial Intelligence Unit
HMRC	Her Majesty's Revenue and Customs
IBA	International Bar Association
ICIJ	International Consortium of Investigative Journalists
IMF	International Monetary Fund
LPP	Legal Professional Privilege
LSAG	Legal Sector Affinity Group
MLR	Money Laundering Regulations
MLRO	Money Laundering Reporting Officer
MTIC	Missing Trader Intra-community Fraud
NCA	National Crime Agency
OCCRP	Organized Crime and Corruption Reporting Project
OECD	Organisation for Economic Co-operation and Development
OPBAS	Office for Professional Body Anti-Money Laundering Supervision
PEP	Politically Exposed Person
POCA	Proceeds of Crime Act
RART	Regional Asset Recovery Team
ROCU	Regional Organised Crime Unit
SDT	Solicitors Disciplinary Tribunal
SSDT	Scottish Solicitors' Discipline Tribunal
SAR	Suspicious Activity Report
SFO	Serious Fraud Office

SRA	Solicitors Regulation Authority
TCSP	Trust and Company Service Provider
TPMA	Third Party Managed Account
UK	United Kingdom
UKFIU	National Financial Intelligence Unit (UK)
UN	United Nations
UNODC	United Nations Office on Drugs and Crime
US	United States
VAT	Value Added Tax
WEF	World Economic Forum

Cases

R v Duff (Jonathan Michael) [2002] EWCA Crim 2117

R v Noel Ward, Raymond Brown, Andrew John Young,
Ian Ronald Colphon [2005] EWCA Crim 1972

R v Griffiths (Philip) [2006] EWCA Crim 2155

Sylvia Allpress, Deborah Symeou, Miguel Casal, Paul Winter Morris,
Stephen Martin v R [2009] EWCA Crim 8

R v Rashid Farid, Mohammed Ali, Imran Hussain, Mohammed
Rafiq, Mohammed Jahangir Farid, Abid Razman
[2009] EWCA Crim 1731

R v Aminat Adedoyin Afolabi [2009] EWCA Crim 2879

Crown Prosecution Service, Secretary of State for the Home
Department v Varsha Bhadresh Gohil, Bhadresh Babulal Gohil
[2012] EWCA Civ 1550

R v James Onanefe Ibori [2013] EWCA Crim 815

HMA v Richard Sutton Housley and Caroline Jane Laing
[2013] (Scotland)

Solicitors Disciplinary Tribunal cases

Case No. 8648/2002 (Duff)
Case No. 8938/2003 (Winter-Morris)
Case No. 9262/2005 (Obidi)
Case No. 9688–2007 (Griffiths)
Case No. 10063–2008 (Hyde)
Case No. 10444–2010 (Krestin)
Case No. 10547–2010 (Farid)
Case No. 10501–2010 (Taylor)
Case No. 10395–2009 (Blok)
Case No. 10069–2008 (Afolabi)
Case No. 10727–2011 (Khan)
Case No. 10872–2011 (Wilcock)
Case No. 10927–2012 (Gohil)
Case No. 10409–2009 (Thorburn-Muirhead)

Scottish Solicitors' Discipline Tribunal cases

Acknowledgements

This book has been a long time in the making. Curiosity about the concept of 'professional enablers', which began to appear within organised crime policy and policing discourse in the UK about a decade ago, led to my PhD research on the role of professionals in the facilitation of money laundering, carried out at the University of Manchester between 2012 and 2016. Over the following three years, in between work on other research projects and starting a lectureship at Lancaster University, the book slowly took shape.

I have been lucky enough to have the support and encouragement of a number of people over the course of this research and writing journey, and there are some key people that I would like to thank. First, my primary PhD supervisor, Jon Spencer, for his guidance, patience and wisdom over a number of years. Bill Hebenton completed my supervisory team, and was always on hand to ask challenging questions to develop my thinking. My PhD examination team of Wim Huisman and Nick Lord provided invaluable feedback on my thesis, which helped to shape its development into this book. Colleagues and friends at the University of Manchester and Lancaster University have lifted me up and kept me going along the way, especially Rose Broad, Cerian Griffiths and Sarah Kingston. Family and friends have been patient and understanding when I have not been as present as I would like to have been. Finally, I am immensely grateful to Colin King and Nick Lord for providing thoughtful, challenging and constructive feedback on earlier drafts of this book.

The research for this book would not have been possible without the generosity of those who gave their time for interviews, or provided advice or assistance with access to interview participants, and their enthusiasm for the improvement of knowledge and understanding in this area. I would also like to acknowledge the PhD funding provided by the Economic and Social Research Council.

The issues covered in this book are constantly evolving, with, for example, regular updates to national and international anti-money laundering directives and regulations and changes to the wider regulatory landscape. As far as possible, the book was up-to-date in terms of policy, legislative and regulatory frameworks at the point that I finished writing it mid-2019. I have no doubt that between that time and its publication date there will have been further developments.

1   Introduction

In 2010, Bhadresh Gohil, a London-based solicitor, was convicted of a range of offences under the Proceeds of Crime Act (POCA) 2002. The charges were related to the laundering of millions of dollars defrauded from the people of Delta State in Nigeria by its then governor, James Ibori. Ibori was jailed for 13 years in 2012 for frauds totalling nearly $77 million, including a $37 million fraud relating to the sale of Delta State's share in a mobile phone company. It was involvement in the laundering of the proceeds of this particular offence for which Bhadresh Gohil was convicted. Gohil was found to have created a series of complex financial transactions to move and conceal the origins of funds on behalf of Ibori, involving off-shore trusts and shell companies, and allowed his firm's client account to be used for the transfer of criminal proceeds. He was also found to have facilitated the purchase of a $20 million Challenger jet on behalf of Ibori, concealing Ibori's ownership of the jet by devising 'a sophisticated money laundering scheme to ensure that the ownership of the jet was made as complicated and as obscure as possible'.[1] Gohil was sentenced to a total of ten years' imprisonment for various offences including money laundering and conspiracy to defraud. He was subsequently struck off the roll of solicitors in the UK by the Solicitors Disciplinary Tribunal.[2]

In 2012, Andrew Tidd, a conveyancing solicitor[3] from a medium-sized legal practice in Liverpool, UK, was convicted under the offence of 'Failure to disclose: regulated sector'. The 'failure to disclose' offence, set out in section 330 of POCA 2002, contains provisions to enforce the disclosure of suspicious transactions by members of particular sectors considered to be vulnerable to money laundering (e.g. lawyers, accountants, estate agents, trust and company service providers), making it a criminal offence to fail to disclose knowledge or suspicion that another person was engaged in money laundering. Over a four-year period, Andrew Tidd had acted in several transactions for a client, including conducting

---

1 *R v James Onanefe Ibori* [2013] EWCA Crim 815, para. 14.
2 Solicitors Disciplinary Tribunal Case No. 10927–2012; *R v James Onanefe Ibori* [2013] EWCA Crim 815.
3 Conveyancing refers to the legal and administrative work required for the transfer of property.

the conveyancing for the purchase of two residential properties. The £26,000 paid as deposits for the two properties is believed to have come from criminal activity. Following his conviction, Tidd appeared before the Solicitors Disciplinary Tribunal. Both the trial court and disciplinary tribunal concluded that Tidd had 'not known or, indeed, suspected that [his client] was involved in money laundering', but 'had information which . . . gave reasonable grounds for knowing or suspecting' such involvement.[4] On this basis, Tidd was convicted on five counts of 'failure to disclose' suspicions of money laundering and sentenced to four months' imprisonment, suspended for 12 months. At the disciplinary tribunal hearing, he was ordered to pay a fine of £2,500, but he was not struck off the roll of solicitors.[5]

In both of these cases, the solicitor played a role in the way that their client used, moved or concealed the origins of the proceeds of crime. The form this role took, the actions and processes involved, and the amount and source of the criminal proceeds all vary. However, both Bhadresh Gohil and Andrew Tidd can be considered to have in some way *facilitated money laundering* on behalf of their clients by way of their position as *legal professionals*.[6]

The facilitation of money laundering by legal professionals

The role of legal professionals in the laundering of criminal proceeds generated by others has become a priority concern for intergovernmental bodies, law enforcement authorities and policy makers at both the national and international level. At the international level, this concern can be traced back to the statement adopted at the 1999 G8 Conference on Combating Transnational Organized Crime, in Moscow, which highlighted 'those professionals, such as lawyers, accountants, company formation agents, auditors, and other financial intermediaries who can either block or facilitate the entry of organized crime money into the financial system' (Moscow Communiqué 1999, para. 7). The statement suggested that such 'gatekeepers' to the financial system should become subject to the anti-money laundering requirements already faced by banks and other financial institutions (Moscow Communiqué 1999, para. 32). Four years later, the Financial Action Task Force (FATF) Recommendations on money laundering were revised to extend responsibility for performing customer due diligence and reporting suspicious activity to certain non-financial businesses and professions, including lawyers, notaries and other independent legal professionals; accountants; trust and company service providers; and real estate agents (FATF 2003).

---

4 Solicitors Disciplinary Tribunal Case No. 11178–2013, para. 13.3.

5 Solicitors Disciplinary Tribunal Case No. 11178–2013.

6 These cases are just two examples of solicitors' involvement in the facilitation of money laundering, selected to highlight some of the different ways that this can occur. These and other cases will be discussed further throughout the book.

The FATF has subsequently published a number of reports highlighting the vulnerability of the legal profession to being exploited for the purposes of money laundering (e.g. FATF 2008, 2013).

In the UK, the government's 2013 *Serious and Organised Crime Strategy* first drew attention to the '[c]omplicit, negligent or unwitting professionals in the financial, accountancy and legal professions' that 'facilitate money laundering on behalf of organised criminals' (Home Office 2013: 14), describing how these 'professional enablers' help organised crime groups to invest in property or set up front businesses to launder the proceeds of their crimes (Home Office 2013: 48). More recently, UK threat and risk assessments have concentrated on the role of professional enablers in relation to economic crime rather than 'traditional' organised crime, with a particular focus on their involvement in 'high-end' money laundering (e.g. NCA 2015, 2018, 2019; HM Treasury/Home Office 2015, 2017). High-end money laundering, distinguished from the 'cash-based' money laundering carried out by groups involved in illicit market activity such as drug distribution, for example, is associated primarily with serious frauds, overseas corruption and tax evasion (NCA 2014) and is defined as 'the laundering of large amounts of illicit funds through the financial and professional services sectors' (NCA 2018: 39). Of particular concern in relation to high-end money laundering is the use of corporate structures to conceal the origin and ownership of funds, the movement of illicit funds through complex financial arrangements and offshore jurisdictions, exploitation of capital markets, and investment in the super-prime property market.

In 2015, the UK published its first *National Risk Assessment of Money Laundering and Terrorist Financing* (HM Treasury/Home Office 2015), followed by a national action plan intended to reform anti-money laundering and counter-terrorist financing measures (Home Office/HM Treasury 2016). In 2017, a follow up *National Risk Assessment* was produced, to assess the implementation of the action plan and lay out the areas of most concern in relation to money laundering and terrorist financing (HM Treasury/Home Office 2017). The document assessed legal services to be at 'high risk of exploitation for money laundering', suggesting that the areas that present the greatest risk are trust and company service provision, conveyancing and client account services (HM Treasury/Home Office 2017: 49). The potential for legal professionals' services or skills to be used for money laundering purposes is also a significant concern for the profession itself, and preventing its members from becoming involved in money laundering has become a priority for the legal profession and those who regulate it. Legislative and regulatory frameworks that emerged out of the global anti-money laundering regime have imposed a number of obligations on legal professionals, aimed at preventing their involvement in money laundering (alongside the criminalisation of money laundering; see Chapter 2). These preventative obligations have significant potential implications, as lawyers and other 'regulated' professionals can face serious consequences for failing to meet them. Thus, legal professional and regulatory bodies put considerable effort into identifying potential money laundering risks and 'red flags' within the sector, and advising their members on how to avoid these risks (see, for example, IBA 2014; LSAG 2018; SRA 2018a).

Aims of the book

Despite the concern surrounding the involvement of legal professionals in the facilitation of money laundering, and the proliferation of measures intended to prevent and control it, there has been little empirical research or other academic attention focused on this area. Much of the existing literature discusses legal professionals' role in money laundering in the context of them providing assistance to organised criminals more widely (Chevrier 2004; Di Nicola and Zoffi 2004; Lankhorst and Nelen 2004; Levi, Nelen and Lankhorst 2004; Middleton and Levi 2004, 2015; Nelen and Lankhorst 2008), or in relation to other forms of wrongdoing by the legal profession, such as mortgage or investment fraud and theft of client money (Middleton 2008; Middleton and Levi 2004, 2015). Bell (2002) considered cases of lawyers convicted of money laundering offences in the UK and the US, describing the services provided by the legal profession that may be of use to those wishing to launder criminal proceeds. Schneider (2005) and Cummings and Stepnowsky (2011) provided the primary previous empirical examinations of the nature and extent of lawyers' involvement in money laundering, in Canada and the US respectively, while Soudijn (2012; see also Soudijn 2014) examined 'financial facilitators' more broadly, looking at cases of assistance provided to criminals in relation to money laundering by a variety of actors in the Netherlands. Others have focused on legal professionals' understanding and interpretation of their 'gatekeeper' role. For example, Helgesson and Mörth (2016, 2018, 2019) conducted interviews with lawyers in Sweden, France and the UK to examine their views on their anti-money laundering obligations, and Kebbell (2017) addressed this aspect with transactional lawyers at some of the largest law firms in the UK.

The potential for legal professionals to facilitate the laundering of the proceeds of serious organised and economic crimes, the vulnerability of the profession to exploitation by individuals in possession of criminal proceeds and the considerable reach of the legislative, regulatory and policy frameworks which have been developed to prevent this mean that there is a clear need for research and analysis in this area. This book provides the most significant empirical and theoretical contribution to the subject to date, but also highlights a number of remaining analytical, conceptual and theoretical gaps and develops an agenda for further research. The book considers the *nature* of legal professionals' involvement in the facilitation of money laundering, and its *control* through criminal justice and regulatory mechanisms, combining empirical data and theoretical debates to provide new insights into this under-researched and under-theorised area. It challenges conceptualisations of the facilitation of money laundering which suggest a singular phenomenon and decontextualise the actions and decision-making involved, drawing attention to the situated nature of these actions and the factors that shape them. By analysing relevant legislation and regulations, as well as the array of professional, regulatory and criminal justice bodies involved in the current response to the facilitation of money laundering by legal professionals in the UK, this book raises questions about the effectiveness and appropriateness of this response and its implications for legal professionals. Finally, the book identifies a range of potential strategies for controlling the facilitation of money laundering.

The book is based partly on empirical research carried out between 2012 and 2015, which collected and analysed data on a number of cases of solicitors convicted for offences related to their involvement in the laundering of the proceeds of crimes committed by others, alongside data from qualitative interviews with individuals working in the criminal justice system, relevant regulatory and professional bodies, and the legal profession itself. This is combined with analysis of current (at time of writing) legislative and regulatory frameworks (UK and international), and relevant policy documents from government, law enforcement organisations, and professional and regulatory bodies. The theoretical and conceptual framework for the analysis, which is detailed in Chapter 3, draws on research and scholarship in the fields of 'organised crime' and 'white-collar crime', and locates legal professionals' involvement in money laundering at their intersection.

Scope of the research: the legal profession and the UK context

Concern about the facilitation of money laundering relates to a broader range of occupations than just the legal profession, and there are themes within this book that will apply across this range. However, there are a number of issues which are specific to the legal profession and legal professionals, and a focus on this particular group allows these to be fully explored. The book focuses primarily on the UK; while it takes account of wider contexts such as the global anti-money laundering regime and EU-level legislative frameworks, most of the data and analysis relate to the UK. There is some variation in the structure of the legal profession and its regulation, and in policing structures, between different parts of the UK, but there are commonalities in relation to the nature and control of the facilitation of money laundering. The empirical work for this book was carried out across the jurisdictions of England and Wales and Scotland. The book highlights where regulatory and policing structures differ, but in the main considers the nature of legal professionals' involvement in money laundering as a common phenomenon.

There are various types of legal professionals, and the roles they play and titles they are given differ between countries. The terms 'legal professional' and 'lawyer' are used interchangeably throughout this book. Within the UK legal system, there are two main categories of lawyer: solicitors and barristers (in Scotland, barristers are known as advocates). Solicitors form the largest part of the legal profession; they provide expert legal advice and assistance on a range of matters, and usually have direct contact with clients. Barristers are legal advisors and courtroom advocates, representing clients in court. While barristers fall under the scope of anti-money laundering regulations, the risk of money laundering and focus of anti-money laundering policies are more relevant for solicitors, as they handle clients' money and participate in certain transactions and services. The UK Money Laundering Regulations, following the FATF Recommendations, apply to 'independent legal professionals' – which they define as 'a firm or sole practitioner who by way of business provides legal or notarial services to other persons' – when participating in financial or real property transactions concerning:

(a) the buying and selling of real property or business entities;
(b) the managing of client money, securities or other assets;
(c) the opening or management of bank, savings or securities accounts;
(d) the organisation of contributions necessary for the creation, operation or management of companies; or
(e) the creation, operation or management of trusts, companies, foundations or similar structures.

Participation in such a transaction refers to 'assisting in the planning or execution of the transaction or otherwise acting for or on behalf of a client in the transaction'.[7]

Key arguments and conclusions

Three key arguments are developed through the course of this book:

1 The facilitation of money laundering by legal professionals is not a homogenous phenomenon. It is complex and multi-faceted, with variation in: the action (or non-action) for which professionals can be considered to have facilitated money laundering, and for which they can be convicted of a money laundering offence; the nature, purpose and complexity of the transactions or processes involved; the nature and form of the criminal proceeds; the relationship between the professional and the predicate offender; the benefit received by the professional for their role in the laundering; and the degree of complicity, knowledge and intent involved. Conflating the range of actors, actions and relations into singular concepts or descriptions is unhelpful for analysis and policy development.
2 Consideration must be given to the various decisions taken by legal professionals in the course of their routine occupational role which may lead to their involvement in the facilitation of money laundering, and to the situational contexts which shape these decisions. These decisions – about clients,

---

7 The Money Laundering, Terrorist Financing and Transfer of Funds (Information on the Payer) Regulations 2017, Reg.12.

funds, transactions and services – will be influenced by a range of factors, including: the nature of the firm in which the legal professionals works; their relationships with other relevant actors; the structures, processes and transactions of the legal profession; the nature of the market for legal services; and the wider legislative, policy and regulatory environment. Future research and analysis should aim for greater understanding of these various contexts, how they interact with each other and influence individual action and decision-making, and thus how they shape the facilitation of money laundering.

3   Variation in the nature of legal professionals' involvement in the facilitation of money laundering, and the challenges and limitations inherent in individual preventative strategies and responses, means that a combination of approaches will be required for effective and proportionate control. Such approaches should be based on strategies for: deterring misconduct; promoting compliance with Money Laundering Regulations and professional standards, rules and regulations; inhibiting opportunity/vulnerability structures; and influencing the decisions taken by legal professionals when providing services or conducting transactions that could act to facilitate money laundering. Further research and analysis is needed to identify the full range of opportunity/vulnerability structures within the legal profession and the relevant points of decision-making, and to understand the nature, relationships, priorities and challenges of the current regulatory environment.

Research methodology

Previous empirical research on the facilitation of money laundering by legal professionals has been primarily quantitative and descriptive (e.g. Schneider 2005; Cummings and Stepnowsky 2011), exploring the frequency of lawyers' involvement in transactions used to launder criminal proceeds and the types of transactions they are involved in. The research on which this book is based took a methodological approach that aimed to build on and go beyond what has been done before. It employed a qualitative research design, examining data from a number of different sources in order to appreciate multiple perspectives and triangulate knowledge produced in different ways, and at different levels (Flick et al. 2012). Data were collected from various sources on 20 cases of UK solicitors who had been convicted for facilitating money laundering between 2002 and 2013.[8]

8 There is no specific offence of 'facilitating money laundering' in UK law. I use the term 'convicted for facilitating money laundering' in this context to refer to the following, which was used as the inclusion criteria for the selected cases: 'Solicitors that had been convicted of money laundering offences (under Proceeds of Crime Act 2002, Drug Trafficking Act 1994 or Criminal Justice Act 1993) between 2002 and 2013, where the offences committed were related to their professional position or role, and involved the facilitation of the laundering of the proceeds of crimes committed by others'. There is clearly a subjective element to these

These data included Solicitors Disciplinary Tribunal transcripts, Court of Appeal transcripts, media reports, press releases, and other publicly available reports and articles. In addition, interviews were conducted with law enforcement personnel working in financial investigation units or organised crime policing units ($n = 9$), members of relevant professional and regulatory bodies ($n = 3$), a prosecutor specialising in money laundering investigations and asset recovery ($n = 1$), and practising solicitors ($n = 3$). All interviewees were based in the UK. Analysis of these data was combined with analysis of legislative and regulatory frameworks (UK and international), and relevant policy documents from government, law enforcement organisations, and professional and regulatory bodies.

Identifying cases of lawyers who had been convicted for facilitating money laundering proved to be a challenging, complex and time-consuming process. Data are not routinely collected on professionals involved in money laundering in any structured or analysable way by either law enforcement, the criminal justice system more broadly, or the relevant professional or regulatory bodies. The regulatory bodies do not keep categorised records that would be searchable for, say, those members of their profession that have been convicted of a money laundering offence. The Solicitors Regulation Authority, for example, could provide a list of those of their members who had been 'struck off' the roll of solicitors, or who had been convicted of a criminal offence, but not specifically for this type of misconduct. Similarly, everybody who had been convicted of a criminal offence under the relevant money laundering legislation could have been identified, but this would not have identified which of those individuals were legal professionals. Therefore, a number of different sources – none of which could be considered comprehensive – were used to identify as many relevant cases as possible within the timeframe of interest. This included a search of the Westlaw legal database for any cases involving 'money laundering' since 1 January 2002; a search of the transcripts of all disciplinary hearings from 2002 from the Solicitors Disciplinary Tribunal and Scottish Solicitors' Discipline Tribunal; a search of media reports and databases; and the review of an FATF (2013) report identifying examples of legal professionals involved in money laundering in FATF member states. Solicitors Disciplinary Tribunal and Scottish Solicitors' Discipline Tribunal transcripts are held as PDF documents on the respective websites. They cannot be searched for cases specifically relating to money laundering, so

---

criteria and there are debates to be had about what or who should be included in research on this subject. For example, including conviction in the criteria means that lawyers who receive a regulatory sanction only are not included, and may create a dataset that omits cases that are more difficult to prosecute. However, not basing the analysis on convicted professionals would increase the subjectivity of the inclusion criteria and create further issues in the identification of cases. The section 328 offence in POCA 2002 refers to involvement in 'an arrangement which . . . facilitates . . . the acquisition, retention, use or control of criminal property by or on behalf of another person'. It is therefore the closest single offence to 'the facilitation of money laundering', but relying only on convictions for this offence would lead to a much narrower analysis. These issues will be addressed further throughout the course of the book.

all transcripts within the relevant timeframe were downloaded and searched using the PDF word search function for reference to 'proceeds of crime' and 'money laundering'. The resulting transcripts were read in full to identify those that fit the inclusion criteria. Likewise, all transcripts identified through Westlaw with the Subject/Keyword = 'money laundering' were read in full to identify those suitable for inclusion. *Google News, ukpressonline* and the *Guardian/Observer Archive* were searched using the terms: 'solicitor money laundering', 'lawyer money laundering' and 'legal professional money laundering'.

The case data presented and analysed in this book were all taken from publicly available sources.[9] As such, they have not been anonymised and no names have been changed. Anonymising the cases while still being able to fully explore the data would have been impossible, and changing the names of those involved would not have prevented identification of the cases. In some parts of the book, data have simply been presented as taken from one or more of the relevant sources. In others, the case data have been analysed and synthesised to explore themes and develop overarching arguments about the nature of the facilitation of money laundering. In Chapter 4, summaries of all the cases are presented; these were created by amalgamating data from all sources available for each case to provide as accurate a picture as possible of each case, based on the available information. The interview data have been anonymised, with all references to names, organisations and locations removed. The following codes are used throughout the book to identify the role of the interviewee being quoted:

LE: member of law enforcement
SA: member of a supervisory authority (i.e. professional/regulatory body)
CPS: prosecutor
S: solicitor

Gathering data from a range of sources enabled a more comprehensive analysis of a phenomenon that is complex and multi-layered than would have been possible with a single approach or source of data. For example, it allowed for consideration of the perspectives of actors in criminal justice, regulatory and professional bodies and the legal profession itself, and identification of areas of convergence and divergence in the different perspectives (including by comparing the views of those in the police and regulatory bodies with the professionals who may be subject to their enforcement and regulation, and those in law enforcement with those in regulatory and professional bodies). It also enabled the conclusions of professional disciplinary tribunals to be analysed alongside perspectives from criminal

---

9 For each case, one or more of the following was used: Court of Appeal of England and Wales transcript; Solicitors Disciplinary Tribunal transcript; Scottish Solicitors' Discipline Tribunal transcript; Judiciary of Scotland Sentencing Statement; press release published by e.g. police forces, Serious Fraud Office (SFO), Her Majesty's Revenue and Customs (HMRC); newspaper or other media article; other article or report from e.g. publications by legal professionals or professional bodies.

trials, and views from the prosecution service to be contrasted with those from police bodies involved in investigation and enforcement. Furthermore, analysis of legislation and policy documents meant that the research could locate the actions and perspectives of different actors within their legislative, regulatory and policy contexts. Unfortunately, there is one perspective that is largely missing from the research: that of legal professionals involved in the facilitation of money laundering. Attempts were made to gain access to solicitors involved in the cases analysed, to request interviews, but none of these were successful. Speaking directly to professionals convicted for facilitating money laundering should be a goal for future empirical research in this area.

The research adopted an 'adaptive theory' approach to the use of data and theory, which focuses on the interconnections between individual activity and the social structures and systems in which it takes place, and stresses the importance of an ongoing relationship between theory and data throughout the research process (see Layder 1998). In line with this approach, data collection and analysis did not take place as discrete phases, subsequent to consideration of the literature and theoretical perspectives. Instead, processes of data collection, reflection on the data, and engagement with literature, theory, legal frameworks and policy documents were interwoven and shaped further data collection in an ongoing process. Once all the data had been collected, a more systematic process of analysis was initiated, following the principles of thematic analysis and incorporating four phases, based on those suggested by Braun and Clarke (2006): familiarisation with the data; generation of initial codes; review of codes and identification of themes; review and finalisation of themes. In line with adaptive theory, themes and patterns in the data were allowed to emerge inductively whilst also being shaped by existing theoretical and analytical frameworks.

Structure of the book

Following this introduction to the book, Chapter 2, 'Money laundering and the anti-money laundering regime', provides background and context to the analysis contained in subsequent chapters, discussing the origins and rise of the concept of money laundering and the extensive global anti-money laundering regime that has developed in response to the perceived threat from 'dirty money'. The strict meaning of money laundering is the act of concealing the origins of the proceeds of criminal activity, in order to provide them with a false appearance of legitimacy. However, the concept of money laundering has broadened significantly, both in popular usage and in international anti-money laundering conventions and national legislation. In effect, it now includes any activity involving the proceeds of crime, including acquiring, spending, moving or disposing of criminal property, and any financial transaction conducted by an individual or group involved in illegal activity. This means that the ways in which legitimate professionals could facilitate or become involved in money laundering are similarly wide-ranging. The construction of money laundering as a major global threat has led to the development of an extensive range of legislative, regulatory and policy frameworks, guidelines, standards and institutions aimed at its prevention. This includes the enlistment of those within certain occupational sectors into the anti-money laundering 'fight', by requiring them to meet certain preventative obligations, including reporting suspicions of money laundering and taking adequate steps to 'Know Your Customer'. This has significant implications for individuals within these occupations, including legal professionals, due to the scope of anti-money laundering legislation, under which they can face severe penalties for not fulfilling their obligations. Chapter 2 finishes by providing an overview of the relevant money laundering legislation within the UK.

Chapter 3, 'Framing the research: "organised crime" or "white-collar crime"?', develops a theoretical and conceptual framework for the analysis and discussion that follows in the remainder of the book. It shows that the involvement of legal professionals in the facilitation of money laundering can be seen both as a form of 'white-collar crime' and as a component of 'the organisation of crime for profit', and thus draws together these two concepts to create an integrated framework for understanding the nature of this involvement. The occupational position of legal professionals, which imparts certain skills, expertise and status, and provides access to services and transactions that can be used to launder the proceeds of crime, means that those who facilitate money laundering can be considered to have committed 'white-collar crime', defined by Croall (2001: 17) as 'an abuse of a legitimate occupational role which is regulated by law'. Applying theories and concepts from the field of white-collar crime research and scholarship draws attention to the situated nature of the actions of lawyers who facilitate money laundering, and the need to take account of their occupational and organisational contexts, the opportunities for misconduct that these can provide, and the wider macro-level factors that can shape these contexts and individual-level behaviours. Conceptualising lawyers' involvement in the management of criminal proceeds as part of the organisation of the crime for profit that generated these proceeds, on the other hand, directs us towards questions about the nature of the processes, behaviours, actors and relations (including the relationship between the lawyer and the client/the predicate offender, and between these actors and those responsible for regulation, enforcement, prosecution and prevention) involved. The subsequent chapters integrate this theoretical framework with the empirical data to explore the nature and control of lawyers' involvement in the facilitation of money laundering.

Chapter 4, 'The nature of facilitation: diversity, complexity and context', summarises and attempts to categorise the 20 cases of solicitors convicted for facilitating money laundering based on the 'means of facilitation'. The majority of the cases involved the purchase of residential property using the proceeds of crime or the use of the solicitor's firm's client account to conduct transactions involving the proceeds of crime, or to move these funds from one place to another. However, many of the cases were less easy to categorise, falling broadly within the provision of legal and/or financial services, but demonstrating the range of behaviours which can be considered as the facilitation of money laundering, and for which legal professionals can be convicted of money laundering offences. Within all the categories there was variation in terms of the action (or non-action) of the solicitor, the transactions and processes involved, the purpose and complexity of the transactions, the relationship between the solicitor and their client, and the nature and form of the criminal proceeds. The chapter warns against seeing 'the facilitation of money laundering' as a singular phenomenon, therefore, and argues for moving beyond descriptions of actions and processes, to understand the *contexts* of these actions, the decisions they involve and the factors that shape them.

Chapter 5, 'Opportunity and vulnerability: factors influencing lawyers' involvement in money laundering', considers some of these factors. First, it focuses on how the occupational context and organisational settings of the legal profession can provide *opportunities* for those wishing to assist others to launder their criminal proceeds, and make individuals within the profession *vulnerable* to exploitation for the purposes of laundering. The chapter highlights the essential similarity of transactions that serve to launder criminal proceeds to legitimate transactions that legal professionals carry out as part of their normal occupational role, and the legitimate and specialised access they have to functions and processes that can facilitate money laundering. This allows transactions with non-legitimate funds to be hidden amongst, and be 'parasitical' on, legitimate activity (Benson, Madensen and Eck 2009: 185; Benson and Simpson 2018). The chapter also considers whether the size and complexity of the organisation in which legal professionals work could influence the likelihood of their becoming involved in money laundering; the implications of autonomy and a lack of internal oversight on misconduct by legal professionals; the potential risks associated with new forms of organisation providing legal services; and whether principles of confidentiality and legal professional privilege may shield interactions between lawyers and their clients that facilitate money laundering from external scrutiny. Finally, Chapter 5 examines how the nature of a legal professional's relationship with the predicate offender, and the potential financial or commercial benefit, could influence their role in the facilitation of money laundering.

The degree of complicity, knowledge and/or intent underpinning this role is complex. Chapter 6, 'On the "borders of knowingness": understanding complicity, knowledge and intent', discusses the various ways that involvement in the facilitation of money laundering has been conceptualised in academic and official literature in relation to the complicity, knowledge and intent of the professional involved, and highlights the difficulty in trying to understand and describe these concepts in an accurate or meaningful way. Between fully complicit participation in laundering, as a result of an active, knowing choice to assist the predicate offender, and the exploitation of a completely innocent legal professional, lie the 'borders of knowingness' on which involvement in the facilitation of money laundering often exists. Here, there may not have been the intention to facilitate money laundering, but may have been a degree of knowledge or suspicion about the client, their funds or the transactions or services requested. This chapter therefore reiterates the need to consider the points of decision-making for legal professionals when dealing with clients or conducting financial or commercial transactions, and the situational contexts that shape the decisions taken.

Chapter 6 also examines the ways that the complicity, knowledge and intent of the convicted solicitors analysed in the research were characterised by the courts and disciplinary tribunals that heard their cases. While some appeared to have been complicit, active participants in the laundering, or had chosen 'deliberately to turn a blind eye' to suspicions about the origins of their clients' funds, others were described as being 'unwittingly drawn into' the money laundering offence, not 'aware of' or not 'actively involved in' the laundering, or as having 'not known or, indeed, suspected' that their client was involved in laundering. Despite this, they were convicted of criminal offences which hold a maximum penalty of 14 years' imprisonment. This is possible because of the wide scope of the legislation used to prosecute such activity in the UK, which allows for conviction without criminal intent or even, in certain circumstances, without actual knowledge or suspicion that laundering was taking place. Chapter 7, 'Knowledge and suspicion in the legislative framework' examines provisions relating to 'knowledge' and 'suspicion' in POCA 2002 to show that UK anti-money laundering legislation goes beyond the international frameworks from which it was derived, which focus on those who have *intentionally* laundered criminal proceeds. While interviewees involved in the investigation and prosecution of professionals suspected of facilitating laundering supported the inclusion of provisions that allow for conviction without actual knowledge or criminal intent, the chapter argues that the far-reaching nature of anti-money laundering legislation in the UK has significant implications for those working in the legal profession, whose occupational role means they are likely to come into contact with illicit funds and individuals wishing to launder them, and who face serious potential consequences for failing to fulfil their 'gatekeeper' obligations.

In Chapter 8, 'Criminal justice and regulatory responses to the facilitation of money laundering', attention moves to the response to the facilitation of money laundering by legal professionals in the UK, which involves both criminal justice and regulatory systems and processes. The chapter analyses data from interviews with members of relevant professional and regulatory bodies, law enforcement and the Crown Prosecution Service (CPS), alongside documents relating to the role and responsibilities of the Solicitors Regulation Authority (SRA), the body responsible for regulating solicitors in England and Wales. It provides a comprehensive overview of the current response to (suspected) involvement in money laundering, and discusses the challenges and complexities that this entails. The chapter raises concerns about the working relationship between regulators, police and prosecuting authorities, suggesting that this has implications for their ability to provide an effective, collaborative response.

The concluding chapter, Chapter 9, 'Understanding and controlling the facilitation of money laundering: a research and policy agenda', draws together the key findings and arguments of the book, develops an agenda for future research and analysis, and discusses potential strategies for controlling the facilitation of money laundering. It proposes an analytical framework, based on Diane Vaughan's (e.g. 1983, 2002) theory of organisational misconduct but adapted to apply specifically to the facilitation of money laundering by legal professionals, in line with the findings developed through the course of the book. This framework is intended to direct analytical focus and future empirical investigation in this area. It identifies the multi-level situational contexts that will shape the individual action and decision-making of legal professionals which can lead to their involvement in money laundering, and suggests the gaps in our understanding of these contexts, how they interact and how they influence behaviour which are worthy of further consideration. The second half of the chapter focuses on strategies for controlling the facilitation of money laundering. It discusses a number of different strategies, their challenges and limitations, and suggests that a combination of approaches is required, focused on encouraging compliance with Money Laundering Regulations and professional standards; deterring misconduct; inhibiting opportunity/vulnerability structures; and influencing the decisions taken by legal professionals when providing services or conducting transactions that could act to facilitate money laundering.

2 Money laundering and the anti-money laundering regime

Introduction

Since its emergence in the second half of the twentieth century, the concept of money laundering has become firmly entrenched in political, public and policy discourse. Intergovernmental bodies, national governments and law enforcement organisations regularly draw attention to the 'problem' of money laundering, the threat it poses and the need for rigorous legislative, regulatory and policing initiatives to counter this threat. Preventing the infiltration of illicit funds into the legitimate economy, and making it harder for those involved in criminal activity to enjoy the financial benefits of their crimes, has become a priority for the international community and individual nation-states. A number of United Nations (UN) and Council of Europe Conventions have focused on or referred to the laundering of the proceeds of drug offences and other crimes for profit, and several major intergovernmental bodies, such as the UN, World Bank, International Monetary Fund (IMF) and Organisation for Economic Co-operation and Development (OECD), have stated intentions to address money laundering and designated programmes for doing so. In 1989, the Financial Action Task Force (FATF) was established, with the primary aim of dealing with the 'threats of money laundering' (FATF 2010: 3) and responsibility for developing worldwide anti-money laundering (and, since 9/11, counter-terrorist financing) standards, issuing recommendations and assessing the compliance of nation-states with those recommendations. This followed the Basel Committee on Banking Supervision – which sets global standards for the regulation of banks – adopting a *Statement of Principles on the Prevention of Criminal Use of the Banking System for the Purpose of Money Laundering* in December 1988. Subsequently, banks and other financial institutions, as well as those working in, for example, legal, accountancy and real estate sectors, have come under increasing pressure to play a role in the identification and prevention of money laundering, and considerable effort and resource is dedicated to compliance with anti-money laundering obligations.

This chapter provides background and context to the analysis contained in the remainder of the book. First, it (briefly) discusses the emergence of the concept of money laundering, its construction as a major global threat and some of the key legislation enacted to try to eliminate this threat. It considers the definition of 'money laundering', and the way the concept has broadened so that – in effect – it includes any activity that involves the proceeds of crime, including acquiring, spending, moving or disposing of criminal proceeds, and any financial transaction conducted by an individual or group involved in criminal (or terrorist) activity. This broadening of the concept of money laundering allows for diversity in the ways by which legitimate actors can play a role in *the facilitation of* money laundering. Second, the chapter considers the extensive global anti-money laundering regime that has developed since the late 1980s in response to the perceived threat from 'dirty money', and the implications of this regime for those designated as 'gatekeeper professionals', including the legal professionals that are the focus of this book. It discusses how the global anti-money laundering regime has manifested in the UK, outlining the evolution of relevant legislation (Proceeds of Crime Act [POCA] 2002 and the various Money Laundering Regulations), the significance of this legislation for lawyers and other regulated professionals, and its relationship to international legislative frameworks and standards.

Money laundering: fears and foundations

Strictly speaking, money laundering is the act of concealing the origins of the proceeds of criminal activity and thus providing them with the appearance of legitimacy. The term 'laundering' reflects the notion that 'dirty' money is being 'cleaned', allowing those who generate criminal proceeds to make use of them in the legitimate economy, and therefore realise the financial benefit of their crimes. The concept of money laundering began its rise to prominence in the latter part of the twentieth century. Concern about the flow of funds from the US to offshore tax havens (both 'dirty' money primarily from the sale of illegal drugs and money generated through legal means but not declared for tax purposes) led to the introduction of the US Bank Secrecy Act in 1970 (see van Duyne, Harvey and Gelemerova 2018). The Bank Secrecy Act was designed to allow better monitoring of cash flows; it created the requirement for financial institutions to maintain records and submit reports to the authorities on 'suspicious' account or transaction activity or on any transaction that exceeded $10,000 (van Duyne, Harvey and Gelemerova 2018). At this point, the term 'money laundering' had not yet been adopted – its first public use came in 1973, when it was used during the Watergate scandal in relation to the 'laundering' of Nixon's illegal campaign funds (Gelemerova 2011), and it became established in policy discourse during the 1980s. In 1984, the President's Commission on Organized Crime, established by Ronald Reagan the previous year, published a report focusing on the profits made by those involved in 'organised crime' activities. *The Cash Connection: Organized Crime, Financial Institutions, and Money Laundering* described money laundering as 'the keystone of organized crime' and recommended measures to 'dislodge that keystone, and thereby to cause irreparable damage to the operations of organized crime' (President's Commission on Organized Crime 1984: 63). The emergence of measures to prevent money laundering, therefore, originated both from a concern about the loss of tax revenues and a desire to disrupt organised crime and prevent those involved from profiting from their illegal activity.

In 1986, the US introduced the Money Laundering Control Act, which made laundering a federal crime. The US was the second country to make money laundering a criminal offence – it had been criminalised in Italy in 1978, as part of the Italian state's ongoing activities against the Mafia and the Brigate Rosse (Red Brigades). The stated aim of the Money Laundering Control Act was to criminalise 'the process by which one conceals the existence, illegal source, or illegal application of income, and then disguises that income to make it appear legitimate' (President's Commission on Organized Crime 1984: vii), and prevent criminal groups from being able to use illicit profits to expand their criminal activity (see Gurulé 1995 for an overview of the Act). While the Money Laundering Control Act criminalised the laundering of the proceeds of a range of specified criminal activities, including extortion, bribery and fraud, its primary focus was the proceeds of drug trafficking.

Concern over the illegal drugs trade and funds associated with it became one of the main drivers of the significant international mobilisation against money laundering that followed the enactment of the Money Laundering Control Act, and the primary justification for the expansion of powers and institutions aimed at controlling laundering that this entailed. The global 'fight' against money laundering became inextricably linked to the 'war on drugs' during the 1990s, as well as to the growing concern about 'transnational organised crime' and its impacts, particularly in Europe and the US. 'Follow the money' approaches, which involved measures aimed at confiscating criminal proceeds as well as preventing laundering, were also driven by the notion that those involved in organised crime should not profit from their illegal activities. From these origins, the concept of money laundering has broadened, and it is no longer associated solely or primarily with drug trafficking or, even, 'organised crime'. It covers an ever-widening range of activities that could be categorised as 'illicit finance', including the management of the proceeds of various crimes for profit and illicit markets, tax evasion, and activities related to the finances for and from bribery and corruption, and is often conflated with terrorism financing (Levi 2010, 2014; Lord and Levi 2016).[1]

Defining money laundering

Within the strict meaning of the term, the key feature of money laundering is the 'false representation of crime money as legitimate earnings' (Gelemerova 2011: 3), and so simple acts of concealment or movement of criminal proceeds

---

1 For more detail on the history and rise of the concept of money laundering, see for example: Blum *et al* 1998; Levi 2002, 2014; van Duyne 2003; Gallant 2005; van Duyne and Levi 2005; Alldridge 2008, 2016; Gelemerova 2009, 2011; Levi and Reuter 2009; Verhage 2009, 2011; Van Duyne, Harvey and Gelemerova 2018.

would not be considered as laundering if they are 'not followed by that very step of false legitimisation' (van Duyne and Di Miranda 1999: 262). References to money laundering from relevant intergovernmental bodies echo this characterisation, highlighting the goal of obscuring the illegal origin of the funds, in order to make use of them and avoid detection:

> Money laundering is the processing of these criminal proceeds to *disguise their illegal origin*. This process is of critical importance, as it enables the criminal to enjoy these profits without jeopardising their source.
>
> (FATF 2019a; emphasis added)

> Money-laundering is the method by which criminals *disguise the illegal origins* of their wealth and protect their asset bases, so as to avoid the suspicion of law enforcement agencies and prevent leaving a trail of incriminating evidence.
>
> (UNODC 2019; emphasis added)

On the face of it, therefore, the concept of money laundering appears quite clear. However, official definitions have demonstrated 'a blurring of the edges of the concept' (van Duyne 2003: 77), leading to a widening of the scope of what constitutes laundering activity beyond the act of legitimising or cleaning 'dirty' money. For example, the 2005 Council of Europe *Convention on Laundering, Search, Seizure and Confiscation of the Proceeds from Crime and on the Financing of Terrorism* (the Warsaw Convention) definition of the crime of money laundering comprises a whole range of actions, including simply the 'acquisition, possession or use' of criminal proceeds:

1   the conversion or transfer of property, knowing that such property is proceeds, for the purpose of concealing or disguising the illicit origin of the property or of assisting any person who is involved in the commission of the predicate offence to evade the legal consequences of his actions;
2   the concealment or disguise of the true nature, source, location, disposition, movement, rights with respect to, or ownership of, property, knowing that such property is proceeds; and, subject to its constitutional principles and the basic concepts of its legal system;
3   the acquisition, possession or use of property, knowing, at the time of receipt, that such property was proceeds;
4   participation in, association or conspiracy to commit, attempts to commit and aiding, abetting, facilitating and counselling the commission of any of the offences established in accordance with this article.[2]

---

2 Council of Europe *Convention on Laundering, Search, Seizure and Confiscation of the Proceeds from Crime and on the Financing of Terrorism* CETS 198 (2005), Article 9.

The US Department of the Treasury definition is much shorter but even broader, stating that: 'money laundering generally refers to financial transactions in which criminals, including terrorist organizations, attempt to disguise the proceeds, sources or nature of their illicit activities' (US Department of the Treasury 2019). This appears to take the concept even further from its strict meaning, beyond reference to the proceeds of crime even, to include any financial transaction conducted or initiated by a criminal or terrorist group.

This broadening of the term can also be seen in national legislative frameworks. In most jurisdictions, the offence of money laundering applies to 'whatever anyone does to hide, transfer or transform the proceeds of any crime, *whether or not this actually legitimises the funds or is intended to do so*' (Levi 2015: 276, emphasis in original). For example, in the UK, money laundering legislation effectively states that a person commits a money laundering offence if he or she:

a) Conceals, disguises, converts or transfers criminal property, or removes it from the jurisdiction;
b) Enters into or becomes concerned in an arrangement which facilitates the acquisition, retention, use or control of criminal property;
c) Acquires, uses or has possession of criminal property.

(POCA 2002, s.327–329)

This reflects the wording of the 2005 Warsaw Convention and the 1988 UN *Convention Against Illicit Traffic in Narcotic Drugs and Psychotropic Substances* (the Vienna Convention), which formed the basis of national anti-money laundering laws in relation to the proceeds of drug production, trafficking and distribution, and which required the criminalisation of:

a) the conversion or transfer of property derived from relevant drug offences;
b) the concealment or disguise of the true nature, source, location, disposition, movement, rights with respect to, or ownership of property derived from relevant drug offences; and
c) the acquisition, possession or use of property derived from relevant drug offences.[3]

Therefore, under such legislation, any activities that would inevitably occur after a crime for profit has been committed, including simply concealing, moving or disposing of the proceeds of crime, or even the acquisition of the proceeds itself, would legally be considered as a laundering offence. Spending the proceeds (i.e. 'lifestyle spending'), even if no attempt had been made to 'clean' or hide the illicit origin of the proceeds, would also fall under the definition of a money laundering offence under this legislation. The broad scope of the meaning

---

3 United Nations *Convention Against Illicit Traffic in Narcotic Drugs and Psychotropic Substances* (1988), Article 3, para. 1: b(i), b(ii) and c(i).

of money laundering, and how it is defined in international conventions and national legislation, means that the ways that legitimate actors (such as legal professionals) could become involved in 'facilitating money laundering' are similarly wide-ranging.

The threat narrative

Since its emergence as a concept and designation as an offence separate from (though inextricably linked to) drug trafficking and other forms of illicit activity, money laundering has been depicted as a significant threat to the integrity and stability of global financial systems and to society more broadly. Within official discourse in the UK, it is seen as a 'critical enabler of serious and organised crime, grand corruption and terrorism', which acts to 'undermine the integrity of [the UK's] financial institutions and markets, enable criminals to hide, store and benefit from the proceeds of their crime, and enable terrorist groups to function, recruit and commit terrorist acts' (Home Office/HM Treasury 2016: 7). The ability of those involved in criminal activity to make use of the proceeds by legitimising them acts to 'incentivise crime by rendering it profitable' and fund further criminality (CPS 2018). It also enables those in possession of laundered funds to infiltrate the legitimate economy and gain power in social structures (see e.g. Savona, Riccardi and Berlusconi 2016). Money laundering is believed to undermine the integrity of the global financial system, with the presence of criminally acquired funds disturbing the normal flow of money through the financial system and negatively impacting the reputational and material strength of banks and financial institutions. It has been described as 'a significant threat' to 'national security, national prosperity and international reputation' in the UK, due to the structural importance of the country's financial services industry 'which may be damaged by the laundering of criminal funds' (NCA 2016: 5). As such, laundering is one of the five national priorities for the UK National Crime Agency (NCA) and appears prominently in official threat assessments, strategy documents and risk assessments (e.g. Home Office 2013; NCA 2014, 2015, 2016; HM Treasury/Home Office 2015, 2017). More widely, the FATF (2019a) suggests that illicit financial flows into developing economies can have a negative impact on their commercial and economic development, due to the damage to their reputation and perceived integrity of their financial sectors, creating a threat to economic stability and democratic processes.

While the actual scale of the threat posed and the extent of money laundering's negative impact on the financial system have been contested (e.g. Naylor 2004; Harvey 2008; van Duyne, Harvey and Gelemerova 2016) – and some have questioned whether the impact of *anti*-money laundering measures actually have a greater impact on developing economies (e.g. Tsingou 2010; Center for Global Development 2015; Ramachandran, Collin and Juden 2018) – the perceived threat from 'dirty money' and its infiltration into the legitimate financial system has led to the development of an extraordinary range of legislative, regulatory and policy frameworks, guidelines, standards and institutions aimed at preventing money laundering. This global anti-money laundering regime incorporates both 'hard' and 'soft' law instruments and involves an array of national and international actors – both public and private – with a role in the prevention and investigation of money laundering. The remaining sections of this chapter will provide an overview of the development of the global anti-money laundering regime,[4] how this has manifested in the UK, and the potential implications of anti-money laundering legislation for legal professionals and others within the regulated sector.

The global anti-money laundering regime and the regulated professions

In December 1988, two years after the introduction of the US Money Laundering Control Act, members of the international community signed the Vienna Convention, which obliged states to 'deprive persons engaged in illicit traffic of the proceeds of their criminal activities and thereby eliminate their main incentive for doing so'.[5] The Vienna Convention was the first international legal instrument that established a specific offence of laundering the proceeds of drug trafficking,[6] and contained the definition of laundering which has informed national legislation worldwide. In the same year, the Basel Committee on Banking Supervision adopted a *Statement of Principles*[7] to highlight concerns about the laundering of criminal proceeds through financial institutions, and to encourage banks to implement a range of procedures to prevent or reduce money laundering. While the Basel Statement was not legally binding, it could be considered as a form of 'soft' law by reinforcing the notion 'that financial institutions are the linchpin to effective money-laundering prevention and detection' and prescribing standards of ethical professional conduct for banks to adhere to in order to achieve this (Alexander 2001: 237). The Vienna Convention and the Basel Principles led to the creation, at the 1989 G7 Summit in Paris, of the Financial

---

4 For further discussion and analysis of the global anti-money laundering regime and its development over the last three decades, see, for example, Gilmore and Mitsilegas 2007; Mitsilegas 2006; Verhage 2011; Alldridge 2016; Bergström 2018; Nance 2018.

5 United Nations Convention Against Illicit Traffic in Narcotic Drugs and Psychotropic Substances (1988), page 1.

6 Subsequent international instruments widened the scope of predicate offences beyond drug trafficking, e.g. Council of Europe *Convention on Laundering, Search, Seizure and Confiscation of the Proceeds from Crime* (1990) (the Strasbourg Convention); United Nations *International Convention for the Suppression of the Financing of Terrorism* (1999); United Nations *Convention against Transnational Organized Crime* (2000) (the Palermo Convention).

7 The Basel Statement of Principles on the Prevention of Criminal Use of the Banking System for the Purpose of Money Laundering (December 1988). The Basel Committee is 'the primary global standard setter for the prudential regulation of banks and provides a forum for cooperation on banking supervisory matters' (Basel Committee Charter, 2018. Available at: www.bis.org/bcbs/charter.htm [Accessed 29 July 2019]).

Action Task Force (FATF), an inter-governmental policy-making body whose initial mandate was to

> assess the results of co-operation already undertaken in order to prevent the utilisation of the banking system for the purpose of money laundering, and to consider additional preventative efforts in this field, including the adaptation of the legal and regulatory systems so as to enhance multilateral judicial assistance.[8]

Since this time, the role of the FATF has evolved, and its current stated purpose is

> to set standards and promote effective implementation of legal, regulatory and operational measures for combating money laundering, terrorist financing and other related threats to the integrity of the international financial system.
>
> (FATF 2019b)

In 1990, the FATF issued 40 Recommendations for action, to be implemented by the governments of its member states, which focused on three key objectives: (1) the improvement of national legal systems, particularly in the area of criminal law; (2) the strengthening of international cooperation; and (3) the enhancement of the role of financial institutions in combating money laundering. Again, the Recommendations were not legally binding, but 'rather a 'soft law' instrument aiming to provide a blueprint for global standards in the field' (Mitsilegas 2006: 199). The most notable impact of the Recommendations can be seen in regard to the third objective: expanding the scope and content of the Basel Principles to suggest that financial institutions commit to implementing a range of policies and procedures to enhance customer due diligence, identification and record keeping. The FATF 40 Recommendations were also hugely influential in the development of subsequent international, regional and, ultimately, national initiatives and legislative changes.

In 1991, the first EU Money Laundering Directive[9] was introduced, bringing the FATF standards to the European sphere. The Directive took a two-pronged approach, focusing on both the criminalisation and the prevention of money laundering. Based on the original FATF Recommendations and using the definition of money laundering from the Vienna Convention, it prohibited the laundering of the proceeds of drug trafficking only, although it gave member states the discretion to extend criminalisation to other offences. However, when the

---

8 G7, Economic Declaration, Paris Summit (16 July 1989) para. 53. Available at: www.g8.utoronto.ca/summit/1989paris/communique/index.html [Accessed 29 July 2019].
9 Council Directive 91/308/EEC of 10 June 1991 on prevention of the use of the financial system for the purpose of money laundering [1991] (First Money Laundering Directive).

Directive was updated in 2001,[10] the criminalisation of laundering the proceeds from offences other than drug trafficking was made mandatory. This reflected revisions that had been made to the FATF's 40 Recommendations in 1996, and was inextricably linked to the emergence of organised crime as a serious threat in international policy discourse and the resultant desire to counter this threat (see Mitsilegas 2006). Following the terrorist attacks of 11 September 2001, the scope of the FATF Recommendations was extended further to include terrorist financing, with the addition of nine Special Recommendations to address terrorist financing by 2004.[11] Following the usual pattern, the European anti-money laundering framework was adapted to take into account the revised Recommendations.

Alongside criminalisation, the second key strand of the EU's Money Laundering Directives is prevention. The First Directive introduced a series of obligations for financial and credit institutions to implement adequate money laundering procedures, policies and training programmes; to carry out appropriate 'customer due diligence' measures, including verifying customers' identities and keeping identification records for five years after the end of the client relationship; to refrain from transactions they knew or suspected were associated with money laundering; to report suspicious transactions to the relevant national authorities; and to not 'tip off' customers that they were being investigated for money laundering. These obligations constituted 'unprecedented changes' in the commercial relationships of financial institutions and their clients (Mitsilegas 2006: 199). The Second Directive, introduced in 2001, extended the preventative obligations beyond the financial sector to include a range of non-financial businesses and professions considered to pose a money laundering risk, such as real estate agents; high-value dealers; auditors, external accountants and tax advisors; and legal professionals. This extension was in response to the growing concern that certain 'gatekeeper professionals' outside of the financial sector were increasingly being exploited by individuals wishing to launder criminal proceeds, acting as intermediaries in money laundering schemes or providing advice to criminals to assist them in the management of their illicit funds. The inclusion of legal professionals in the preventative measures of the anti-money laundering regime proved contentious, with considerable resistance in particular to the reporting obligations of the regime. Concern was raised both by legal scholars (e.g. Gentzik 2000; Xanthaki 2001; Mitsilegas 2006; Gallant 2013) and by legal professional associations (see Kirby 2008; Terry 2010) about the implications of reporting duties and other anti-money laundering prevention measures for the confidential nature of the lawyer-client relationship and defendants' rights to a legal defence

---

10 Directive 2001/97/EC of the European Parliament and of the Council of 4 December 2001 amending Council Directive 91/308/EEC on prevention of the use of the financial system for the purpose of money laundering [2001] (Second Money Laundering Directive).
11 The first eight Special Recommendations were introduced in 2001, with the ninth Special Recommendation being added in 2004.

and due process, and the potential risk to professionals who come into contact with 'dirty' money. While in some countries (such as Canada),[12] these objections led to lawyers being exempted from the reporting obligations, national legislation in other countries (including the UK) was adapted to include lawyers within their anti-money laundering framework.

There have been four subsequent EU Money Laundering Directives. The Third Directive[13] of 2005 extended the scope of the anti-money laundering regime to include activities related to terrorist financing (in line with the revised FATF Recommendations) and made trust and company providers subject to the Directive's preventative obligations, amongst other changes. This was followed by the Fourth Directive,[14] required to be implemented by 26 June 2017, which gave effect to the latest version of the FATF Recommendations, issued in February 2012. The Fourth Directive contained a number of new developments, with a greater emphasis on a risk-based approach to anti-money laundering, requirements for more transparency around beneficial ownership, and changes to customer due diligence measures. This Directive was quickly amended by the Fifth Money Laundering Directive,[15] agreed to in May 2018, which added some new provisions rather than making wholesale changes. These provisions focused on the regulation of virtual currencies, greater access to and sharing of information, and further increased transparency in relation to beneficial ownership of companies and trusts (primarily driven by the 'Panama Papers' revelations). Only five months later, the Sixth Money Laundering Directive was adopted, aiming, amongst other things, to harmonise the definition of money laundering and predicate offences across member states, extend criminal liability to legal persons, and impose minimum penalties for money laundering offences.[16] While the changes brought about in subsequent Directives have had implications for legal professionals, their obligations and working practices, it was the Second Directive, which required

---

12 In 2015, the Supreme Court of Canada found that the reporting requirements were a breach of the constitutional right to attorney-client privilege. The exemption of legal professionals within Canada from the reporting requirements is considered by the FATF to be 'a serious impediment to Canada's efforts to fight money laundering' (FATF 2016, para. 27).

13 Directive 2005/60/EC of the European Parliament and of the Council of 26 October 2005 on the prevention of the use of the financial system for the purpose of money laundering and terrorist financing [2005] (Third Money Laundering Directive).

14 Directive (EU) 2015/849 of the European Parliament and of the Council of 20 May 2015 on the prevention of the use of the financial system for the purposes of money laundering or terrorist financing [2015] (Fourth Money Laundering Directive).

15 Directive (EU) 2018/843 of the European Parliament and of the Council of 30 May 2018 amending Directive (EU) 2015/849 on the prevention of the use of the financial system for the purposes of money laundering or terrorist financing, and amending Directives 2009/138/EC and 2013/36/EU [2018] (Fifth Money Laundering Directive).

16 Directive (EU) 2018/1673 of the European Parliament and of the Council of 23 October 2018 on combating money laundering by criminal law [2018] (Sixth Money Laundering Directive). EU member states are expected to transpose this Directive into national law by December 2020. At the time of writing, the Sixth Money Laundering Directive had not yet been transposed into UK law.

member states to incorporate 'Designated Non-Financial Businesses and Professions' (DNFBPs) into their anti-money laundering frameworks and subject them to the 'Know Your Customer' and reporting requirements that had previously only applied to financial institutions, which was the landmark moment for such professionals in the global anti-money laundering regime. These requirements were implemented in UK law by way of the 2003 Money Laundering Regulations. Provisions introduced by the first four EU Money Laundering Directives have been transposed to the UK through successive Money Laundering Regulations (1993, 2003, 2007 and 2017), which implement the main preventative measures of the EU Directives, and the Proceeds of Crime Act (POCA) 2002, which established the primary criminal money laundering offences in the UK.

Money laundering regulations

The UK Money Laundering Regulations set out the administrative requirements for the anti-money laundering regime within the 'regulated sector', by requiring specified business sectors to 'apply risk-based customer due diligence measures and take other steps to prevent their services being used for money laundering or terrorist financing'.[17] The most recent iteration is the Money Laundering, Terrorist Financing and the Transfer of Funds (Information on the Payer) Regulations 2017 (hereafter 'the Regulations' or MLR 2017), which came into effect on 26 June 2017, replacing the Money Laundering Regulations 2007 and the Transfer of Funds (Information on the Payer) Regulations 2007. The 2017 Regulations did not make wholesale changes to the previous version; they maintain the same overarching purpose, with some new features to reflect the provisions of the Fourth EU Money Laundering Directive, including an extension of the 'risk-based approach'. The Regulations apply to the following sectors:

- Credit institutions
- Financial institutions
- Auditors, insolvency practitioners, external accountants and tax advisors
- Independent legal professionals
- Trust or company service providers
- Estate agents
- High value dealers
- Casinos

As one of the regulated sectors, therefore, legal professionals are required to comply with a number of measures to 'know their clients' and monitor the use of their services, including risk assessment, customer due diligence and record-keeping measures and the implementation of adequate policies, systems and

17 Explanatory Memorandum to The Money Laundering Regulations 2007. Available at: www.legislation.gov.uk/uksi/2007/2157/memorandum/contents [Accessed 29 July 2019].

procedures. They are also required to be supervised for anti-money laundering purposes by a designated supervisory authority. Non-compliance with certain parts of the Regulations is considered a criminal offence, punishable by up to two years' imprisonment, a fine or both (MLR 2017, Reg 86).

Risk assessment

In line with the risk-based approach emphasised in the Fourth EU Money Laundering Directive, aimed at directing resources to areas of greatest risk, a focus on risk assessment measures is a key feature of the 2017 Money Laundering Regulations, and should provide the 'cornerstone' of a law firm's anti-money laundering framework (Law Society Scotland 2017). Under Regulation 18, legal professionals must carry out and maintain a written firm-level risk assessment to identify and assess the risk of money laundering and terrorist financing that their firm faces. In carrying out this risk assessment, the firm must take into account the nature and location (sector and jurisdiction) of its client base; the countries or geographic areas in which it operates; the products and services it provides; its transactions; and its delivery channels. It should also take account of the risk assessment carried out by the relevant supervisory authority.

Customer due diligence

Legal professionals must undertake customer due diligence measures, which involve verifying the identity of their clients and obtaining information on the nature and purpose of the intended business relationship or transaction. Where the client is an entity or legal arrangement, they are also expected to verify the identity of the beneficial owner(s) and, where relevant, the underlying client, and take reasonable measures to understand (and document) ownership, governance and constitutional structures of the entity (MLR 2017, Reg 28). The requirements to understand the nature and ownership of corporate body clients are more stringent and prescriptive in the 2017 Regulations than they were in the 2007 version, reflecting growing concern about the use of corporate vehicles and associated obscuring of ownership to facilitate money laundering and other economic crimes. Furthermore, the circumstances in which 'Simplified Due Diligence' is permitted are now more restrictive than under the 2007 Regulations. Regulation 37 allows Simplified Due Diligence where it is determined that the business relationship or transaction presents a low risk of money laundering or terrorist financing, but a range of risk factors must be considered when deciding if this is the case, including customer and geographical factors. Regulation 33, on the other hand, details circumstances in which 'Enhanced Due Diligence' measures must be applied, including any transaction or business relationship involving a 'politically exposed person (PEP)' (or family member or associate of a PEP), or any situation that presents a higher risk of money laundering or terrorist financing. The 2017 Regulations include a 'black list' of high-risk jurisdictions; association with any of these makes Enhanced Due Diligence compulsory.

Keeping records

Legal professionals must also keep a record of the information obtained on the customer's identity and business, along with supporting documentation, for a period of five years (MLR 2017, Reg 40), deleting it after this period for data protection reasons, unless there is a valid business justification and client consent not to do so.

Implementation of adequate systems, policies, controls and procedures

Legal professionals must establish and maintain appropriate written policies, controls and procedures to mitigate and manage effectively the risks of money laundering and terrorist financing identified in any risk assessment they carry out (MLR 2017, Reg 19). These should include measures for conducting customer due diligence, reporting and record-keeping, risk assessment and management, and training of staff. Regulation 24 requires that staff must be provided with appropriate anti-money laundering and counter-terrorism financing training, and evidence of this training must be recorded and maintained. Under Regulation 21, all organisations within the regulated sector must have a 'nominated officer' responsible for receiving disclosures of suspicious activity from members of the organisation and making disclosures to the relevant authorities (as required by Part 7 of POCA 2002 and Part 3 of the Terrorism Act 2000). At the present time, the relevant authority for making disclosures to is the National Crime Agency (NCA).

Supervision of the regulated sector

Members of the regulated sector are required to be supervised by a designated supervisory authority to ensure their compliance with the Regulations. The role of the supervisory authority is to effectively monitor the persons it is responsible for; take necessary measures to ensure their compliance with the requirements of the Regulations; and report any suspicions or knowledge that a person it is responsible for is or has engaged in money laundering or terrorist financing to the NCA (MLR 2017, Reg 46). The supervisory authority must adopt a risk-based approach to supervision, by identifying and assessing the international risks of money laundering and terrorist financing to which its sector is subject; ensuring its employees and officers have access to information on money laundering and terrorist financing risks; and basing the operation of its supervisory activities on the risk profiles it has prepared for the sector. It must also review the risk assessments carried out by members of its sector, and assess the adequacy of the policies, controls and procedures that have been implemented (LSAG 2018: 120).

Within the Money Laundering Regulations, the designated supervisory authorities for those that belong to the regulated professions are their professional bodies. For the legal profession in the UK, there are nine named supervisory authorities.[18] Subsequent to the enactment of the 2007 Regulations, the representative and regulatory roles of the Law Society (the professional body for solicitors in England and Wales) were split, and the Solicitors Regulation Authority (SRA) was established. While the Law Society retains the representative function, the SRA acts as the regulatory and disciplinary body for solicitors in England and Wales, and so, in effect, plays the role of supervisory authority for solicitors in relation to the Money Laundering Regulations in this jurisdiction. In Scotland and Northern Ireland, this separation between representation and regulation did not take place and so the regulatory and disciplinary role remains as the remit of, respectively, the Law Society of Scotland and the Law Society of Northern Ireland. These Law Societies, therefore, are the designated supervisory authorities for solicitors in Scotland and Northern Ireland. Concern about the wide range of professional bodies acting as supervisory authorities in relation to anti-money laundering in the UK, and the lack of consistency and information-sharing between them, led to the introduction in 2018 of the Office for Professional Body Anti-Money Laundering Supervision (OPBAS). OPBAS oversees the 22 professional body supervisors listed in Schedule 1 of the 2017 Regulations (as well as the three regulatory bodies with delegated responsibility for anti-money laundering supervision, such as the SRA), with the aim of improving the consistency of their supervisory practices in relation to anti-money laundering and facilitating collaboration and information-sharing between each other, other supervisors in the anti-money laundering framework, and law enforcement. The supervision and regulation of the legal profession in relation to money laundering in the UK, and some of the challenges involved in this, will be discussed fully in Chapter 8.

Proceeds of Crime Act 2002

The Money Laundering Regulations apply only to those considered as members of certain 'regulated sectors' under the anti-money laundering regime. The Proceeds of Crime Act (POCA) 2002, which came into force on 24 February 2003, establishes the primary criminal money laundering offences in the UK and applies to all persons. Prior to the enactment of POCA 2002, laundering offences were covered by two different Acts: laundering the proceeds of drug trafficking was an offence under the Drug Trafficking Act 1994, and laundering the proceeds of other crimes was covered by the Criminal Justice Act 1988.

---

18 Chartered Institute of Legal Executives; Council for Licensed Conveyancers; Faculty of Advocates; Faculty Office of the Archbishop of Canterbury; General Council of the Bar; General Council of the Bar of Northern Ireland; Law Society; Law Society of Northern Ireland; Law Society of Scotland (MLR 2017, Reg 7).

Sections 327, 328 and 329

The three principal money laundering offences are contained within Part 7 of POCA 2002, in sections 327, 328 and 329. Section 327 covers the offence of concealing, disguising, converting or transferring criminal property, or removing criminal property from England and Wales, Scotland or Northern Ireland (POCA 2002, s.327[1]). The references to concealing and disguising criminal property also include concealing or disguising its 'nature, source, location, disposition, movement or ownership or any rights with respect to it' (POCA 2002, s.327[3]). Section 328 focuses on involvement in arrangements *known or suspected to facilitate* money laundering, stating that a person commits an offence if he:

> enters into or becomes concerned in an arrangement which he knows or suspects facilitates (by whatever means) the acquisition, retention, use or control of criminal property by or on behalf of another person.
>
> (POCA 2002, s.328)

Section 329 of the Act provides the third principal money laundering offence, and relates to the acquisition, possession or use of criminal property (POCA 2002, s.329). For all three sections, an offence is not committed if the person makes an 'authorised disclosure' or intended to make such a disclosure but had a reasonable excuse for not doing so, or if the actions involved are related to the enforcement of a provision of the Act or any other enactment relating to criminal conduct or its benefit (POCA 2002, ss.327[2], 328[2], 329[2]). A person convicted of an offence under any of these parts of the legislation is liable to imprisonment for 14 years, a fine or both (POCA 2002, s.334).

An offence of money laundering can be charged on its own, or included on an indictment which contains the underlying predicate offence. In both of these cases, there are two sub-categories: (1) 'own-proceeds' or 'self-laundering', where the person charged with money laundering also committed the predicate crime, and (2) laundering by a person or persons other than those who committed the predicate crime (CPS 2018). The section 327 offence would be the most relevant offence for cases of 'self-laundering', where the person who committed the predicate crime is prosecuted for laundering the proceeds of that crime. The section 328 offence, on the other hand, covers situations where a third party handles money derived from criminal activity, and so would be more appropriate when the individual prosecuted for the laundering offence was not involved in the proceeds-generating predicate offence. The Crown Prosecution Service (CPS 2018) highlights the utility of the section 328 offence for prosecuting those who 'launder on behalf of others', suggesting that it can be used to 'catch' individuals working within professional roles who 'in the course of their work facilitate money laundering by or on behalf of other persons'. Therefore, this particular component of the Act may be 'of considerable concern to those who handle or advise third parties in connection with money and other types of property' (Fortson 2010: 181), including legal professionals.

'Failure to Disclose: Regulated Sector' (section 330)

In addition to the primary money laundering offences laid out in sections 327, 328 and 329, there is a further part of the Act that is of particular relevance to the subject of this book. Section 330 contains the offence of 'Failure to Disclose: Regulated Sector', which lays out provisions to enforce the disclosure of suspicious transactions by members of the regulated sector, including legal professionals. Further provisions in the Act relate to the disclosure of suspicious transactions in non-regulated sectors, but the requirements for those in the regulated sector are more stringent than those in the non-regulated sector. According to section 330 of POCA 2002, persons commit an offence if:

- they know or suspect, or have reasonable grounds to know or suspect, that another person is engaged in money laundering; and
- the information or other matter on which their knowledge or suspicion is based, or which gives reasonable grounds for such knowledge or suspicion, comes to them in the course of a business in the regulated sector; and
- the person does not make the required disclosure as soon as is practicable after the information or other matter comes to him.

Section 330 of POCA 2002 thus creates *positive obligations* on individuals employed in the regulated sector, compelling them to make money laundering disclosures and making it a criminal offence to fail to do so. The potential implications of the anti-money laundering regime and resultant legislative framework for legal professionals and other members of the regulated sector, therefore, are significant. Under the Money Laundering Regulations, they must adhere to an ever-increasing array of duties and obligations (often poorly defined or lacking in clarity), with a failure to meet these obligations leading to the possibility of criminal sanctions. In addition, involvement in the laundering of criminal proceeds generated by others, or failing to disclose knowledge or suspicion that a client was engaged in laundering, can result in prosecution under POCA 2002. These implications will be explored in more depth throughout the course of the book.

Conclusion

The legislative and regulatory framework in relation to money laundering in the UK, and the global anti-money laundering regime from which this derived, provides important context for the examination of the nature and control of legal professionals' involvement in the facilitation of money laundering contained in this book. As will be seen in later chapters, the regulatory environment in which legal professionals operate, shaped by the designation of such professionals as 'gatekeepers' to the financial system and potential 'professional enablers' of money laundering, and consisting of an array of legislation, regulation and control agencies (criminal justice, professional and regulatory bodies), can influence both the actions and decision-making that can lead to involvement in money laundering and the way in which 'the facilitation of money laundering' is constructed and penalised. The nature of the immediate regulatory environment and associated legal frameworks is intrinsically linked to the global anti-money laundering regime, and the policies, procedures and institutions which this comprises, which is founded in the perception of money laundering as a significant crime problem, driver of serious criminality, and threat to the integrity of the global financial system. The implications for legal professionals of national regulatory and legislative frameworks aimed at preventing regulated professionals from becoming involved in money laundering, therefore, cannot be separated from the threat narrative around 'dirty money' and the policies that have emerged from this.

3 Framing the research

'Organised crime' or
'white-collar crime'?

Introduction

As the history of the concept shows, the 'problem' of money laundering has primarily been framed in relation to 'organised crime', and anti-money laundering policy as a way of preventing 'organised criminals' from realising the benefits of their crimes. More recently, discussion about the movement and concealment of criminal proceeds has increasingly been associated with financial or 'white-collar' crimes, such as corruption and tax evasion (and, since 2001, regularly conflated with terrorist financing, despite key differences). The role of legal professionals (and other providers of financial or commercial services) in the facilitation of money laundering, therefore, has also been predominantly framed in terms of the assistance this provides to those involved in organised crime. Most of the academic literature in this area considers money laundering as one aspect of organised crime where lawyers can provide assistance (e.g. Chevrier 2004; Di Nicola and Zoffi 2004; Lankhorst and Nelen 2004; Middleton and Levi 2004, 2015), and empirical examination of cases of facilitation refer to the laundering of the proceeds of drug trafficking and other organised criminal activities (e.g. Bell 2002; Schneider 2005). Similarly, introduction of the concept of 'gatekeeper professionals' and the co-opting of 'designated non-financial businesses and professions' into the anti-money laundering regime were based on the concern that such professionals were in a position to allow organised criminals to access the legitimate financial system (see Chapters 1 and 2). The term 'professional enablers' has become popular in official discourse in the UK to refer to legitimate professionals who assist organised criminals in a variety of ways, and has been used primarily in government 'Serious and Organised Crime Strategy' documents (e.g. Home Office 2013) and national strategic assessments of organised crime (e.g. NCA 2016, 2018). Again, reflecting the increasing focus on money laundering in relation to high-level financial or white-collar crimes, more recent threat and risk assessments and strategy documents in the UK have focused on the role of professional enablers in these forms of criminal activity, concentrating on what is characterised as 'high-end' money laundering, which is defined in part by its reliance on access to the professional skills of lawyers, accountants and other professionals (e.g. HM Treasury/Home Office 2017; NCA 2018).

This chapter considers how lawyers' involvement in the facilitation of money laundering should be framed for the purposes of criminological research and analysis, and thereby develops a theoretical and conceptual framework for the discussion that follows in the remainder of the book. It argues that the role played by lawyers in the management of criminal proceeds should be seen as a part of the organisation of crime for profit, in the same way that all relevant actors (both those holding primarily or ostensibly *legitimate* positions and those involved predominantly in *criminal* activity) should be considered as part of this organisation, and their roles analysed accordingly. This means that account should be taken of the nature of the activities and behaviours involved, the relationships between various actors (including those involved in crime control processes), the wider settings and conditions, and the interactions between these (Edwards and Levi 2008; Levi 2007, 2008a, 2012). However, it is also necessary to pay attention to the legitimate, professional position of lawyers, as it is their skills, expertise and status, and the services and access to transactions that their occupation provides, which create the means and opportunities to help others launder the proceeds of crime. Therefore, lawyers who facilitate money laundering can be considered to have committed 'white-collar crime', broadly and inclusively defined by Croall (2001: 17) as 'an abuse of a legitimate occupational role which is regulated by law'.

This chapter begins by showing how using an integrated framework which draws together the concepts of 'white-collar crime' and 'the organisation of crime for profit' can be used to understand the involvement of lawyers in the facilitation of money laundering. It then summarises the key theoretical perspectives that have been developed to try to explain 'white-collar crime' since the introduction of the concept by Edwin Sutherland in 1937 (see Sutherland 1940, 1945, 1949), highlighting theories and concepts that can be used to provide new insights into the actions of those that facilitate money laundering. Finally, it argues for a multi-level approach to understanding the role of legal professionals in money laundering, which appreciates the situated nature of individual action and decision-making, and takes account of the multi-layered settings in which this action occurs.

The organisation of crime for profit and the management of criminal proceeds

Despite its prevalence in policy and popular discourse, and the considerable attention it has received from politicians, law enforcement, academia and the media, the concept of 'organised crime' remains contested, with no universally accepted definition or common theoretical understanding. The definitions of organised crime adopted by official bodies are often loose and ambiguous, and can vary notably, with a lack of consensus around, for example, the number of offenders required to constitute an 'organised crime group', the material and/or political aims of such groups, and the inclusion of violence, corruption and 'transnational' activity as defining characteristics. Furthermore, while criminologists and others have been endeavouring to provide an effective definition of organised crime for a number of years (see e.g. Maltz 1976; Hagan 1983, 2006; Albanese 2000; Finckenauer 2005; Varese 2010), there remains little agreement on the nature and meaning of the concept within the academic literature in this area.[1] Organised crime has been conceptualised in various ways: as a type of criminality, characterised by continuity, sophistication and rationality in contrast to the compulsive and sporadic nature of other types of crime; in relation to the 'organised' nature of the relationships between offenders, operating in groups or networks rather than alone; and as a 'systemic condition', focusing on the 'concentration of illegitimate power' and the interrelationships between criminals and political and economic elites (von Lampe 2015: 27). So, agreement cannot even be reached on whether the term refers to certain criminal activities or the people engaged in them. Organised crime has been conceived as the provision of illegal goods and services, or as large-scale, well-defined collective organisations engaged in illegal activity. However, as Paoli (2002: 88) argues, the supply of illegal goods and services actually tends to occur in a *disorganised* fashion, carried out by 'small ephemeral enterprises', and the large-scale, long-lasting criminal organisations that do exist (e.g. the Italian Cosa Nostra and Japanese Yakuza) are not exclusively involved in illegal market activities. These 'paradoxes of organised crime' (Paoli 2002: 52) are emblematic of the lack of clarity and consistency that surrounds the discourse in this area.

The lack of definitional consensus or conceptual clarity for 'organised crime' arises from trying to identify as a clear and coherent phenomenon something that encompasses a diverse range of people and activities, and a complex set of relationships. The range of actors and activities that are subsumed under this label 'make it a vague umbrella concept that cannot be used, without specification, as a basis for empirical analyses, theory-building, or policy-making' (Paoli and Vander Beken 2014: 13). As such, there is a growing awareness that the term itself is problematic and 'rarely helpful' (Spencer 2007: 118), being unable to reflect the complexities and ambiguities of the interrelationships between actors and activities involved. Consequently, there has been a move away from the term 'organised crime' in recent years, and from trying to define and explain 'its' nature. Instead, it has been convincingly argued that it is more meaningful to consider the *organisation* of 'serious crimes for gain', or 'crimes for profit', in order to shift 'the analytical focus from explanations of "it" towards building theories of the organisation of serious crimes' (Edwards and Levi 2008: 363). This involves examining how such crimes are organised; the actors, activities and social relations involved; the settings in which offending takes place; the services required from both the licit and illicit worlds; and the interactions of these actors and settings with crime control processes (see Edwards and Levi 2008; Levi 2007, 2008a, 2012). This approach allows for recognition of the heterogeneity of the actors and activities involved, and the relations between them, and enables

---

1 For an overview of the history of the concept of organised crime, and debates about its scope, meaning and legitimacy, see e.g. Paoli and Vander Beken 2014; von Lampe 2015.

investigation of the wider 'social organisation' of serious crimes and those that commit them, including the interrelationships between actors in legitimate and illegitimate spheres (Passas 2002: 31).[2]

In addition, the type of activity encompassed by the phrase 'serious crime for gain', or 'crime for profit', or referred to in discussions of the organisation of such crimes, has broadened beyond what would have traditionally been considered as 'organised crime'. As well as those crimes based on illicit markets in, for example, drugs, tobacco, counterfeit goods, arms and people, we can include criminal activity that takes place within legitimate markets and is committed by those within legitimate occupations or businesses. Such 'white-collar crimes' include fraud, bribery, corruption, embezzlement and offences within financial markets, and by analysing their 'organisation' we can begin to understand how criminal opportunities are presented; how such opportunities are exploited by legitimate actors; the knowledge, skills and expertise required to exploit these; and the wider conditions that facilitate this (Lord and Levi 2016).

The *management of the proceeds* of crimes for profit is an essential part of the way that such crimes are organised. The processes by which criminal proceeds are used, moved and/or concealed vary, from their use in general living expenses, or to purchase property or other assets, to investment in legitimate businesses or concealment through shell companies and complex financial transactions. 'Laundering' in the strict sense of the term – i.e. concealing the origins of criminal proceeds to provide them with a false appearance of legitimacy – may occur as part of the management of criminal proceeds. A range of actors will be involved, in various ways and to varying extents, in the processes by which criminal proceeds are managed, including those that were involved in the predicate offence and others that were not – for example: cash couriers who transport cash proceeds within or across borders; members of a criminal group whose role involves organising the setting up of multiple bank accounts for the deposit of criminal proceeds; a cashier in a currency exchange business who exchanges funds derived from criminal activity into another currency; a bookkeeper who manages the accounts for a cash-intensive business which mixes the profits from licit and illicit activity; or a lawyer who acts as conveyancer in the purchase of a property bought using criminal proceeds, amongst many others.

The involvement of those in legitimate occupational roles – such as bank employees, real estate agents and accountants, as well as the lawyers that this book focuses on – in the management of criminal proceeds can be seen as a point of intersection between the 'legitimate' and 'criminal' spheres (or between the 'upperworld' and 'underworld'): legitimate (even if only outwardly) actors playing a role in criminal activity and having some form of relationship with criminal

---

2 This framework has been applied to, for example, the organisation of human trafficking (Goodey 2008), various financial frauds (Levi 2008a), food fraud (Lord, Flores Elizondo and Spencer 2017), and the finances required for and generated by transnational corporate bribery (Lord and Levi 2016).

actors, *and* criminally derived funds being integrated into the legitimate financial system. The juncture between the legitimate and illegitimate worlds, or 'the points at which criminals and conventional society meet' (Passas 2002: 31), has been widely discussed in the literature on organised crime and criminal markets,[3] and the popular notion of a criminal 'underworld' that is distinct and clearly separated from the rest of society is seen as presenting a false perception of reality, failing to show the interplay between different sections of society (Kostakos and Antonopoulos 2010). Interactions between the criminal and legitimate worlds have been primarily understood in terms of the infiltration by criminals into legitimate industries or economic sectors, with 'organised crime' being seen as a 'predatory force within legitimate enterprise and conventional society' (Morselli and Giguere 2006: 186). The notion of such criminal actors as the dominating or instigating force in the relationship fits with the 'threat image' of organised crime described by van Duyne (2004: 25), but presents a 'false conceptual dichotomy between unproblematic licit economies and the exceptional threats of illicit actors' (Edwards and Levi 2008: 374). Therefore, an alternative perspective has emerged, which focuses on a more complex, symbiotic relationship between legitimate and criminal actors, where legitimate actors can be active, critical participants in criminal networks (Morselli and Giguere 2006; see also, Passas 2002; Kupatadze 2008; Morselli 2009; Kostakos and Antonopoulos 2010).

Considering the organisation of crimes for profit provides a more useful way of thinking about the involvement of lawyers (and other legitimate professionals) in the management of criminal proceeds than a preoccupation with seeing them as enabling 'organised crime'. It directs us towards questions about the social organisation of their involvement in money laundering and relationships between the actors and actions involved, and how this is shaped by the wider conditions and contexts in which it occurs. Furthermore, it allows us to consider the proceeds from a range of serious crimes for gain, including those that would be characterised as 'white-collar' or 'economic' crimes as well as 'organised' crimes.

Legal professionals as white-collar criminals

It is also important, however, to retain a focus on the professional position and occupational context of legal professionals, and take account of these when

---

3 Legitimate actors from a variety of occupational settings have been shown to play a role in the organisation of various forms of crimes, including the airport luggage handlers, pilots, truck drivers, port employees, and transport and logistics firms involved in the distribution of drugs and illicit alcohols (e.g. Lyman and Potter 2000; Gruppo 2003; Zaitch 2003; Kostakos and Antonopoulos 2010; Lord *et al.* 2017); lawyers assisting human smugglers by supplying false identity papers (Nelen and Lankhorst 2008) and in a variety of ways in the cocaine business in Greece (Kostakos and Antonopoulos 2010); and professionals in the financial and real estate sectors aiding criminals in the commission of mortgage frauds (Tusikov 2008; Van Gestel 2010).

considering their involvement in the facilitation of money laundering. It is their role as a professional with particular skills, expertise and status, employed in an occupation that provides certain services and financial transactions, that has led to lawyers (and other similar professionals) being positioned as 'gatekeepers' in the fight against money laundering, and is said to provide the means and opportunity for them to help others launder the proceeds of their crimes (e.g. WEF 2012; Europol 2013; FATF 2008, 2013). Therefore, the concept of 'white-collar crime' and associated theoretical positions can provide an alternative framework for understanding the role of lawyers in the facilitation of money laundering.

The concept of 'white-collar crime' was introduced by the sociologist Edwin Sutherland, during his Presidential Address to the American Sociological Society's annual meeting in Philadelphia in December 1939. Through a series of subsequent publications (e.g. Sutherland 1940, 1945, 1949), Sutherland defined white-collar crime as 'a crime committed by a person of respectability and high social status in the course of his occupation' (1949: 9) and aimed to draw attention to crimes not usually included within the scope of criminology at that time, challenging traditional explanations of criminal behaviour that focused on poverty or social disadvantage. Sutherland's work in this area has been hugely influential, challenging existing perceptions and 'sensitizing' the field of criminology to the crimes of those in positions of power or prestige. However, his definition has been extensively debated and challenged over the years, facing various criticisms related to its ambiguity and inclusion of acts that were not legally crimes, and stimulating questions about whether the focus should be on the characteristics of the *offender* or nature of the *offence* (see e.g. Pontell and Geis 2007; Nelken 2012; Benson, Van Slyke and Cullen 2016). Central to Sutherland's conception of white-collar crime is the high social status and respectability of its perpetrators; this creates 'an imprisoning framework that confuses the offender with the offence' (Pontell and Geis 2007: xiv) and means that social status and class cannot be used as explanatory variables, or their variation measured across cases. Sutherland also failed to differentiate between crime committed by employees against their organisation for their own personal benefit (such as theft or embezzlement) and that committed for the benefit of the organisation (Huisman and Vande Walle 2010). Thus, it has been widely argued that the focus of the concept should be the nature and characteristics of certain offences rather than those carrying them out, thereby 'collaring the crime not the criminal' (Shapiro 1990).

The terms 'organisational crime' and 'occupational crime' have been used as alternatives to 'white-collar crime', in order to move away from a focus on the social status of the offender. 'Occupational crime' is described as offences committed by individuals, for their own benefit, in the course of activity in a legitimate occupation, or offences committed by employees against their employers (Clinard and Quinney 1973; Clinard and Yeager 1980). In contrast to Sutherland's focus on individuals of high social status, occupational crime also includes offences committed by 'blue-collar workers' in connection with their occupations (Clinard and Yeager 1980). Therefore, the key feature of this concept is the location of the offence, with the legitimate occupation providing the context in which the offence occurs. The *occupational context* provides opportunities for criminal activity, which can be exploited regardless of the specific motivation of the offender (Clinard and Meier 2011). It can also provide a degree of 'invisibility' to the offence because the offender is 'legitimately present at the scene' (Croall 2001: 8). The occupational role can play a part in the commission of the offence, with the offender often making use of 'some form of technical or "insider" knowledge', or professional expertise (Croall 2001: 8). The concept of occupational crime, therefore, removes reference to the high social status of the offender, meaning that the focus can be on the opportunities provided by the occupational setting, and the interactions of offenders with this setting, regardless of the class or status of the offender.

The concept of 'organisational crime' as a subcategory of white-collar crime refers to 'crime committed by a legal organisation or a member of that organisation in the course of his occupation in favour of the organisation' (Huisman and Vande Walle 2010: 119). Its defining features, therefore, are the *organisational setting* of the behaviour and its purpose – at least in part – of serving the goals of the organisation. Organisational crime that takes place within the context of a corporation falls under the category of 'corporate crime', defined by Clinard and Quinney (1973: 189) as 'offenses committed by corporate officials for their corporation and the offenses of the corporation itself'. However, organisational crime is wider than just corporate crime; it also includes violations of laws or regulations in public and voluntary organisations, and those committed for the benefit of the state or its agencies (state crime) (Croall 2001). The concept of organisational crime can be taken to include activities that violate non-criminal forms of law and regulations as well as those that constitute a criminal offence, and that result in some form of penalty or sanction other than criminal prosecution.

There have been various other conceptualisations since Sutherland's introduction of 'white-collar crime', including 'corporate crime' (Clinard and Quinney 1973; Clinard and Yeager 1980; Slapper and Tombs 1999), which focuses on the actions of corporations; 'crimes of the powerful' (Pearce 1976), which highlight issues of status, power and class dynamics and include state crime; and 'crimes of the middle classes' (Weisburd et al. 1991) and 'middle class crime' (Karstedt 2016), focusing on the mundane and everyday characteristics of offences classified as 'white-collar'. Croall (2001: 17) considers 'white-collar crime' to be a useful umbrella term, defining it as 'an abuse of a legitimate occupational role which is regulated by law'. This broad and inclusive definition encompasses both organisational and occupational crime, while focusing on the legitimate occupational context, and takes account of activities that are controlled not only by criminal law. Many of the definitions that fall under the broad construct of 'white-collar crime' have 'common analytical features', summarised by Levi and Lord (2017: 726) as 'the focus on unlawful acts and omissions in the course of an occupation and/or in an organisational setting (public or private), the foregrounding of a violation or abuse of trust characterised by some form of deception or dishonesty, and the misuse of otherwise legitimate business or institutional procedures and practices to conceal behaviours'.

This book does not aim to contribute to the debates about the definition of white-collar crime, nor does it make any claims to advance general theories of white-collar crime. Rather, it shows how concepts, theories and ideas from the field of white-collar crime research and scholarship can be used to aid understanding of the involvement of legal professionals in the management of criminal proceeds. It is clear that this issue, and both the actors and activities concerned, fall within the concept of white-collar crime, broadly construed: it entails legitimate professional actors who, in the course of their occupational position and in an organisational setting, are involved in (the facilitation of[4]) unlawful acts or omissions. It could be categorised as both 'occupational crime' and 'organisational crime', as defined above, highlighting the relevance of both the legitimate occupational context and organisational setting of the behaviour, and with potential benefit for both the individual lawyer and the firm in which they work.

An integrated framework

To understand the involvement of lawyers in the management of criminal proceeds, we need to draw together the concepts of 'white-collar crime' and 'the organisation of crime for profit' (Figure 3.1). Considering the organisation of

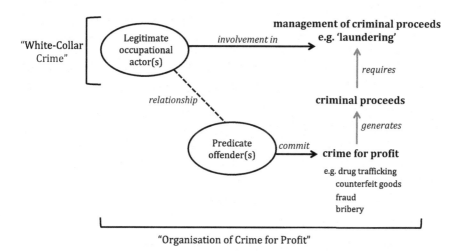

Figure 3.1 Integrating the concepts of 'white-collar crime' and 'the organisation of crime for profit'

4 They are *facilitating* a criminal offence – money laundering – but, because of the nature of money laundering legislation, are also *committing* an offence in many jurisdictions.

crimes for profit (both 'organised crimes' and 'economic' or 'white-collar crimes') allows us to take account of, and ask questions about:

- the relationship between the lawyer and the client(s) whose funds they are helping to legitimise;
- the relationship between these actors and those responsible for regulation, enforcement, prosecution and prevention;
- the processes involved in the commission of the criminal activity (including both the predicate crime and the management of the proceeds generated);
- the nature of lawyers' involvement in these processes;
- the reasons that this involvement is beneficial (or necessary); and
- the wider social-structural contexts in which this takes place.

Using theories and concepts from the field of white-collar crime research and scholarship can help us understand the nature of lawyers' involvement in money laundering, and its control through criminal justice and regulatory mechanisms. This approach emphasises the occupational context and organisational setting of lawyers' actions in the facilitation of money laundering, and highlights the opportunities for criminal activity that these can provide. It also draws attention to the situated nature of individuals' actions and the importance of considering the contexts in which they occur, and provides a framework for exploring strategies for – and the challenges of – controlling the facilitation of money laundering. Using this approach creates new insights and understandings that have been largely missing from previous analyses; these will become evident throughout the course of the book. The remainder of this chapter summarises these theoretical perspectives and argues for the need to incorporate multiple levels (micro, meso and macro) of explanation in order to fully explore the role of lawyers in the facilitation of money laundering, thus providing a theoretical and conceptual framework for the analysis that follows.

Explaining white-collar crime

Attempts to explain white-collar crime, variously defined, have utilised and developed a range of theoretical perspectives, focused on micro, meso and macro levels of analysis.

Individual-level explanations

Many explanations for white-collar crime are focused at the level of the individual, seeking to understand individual decision-making processes and motivations for offending, or identifying certain characteristics, pathologies, or personality traits that may lead to – or at least increase the likelihood of – involvement in these types of offences. There is a range of literature suggesting an association between white-collar offending and certain personality traits, such as ambitiousness, drive, risk-taking, recklessness, narcissism, guile, hubris and the desire for control (e.g. Piquero, Exum and Simpson 2005; Blickle et al. 2006; Elliott 2010; Listwan, Piquero and Van Voorhis 2010; Zona, Minoja and Coda 2012). Alalehto (2003) described white-collar offenders as manipulative, egocentric and extroverted, and Babiak and Hare (2007) suggest that 'snakes in suits' often display typical signs of a narcissistic personality disorder. Of course, many of these characteristics can also be seen in those within 'white-collar' professional positions who are *not* involved in criminal activity, and, indeed, such characteristics are often associated with legitimate business success.

Gottfredson and Hirschi (1990) suggested that individuals with low self-control would be more likely to engage in criminal activity, including white-collar crime. A number of researchers have applied self-control theory to account for various forms of white-collar crime (e.g. Benson and Moore 1992; Hirschi and Gottfredson 1989; Geis 2000; Simpson and Piquero 2002; Friedrichs and Schwartz 2008; Piquero, Schoepfer and Langton 2008), but it has been subject to criticism. The primary criticism of self-control theory as an explanation for white-collar crime is that its focus on individual desires and self-gratification ignores the organisational and cultural context of offending behaviour, and fails to account for crimes that benefit the organisation rather than the individual (Friedrichs 1996; Slapper and Tombs 1999). Portraying those involved as inherently different to non-offenders may serve an ideological function, identifying white-collar offenders as 'rotten apples in the barrel', and suggesting that such behaviour is unavoidable and unrelated to any wider organisational culture, policies or practices (Croall 2001).

Sutherland rejected the notion that white-collar offending could be explained by innate individual characteristics, instead arguing that it was through a process of 'differential association' (Sutherland 1947) that individuals in business settings 'come to accept and adopt behaviours that are favourable to violations of the law in the form of white-collar crimes' (Benson and Manchak 2014: 1). Sutherland's theory of differential association stated that criminal behaviour is learned, and that greater exposure to individuals who approve of criminal behaviour, or attitudes in favour of criminal activity, than to those against law breaking, leads individuals to commit crimes. People learn the rationalisations, motivations and attitudes necessary to engage in criminal activity – as well as the techniques required to carry it out – from their peers (Sutherland 1947). However, Benson and Manchak (2014: 2) suggest that Sutherland's rejection of psychological factors and individual characteristics 'was premature'. While the influence of situational contexts and cultures, and the process of learning from others, are important, they do not explain why some individuals within certain settings commit offences and others do not. They argue, therefore, that individual traits, psychological factors and cognitive processes play a central role in the causes of white-collar offending. Recent research supports this view, providing increasing evidence of the existence of certain personality traits and psychological disorders among white-collar offenders (see Huisman 2016: 440).

Choice

Underpinning many of the individual-level explanations of white-collar crime is the view that crime is a rational choice, motivated by self-interest and based on an evaluation of risk and reward. In line with this view, a number of scholars have explicitly utilised a rational choice framework in their attempts to explain white-collar crime, considering it a 'natural fit' for understanding the decision-making processes of this type of offender (Piquero 2012: 364; see also, Paternoster and Simpson 1993; Shover and Hochstetler 2006; Tomlinson and Pozzuto 2016). With foundations in the utilitarian tradition of criminology and economic models of human behaviour, the rational choice perspective conceives criminal activity as the outcome of rational choices and decisions based on an analysis of risk and reward (Cornish and Clarke 1986, 2002, 2014), carried out by a 'reasoning criminal', who 'considers the risks, effort, and rewards associated with alternative courses of action and selects the one which maximises, or at least gives a reasonable return on, his or her investment of time and energy' (Cornish and Clarke 2002: 43). Individuals offend, therefore, when crime provides the most effective means of achieving the desired benefits.

At its core, rational choice theory assumes that criminal acts are the product of a process of cognition and calculation where 'reasoned actors weigh the costs associated with the potential act against the potential benefits or gains that will be derived from the act' (Piquero 2012: 364). A rational actor model which sees crime in terms of cost-benefit calculations is considered a useful framework for analysing white-collar and corporate crimes, as such crimes are rarely spontaneous or driven by emotion, usually require a degree of foresight and planning, are calculated and deliberative, and are directed towards economic gain (e.g. Braithwaite and Geis 1982; Paternoster and Simpson 1993, 1996; Simpson, Piquero and Paternoster 2002; Piquero, Exum and Simpson 2005; Shover and Hochstetler 2006; Shover, Hochstetler and Alalehto 2013). They represent 'calculated decisions intended to obtain highly valued outcomes illicitly with minimal likelihood of detection and/or punishment' (Tomlinson and Pozzuto 2016: 368).

The rationality of offending decisions, however, is 'bounded' by personal and situational factors, including the personal characteristics, perceptions, emotions and biases of those making the decision; the limits of the information they possess and how they process it; and the situational context in which the decision is being made (see e.g. Simon 1957, 1996; Nee and Meenaghan 2006; Van Gelder 2013, 2017). The application of the rational choice perspective in white-collar crime scholarship, therefore, has developed to incorporate such factors, including the appreciation of the characteristics of the situation in the decision-making process (see Huisman 2017 for discussion). The choices made, and decisions taken, by those involved in white-collar crime are influenced by instrumental and normative considerations, and shaped by micro-, meso- and macro-level factors, including the organisational, social and cultural contexts in which the offending behaviour takes place. The notion of an 'isolated decision maker' is not appropriate for those who work in organisations, because of the inevitable interactions with others within the organisational setting, in which 'the preferences and subjective assessments of the interacting parties are shared and become part of each individual's decision-making gestalt' (Benson, Van Slyke and Cullen 2016: 8). Thus, it is important to use *contextualised* theories of choice, and consider 'the dynamics between choice, organisation, opportunity and context' (Levi and Lord 2017: 731).

Organisation

The organisational context has long been seen as an important factor in the commission of white-collar offences. In 1978, Schrager and Short (1978: 410) highlighted the need to recognise that 'structural forces influence the commission of these offences' and called for an emphasis on 'organisational as opposed to individual etiological factors' in explanations of white-collar offending. Similarly, Slapper and Tombs (1999) argued for a focus on the structural pressures that occur within organisational contexts, which may be more significant in influencing behaviour than the personalities or moral codes of individuals, and may have criminogenic effects. Maurice Punch's work on corporate crime led him to argue that 'the *organizational component* is crucial' (Punch 2011: 103) in white-collar offending, suggesting that an organisation's 'institutional context and culture shape an environment that encourages, colludes or is culpably blind to law-breaking', leading to criminal behaviour within that organisation (Punch 2011: 101; see also Punch 1996). To Punch (2008, 2011), the organisation provides the motives, means, setting and opportunity for corporate misconduct.

Organisational characteristics and dynamics, including structure, culture and strategy, shape the behaviours of those within, and so must be seen as crucial in offending within and by organisations (see e.g. Huisman 2016). Individual-level explanations do not take sufficient account of the role of organisational factors, and how these factors influence individual behaviour and choices. Research has shown the role of organisational culture in misconduct by employees (see Campbell and Göritz 2014 for an overview). The goal-seeking nature of corporations and other organisations may make them inherently criminogenic (Gross 1980; Punch 1996), with reward systems and the 'pressure for profits' promoting law-breaking or unethical behaviour within and by organisations (e.g. Kramer 1982; Slapper and Tombs 1999; Anand, Ashforth and Joshi 2004; Shover and Hochstetler 2006). Furthermore, organisational structures can create 'walls of secrecy and silence' which allow the successful concealment of illegal activity and therefore the inhibition of effective regulation (van de Bunt 2010). Based on her study of the *Challenger* space shuttle disaster of 1986, Vaughan (1996, 1999, 2002) argued that it may be *conformity to* organisational goals and norms, rather than *deviance from* them, that explains organisational misconduct and that the normalisation of deviance within organisations, grounded in organisational processes and characteristics, can lead to mistakes, misconduct and even – as in the case of the *Challenger* shuttle – disaster. The nature of organisations can provide opportunities for misconduct and criminal activity to occur within them, which can be exploited by those who choose to do so.

Opportunity

The 'opportunity perspective' on white-collar crime argues that offending will take place in the presence of opportunities to do so and individuals (or groups) motivated to exploit these opportunities (Benson, Madensen and Eck 2009; Benson and Simpson 2018). Furthermore, different forms of white-collar crime will have particular 'opportunity structures' (Benson, Madensen and Eck 2009), referring to the characteristics of the opportunity, or the conditions or elements that must be in place in order for the offence to be carried out. Opportunities for white-collar crime are formed by their immediate environment, and so within organisational or occupational contexts are related to legitimate business activities or processes. As well as *allowing* offending to take place in such environments, it is suggested that the presence of opportunities can also *cause* white-collar crime by 'provoking criminal behaviour' (Madensen 2016: 382).

Opportunity theories of white-collar crime are grounded in notions of rational choice, and are based on three theoretical perspectives initially developed in relation to other types of offending: routine activity theory, crime pattern theory and situational crime prevention. Routine activity theory states that crime will occur when a motivated offender, attractive target and access to the target come together in the absence of an effective controller, or 'guardian' (e.g. Cohen and Felson 1979; Felson 1986; Eck 1994). In white-collar crime, the 'target' refers to 'particular types of situations in which a person can take advantage of certain categories of economic transactions in such a way as to enrich himself or herself' (Benson and Simpson 2018: 83), rather than a physical target that would be more relevant in forms of 'street' (rather than 'suite') crime. These situations occur within the workplace setting, and so, with white-collar crime, the offenders have 'legitimate access' to the target, by virtue of their occupational role (Benson and Simpson 2018: 85). The role of an effective controller, or 'capable guardian', to prevent individuals taking advantage of opportunities for offending or protect the location of these opportunities – through, for example, regulation or business compliance processes – becomes key. Therefore, a lack of (credible) oversight can increase the likelihood of white-collar crime occurring (Shover and Hochstetler 2006).

In line with crime pattern theory (Brantingham and Brantingham 1993, 2011), potential white-collar offenders become aware of crime opportunities as they 'move through familiar places', conducting their everyday (legitimate) activities (Madensen 2016: 396). Drawing on theories developed in relation to the situational crime prevention perspective (Cornish and Clarke 2002), it is clear that the decision by offenders to take advantage of these opportunities as they come across them in their everyday routine activities will be shaped by: a calculation of risk and reward, the effort required to carry out the offence, the nature of the situational context of the opportunity, and the potential offender's ability to excuse or rationalise his or her behaviour (Madensen 2016: 393).

Wider contexts

The nature of organisations, their cultures, and the opportunities for white-collar crime that occur within them are shaped by their wider social, political, cultural and economic contexts. These factors, therefore, have also been used to explain organisational misconduct. For example, a capitalist economic system is seen by many as a key driver of white-collar offending (see e.g. Pearce and Tombs 1998; Slapper and Tombs 1999). Such a system can drive people towards certain behaviours by 'constantly pushing people with targets to hit, promotions to seek and emotions to avoid, recessions to try and survive, and so on' and so is 'likely to engender corporate crime' (Slapper and Tombs 1999: 162). Indeed, it has been argued that corporate and business crimes could be seen as an 'inevitable consequence of capitalism' (Nelken 2012: 637). Over a century ago, Bonger and Horton (1916) argued that capitalism 'created a moral climate of egoism that inflamed the desire for material success' (Benson, Van Slyke and Cullen 2016: 11), and cultures of competition and enterprise that are endemic to capitalist systems and ideology are seen as criminogenic. The 'enterprise culture' stresses the values of individualism and financial success, and can lead to business practices that 'bend the rules' in the pursuit of profit or personal gain (Sikka 2008: 270). A culture of competition not only sees organisations and individuals seeking a competitive advantage over others, sometimes by illegitimate means, but also instils a 'fear of falling' (Coleman 1995) that leads some to indulge in law-breaking behaviour if success is threatened (Huisman and Vande Walle 2010: 16).

However, there are problems with a perspective that sees white-collar crime as endemic to capitalism, or capitalism as inherently criminogenic. Such a perspective would 'predict too much crime', suggesting illegitimate activity was occurring across the board in capitalist societies, and so failing to explain the relative stability of economic trade (Nelken 2012: 637). In addition, it fails to account for criminal activity in non-profit organisations or industries in societies that do not follow the capitalist model (Croall 2001) and does not allow for law-abidingness working *for* the competitive interests of companies (Lord and Doig 2014). Attempting to explain white-collar crime with a macro-level approach that focuses only on the criminogenic properties of certain cultural or economic environments cannot fully explain why some organisations and some individuals become involved in misconduct and others do not. Other factors, including organisational characteristics and cultures, individual traits, choices and decision-making, and the interactions between them, must also be taken into account.

A multi-level approach

A range of theoretical approaches have been taken in an attempt to understand and explain white-collar and corporate offending. While many focus on either individual, organisational or wider social-structural contexts, there is increasing consensus on the need to consider all levels and the interconnections and interactions between them, in order to fully explain offending behaviour. For example, we need to consider how organisational characteristics (e.g. culture, strategy and structure) interact with the wider industry culture and regulatory environment to produce white-collar crime, and how these factors influence opportunities and individual decision-making (Huisman 2016). A key proponent of the multi-level approach to understanding misconduct within and by organisations was Diane Vaughan (e.g. 1983, 1992, 2002, 2007), who suggested that in order to understand misconduct that is committed in an organisational context, it is crucial to explore the micro-, meso- and macro-levels to consider the relationships and interconnections between the wider environment, the organisational setting, and the behaviour of individuals within. This takes into account the socially organised and situated nature of individual action and thus provides the means of developing a full causal explanation of organisational misconduct (Vaughan 2007).

Vaughan suggested that explanations of white-collar crime that focus on individual motivations and models of rational choice are insufficient as they ignore the 'situational contexts' within which decisions and choices are made, and which influence, to varying degrees, these decisions (see e.g. Vaughan 1996, 1998, 1999, 2002, 2007). She argued that all social action is 'situated action'; that is, that individual actions, meaning and choice are situated within a 'layered social context', influenced not only by their immediate social setting, but also the wider institutional, structural and cultural environment in which this setting is located (Vaughan 2007: 7). Situated action sees individual, organisation and environment coming together to produce events, behaviours and activities (Vaughan 2002). The concept of 'situated action' has its origins in the writing of C. Wright Mills (1940), who argued that people's actions and motivations originate from the situation they are in rather than originating internally from the individual themselves (Suchman 2007). It was later brought to prominence by the anthropologist Lucy Suchman in relation to human-machine interaction and communication. Suchman argued for a better understanding of the situated nature of most human behaviour (Suchman 1987; see also Suchman 2007), using the term to underscore her position that 'every course of action depends in essential ways on its material and social circumstances' (Suchman 2007: 70). She argued that 'actions are always situated in particular social and material circumstances', so 'the situation is crucial to action's interpretation' (Suchman 2007: 176). Vaughan has applied the 'situated action' model of human behaviour to her research on organisational misconduct (most notably, in her extensive study into the organisational decision-making that led to the *Challenger* space shuttle disaster) in order to add context to the decision-making processes of offenders in organisational settings and move away from more individualistic models (Vaughan 1996, 1998, 2002). She argues that the study of misconduct – which can include the violation of rules, norms, and administrative, civil and criminal laws – within and by organisations must take into account the situated nature of individual action, by examining the contexts within which decisions to violate laws or rules are taken and, crucially, the relationship and interactions between individual behaviour and the settings in which it occurred (Vaughan 1996, 1998, 2002). A full theoretical explanation of any particular behaviour, Vaughan suggests, can only be possible by considering, to the greatest extent possible, the situated character of that behaviour, and by understanding the link between rational choice and the social context in which such choices are made, and recognising the importance of the role of social contingencies in decision-making (Vaughan 2007).

Vaughan developed a theory of organisational misconduct (see Vaughan 1983: 54–104), designed to explain violations of laws and regulations by individuals in organisational roles to further the interests of the organisation itself or a subunit of it, which incorporates three main elements:

1   The **competitive environment**, which includes competition from other organisations and the scarcity of resources, which generate pressures upon organisations to violate the law or regulatory norms in order to achieve certain goals.
2   The **regulatory environment**, which relates to the relationship between regulators and those they regulate. The structure of this relationship may mitigate the effectiveness of the regulators in controlling and deterring violations, contributing to individual decisions to violate.
3   **Organisational characteristics**, which provide opportunities to violate. Such characteristics include structures, processes and transactions.

(Adapted from Vaughan 1983, 2002)

This framework emphasises organisational factors and features of the wider environment to explain individual action. Rather than receiving a separate heading in this model, the individual level of analysis is taken to be implicit, with the connection between environment, organisation and individual action forming the basis of the theory (Vaughan 2002). It suggests that the three elements outlined are important influencers of 'violative behavior' in organisations, but also that all elements are interrelated:

the competitive environment provides the structural impetus for misconduct; organizational characteristics provide opportunities; and the regulatory environment, systematically failing because of structurally engendered constraints, encourages individuals to respond to competitive pressures by taking advantage of the socially organised opportunities for deviance that are available in organizations.

(Vaughan 1992: 127)

The framework thus aims to

draw systematic attention to 1) structures and processes in the organizational setting, as they are implicated in individual action, 2) the role of the environment as it impinges upon and is reproduced in the organizational settings, and 3) the relationship between the environment, the organizational setting and the behaviour of individuals within.

(Vaughan 2002: 122)

The causal explanation is revealed, therefore, by the interconnections between the constituent parts, which, when combined, play an influencing role on individual choice, meaning and action (Vaughan 2002).

An approach that appreciates the situated nature of individual action and decision-making and takes account of the multi-layered settings in which this action occurs, and which interact to play a role in shaping individual actions, provides a useful framework for the analysis of white-collar crime and misconduct in an organisational setting. It also, therefore, provides a useful framework for the analysis of the role of legitimate occupational actors in the management of criminal proceeds.

Conclusion

The role played by lawyers in the facilitation of money laundering can be seen both as a form of 'white-collar crime' and as an element of the 'organisation of crime for profit'. Drawing together these concepts provides us with a theoretical and conceptual framework for the analysis of the nature of lawyers' involvement in money laundering and its control through criminal justice and regulatory mechanisms. The actions taken by lawyers should be considered in relation to the multi-layered settings in which they occur, taking account of their situational contexts, the relationships between actors involved, and the dynamics between choice, decision-making, organisation and context. The occupational context and organisational setting of those within the legal profession may provide opportunities to assist those wishing to launder the proceeds of their crimes, and the nature of the relationships and interactions between lawyer, predicate offender, and those responsible for the regulation and control of money laundering and the legal profession, may influence decisions to take such opportunities. The wider environment in which lawyers' involvement in money laundering occurs includes the nature and culture of the legal profession and market for the provision of legal services, the relevant regulatory context and legislative framework, and the global anti-money laundering regime and associated requirements. These factors should also, therefore, form a part of our analytical lens. The following chapters integrate the theoretical and conceptual frameworks developed in this chapter with data on cases of legal professionals convicted for facilitating money laundering on behalf of their clients, and data from interviews with individuals working in law enforcement and other parts of the criminal justice system, relevant regulatory and professional bodies, and the legal profession, to explore the nature and control of lawyers' involvement in the facilitation of money laundering.

4 The nature of 'facilitation'

Diversity, complexity and context

Introduction

This chapter summarises and analyses 20 cases of solicitors convicted for money laundering offences in the UK between 2002 and 2013, where the offences committed were related to their professional position and involved the facilitation of the laundering of the proceeds of crimes committed by others. The cases were identified primarily through searches of databases held by the relevant disciplinary tribunals in the UK (Solicitors Disciplinary Tribunal and Scottish Solicitors' Discipline Tribunal) and the Westlaw legal database, and the data were collated from a range of publicly available sources including Court of Appeal judgments, disciplinary tribunal transcripts, and media and other articles and reports.[1] The case summaries are divided into four categories, related to the means of facilitation of the money laundering.

Much of the literature in this area – both academic and official – focuses on the methods or means by which legal professionals *have facilitated* or *could facilitate* money laundering, considering the services they provide that may be of use to those with criminal proceeds to launder and/or examining known cases of money laundering which involved lawyers (e.g. Bell 2002; Schneider 2005; Middleton 2008; Cummings and Stepnowsky 2011; FATF 2013). Understandably, these methods primarily relate to the role lawyers play as intermediaries in commercial or financial transactions, and can be summarised as follows:

- Purchase or sale of property
- Misuse of client or trust accounts[2]
- Formation, administration and management of companies and other corporate vehicles[3] (e.g. trusts and foundations)

---

1 See Chapter 1 for further details of the methods used to identify and collate these data.
2 Legal professionals in most countries are permitted to hold client funds in a separate account, known primarily as the 'client account' or 'trust account', to be used for the provision of legal services and in accordance with their client's instruction.
3 Corporate vehicles are defined as 'legal entities through which a wide variety of commercial activities are conducted and assets are held' (OECD 2001: 13). They can be used for money

- Use of off-shore tax havens and complex financial constructions
- Providing financial advice
- Providing introductions, or acting as intermediaries, to financial institutions or other legal, financial or property service providers
- Creating false legal documentation

The cases identified in this research primarily involved the solicitor acting in the purchase or sale of residential property or using his or her firm's client account to facilitate transactions involving funds derived from criminal activity, or to move such funds from one place to another. Other cases involved the transfer of ownership of commercial property to an off-shore company, the movement of funds into off-shore trusts and shell companies, and a variety of actions which fall broadly under the provision of legal and/or financial services.

The cases highlight the *diversity* in the ways that legal professionals can be considered to have facilitated money laundering, and for which they can be convicted of a money laundering offence. Even though they have been grouped and separated into categories, there is variation even within groups in terms of the actions (or non-action) of the lawyers, the transactions and processes involved, the purpose and complexity of the transactions, the relationship between the lawyer and his or her client (the predicate offender), and the nature and form of the criminal proceeds. This demonstrates the importance of not seeing 'the facilitation of money laundering' as a singular phenomenon, and avoiding the temptation to 'lump together' all the ways in which professionals are involved in the management of criminal proceeds. The chapter also, therefore, highlights the inherent problems with trying to categorise cases in this way. As well as masking the heterogeneity of the actors, behaviours and relations, a focus on descriptive categories of methods of 'facilitation' acts to decontextualise the actions and decision-making involved. Instead, we need to look beyond methods or techniques of 'facilitation' to appreciate and understand the *contexts* of the actions and choices of legal professionals, which lead to their involvement in money laundering on behalf of others.

The cases

Table 4.1 provides an overview of the solicitors identified as having been convicted for money laundering offences in the UK between 2002 and 2013, where the offences committed were related to their professional position and involved the facilitation of the laundering of the proceeds of crimes committed by others. The Table provides background information on the solicitors, the date(s)

---

laundering purposes in a variety of ways, due primarily to their ability to conceal or confuse the links between offenders and the proceeds of their crimes by hiding their true or ultimate 'beneficial owner' (see e.g. Does de Willebois *et al.* 2011; Transparency International 2017; Lord, van Wingerde and Campbell 2018).

Table 4.1 Solicitors convicted of money laundering offences in the UK between 2002 and 2013

Case No.	Name	Occupation	Male/Female	Age at Conviction	Time in Profession	Date of Conviction	Sentence Received	Disciplinary Sanction Received
1	Jonathan Duff	Solicitor	Male	43	18 years	01/07/2002	6 months' imprisonment	Struck off
2	Paul Winter Morris	Solicitor	Male	54	28 years	12/03/2003	5 years' imprisonment	Struck off
3	Andrew Young	Solicitor	Male	39	14 years	09/09/2004	27 months' imprisonment	No record
4	Peter Obidi	Solicitor	Male	44	4 years	08/10/2004	6 months' imprisonment	Struck off
5	Brian Dougan	Solicitor	Male	48	Unknown	22/05/2006	3 months' imprisonment	No record
6	Philip Griffiths	Solicitor	Male	45	21 years	19/06/2006	6 months' imprisonment	Struck off
7	Gerard Hyde	Solicitor	Male	55	29 years	02/03/2007	42 months' imprisonment	Struck off
8	Jonathan Krestin	Solicitor	Male	60	31 years	19/11/2008	£5,000 fine	Severe reprimand
9	Mohammed Jahangir Farid	Trainee Solicitor	Male	25	Unknown	02/04/2009	4 years' imprisonment	Prohibited from being employed as/by a solicitor
10	Rachel Taylor	Assistant Solicitor	Female	29	5 years	22/05/2009	39 weeks' imprisonment (suspended); 200 hours community work; £5,015 fine	Suspension (12 months)

(Continued)

Table 4.1 (Continued)

Case No.	Name	Occupation	Male/Female	Age at Conviction	Time in Profession	Date of Conviction	Sentence Received	Disciplinary Sanction Received
11	Anthony Blok	Solicitor	Male	72	49 years	30/06/2009	4 years' imprisonment	Prohibited from having name restored to roll
12	Aminat Afolabi	Solicitor	Female	41	2 years	14/07/2009	18 months' imprisonment	Struck off
13	Shadab Khan	Solicitor	Male	38	12 years	30/09/2009	4 years' imprisonment	Struck off
14	Martin Wilcock	Solicitor	Male	50	11 years	22/09/2010	£2,515 fine	Suspension (3 months)
15	Bhadresh Gohil	Solicitor	Male	46	18 years	22/11/2010 and 06/12/2010	10 years' imprisonment	Struck off
16	James Thorburn-Muirhead	Solicitor	Male	63	37 years	19/02/2011	16 months' imprisonment	Struck off
17	Nicholas Heywood	Solicitor	Male	45	21 years	12/12/2011	12 months' imprisonment	Struck off
18	Andrew Tidd	Solicitor	Male	52	27 years	06/02/2012	4 months' imprisonment (suspended)	£2,500 fine
19	Richard Housley	Solicitor	Male	57	Unknown	29/01/2013	4 years' imprisonment	Struck off
20	Andrew Wormstone	Solicitor	Male	43	20 years	07/02/2013	30 months' imprisonment	Struck off

they were convicted, the type of sentence they received following conviction, and the nature of the disciplinary sanction imposed by their relevant disciplinary tribunal.[4] The sanctions received included being 'struck off' the roll of solicitors; being prohibited from having their name restored to the roll of solicitors (having previously removed it voluntarily); being prohibited from being employed or remunerated in connection with practice as/by a solicitor or recognised body; or receiving a reprimand, sanction or fine. Further information on the cases, including full details of the offence(s) each solicitor was convicted for and sentence they received, can be found at the Appendix.

Categorising the means of facilitation

Analysis of cases of solicitors convicted for money laundering offences in the UK shows the wide range of actions for which they can be considered to have facilitated money laundering on behalf of their clients. While many of the cases involve methods of facilitation that we might expect to find, such as the use of client accounts and conveyancing processes, others are less easy to categorise, and the data highlight the heterogeneity of the actions, behaviours, transactions, actors and relationships involved. The cases have been allocated to the following four categories: (1) buying or selling property; (2) (mis)use of client account; (3) corporate vehicles and offshore accounts; and (4) other legal or financial services. Each case summary has been compiled by amalgamating data from a variety of publicly available sources (including Court of Appeal transcripts; Solicitors Disciplinary Tribunal transcripts; media reports; law enforcement, regulator and prosecuting authority press releases; reports, articles and other legal professional publications) to provide an overview of the case and relevant points. As such, they represent my interpretation of the case, based on the data available. It should be noted that the amount and quality of the data available for each case varied; for some it was very limited, while for others the data contained considerable detail. Table 4.2 details the different sources used, referenced under each case summary.

Buying or selling property

In six of the cases identified, the solicitor had been convicted for acting in the purchase or sale of residential property, by individuals using the proceeds of crime to purchase a property or multiple properties, or selling property that had been bought using the proceeds of crime and was thus considered to be a criminal asset. The role of the convicted solicitor in these cases was in the conveyancing: conducting the legal and administrative work required for the transfer of property.

---

4 Richard Housley practised in Scotland and so was sanctioned by the Scottish Solicitors' Discipline Tribunal; all others for whom a record was available were sanctioned by the Solicitors Disciplinary Tribunal (England and Wales).

Table 4.2 Sources used to inform case summaries

Reference	Description
CoA	Court of Appeal of England and Wales transcript
SDT	Solicitors Disciplinary Tribunal transcript
SSDT	Scottish Solicitors' Discipline Tribunal transcript
Sentencing Statement	Judiciary of Scotland Sentencing Statement
Press Release	Press release(s) published by e.g. police forces, Serious Fraud Office (SFO), Her Majesty's Revenue and Customs (HMRC)
Media	Newspaper or other media article(s)
Article	Other article(s) or report(s), for example, in publications by legal professionals or professional bodies

Case 5: Brian Dougan

Brian Dougan, a 48-year-old solicitor from County Armagh, Northern Ireland, was convicted in July 2006 at Liverpool Crown Court of converting or transferring the proceeds of criminal conduct, under section 93 of the Criminal Justice Act (CJA) 1988. His conviction related to funds he handled on behalf of Thomas McCague, convicted of involvement in a major fuel fraud. Dougan acted for McCague in the purchase of 11 properties. It was estimated that £66,500 of the proceeds of McCague's criminal activity were used as deposits for the purchase of these properties, and this money was believed to have been transferred through Dougan's firm's client account. Dougan was sentenced to three months' imprisonment following his conviction, and was issued with a confiscation order for the £66,500.

(Sources: Press Release, Media, Article)

Case 6: Philip Griffiths

Philip Griffiths acted as conveyancer in the sale of a property owned by Peter and Donna Davis, who had been convicted for involvement in a drug trafficking conspiracy. Following their conviction in 2004, the Davises sold the property (their primary asset) in what was considered to be an attempt to thwart confiscation proceedings. They had purchased the property for £83,000, with a mortgage of £43,000 arranged by Leslie Pattison, an estate agent. When they sold the property, it was valued at £150,000, but they sold it to Pattison for £43,000. Griffiths acted in this sale, having been asked to do so by Pattison, whom he had known for a number of years. Griffiths had previously acted for the Davises in another property sale in 2001, and had later been served with a production order in relation to that transaction, suggesting that he had known that they were being investigated for drug trafficking at the time of the transaction for which he was convicted. Griffiths stated that Pattison had told him that he was buying out the mortgage to help some friends who were in financial difficulties.

Griffiths was charged with entering into a money laundering agreement, but was acquitted of this charge and instead convicted of failing to make a required disclosure to the authorities, under section 330 of POCA 2002. It was accepted by the Court that he had reasonable grounds for knowledge or suspicion that another person was engaged in money laundering, but not that he had actual knowledge of the laundering. Griffiths was sentenced to 15 months' imprisonment, which was later reduced to six months on appeal. He was struck off by the Solicitors Disciplinary Tribunal on 24 July 2007.

(Sources: SDT, CoA, Article)

Case 12: Aminat Afolabi

Aminat Afolabi was involved in the conveyancing of a property bought, and later sold, by a company controlled by her husband, who was subsequently convicted for fraud offences. She was convicted in June 2009 of three counts of entering into or being concerned in a money laundering arrangement contrary to section 328 of POCA 2002, and one offence of acquiring criminal property contrary to section 329 of POCA 2002. In December the same year, the Court of Appeal quashed the convictions on two of the counts under section 328.

Afolabi set up a firm of solicitors prior to becoming qualified. Until she became qualified she was practice manager of the firm; after she was admitted as a solicitor in April 2007, she became a partner at the firm. The conviction which remained under POCA 2002 section 328 arose from the sale of the property by her husband's company, for which Afolabi was involved in the conveyancing (the conveyancing had been done by another partner in the firm). Subsequent to the sale, Mr Afolabi was convicted for fraudulent activities and received a substantial prison sentence; the property in question had been purchased using funds derived from his criminal activity. Aminat Afolabi's conviction under POCA 2002 section 329 arose from a series of money transfers made to her from her husband. She was sentenced to 18 months imprisonment, and was struck off by the Solicitors Disciplinary Tribunal on 12 January 2012.

(Sources: SDT, CoA)

Case 13: Shadab Khan

Shadab Khan was convicted in September 2009 on one count of money laundering and two counts of failing to disclose knowledge or suspicion of money laundering. The offences for which Khan was convicted were related to conveyancing work he had carried out for Khalid Malik, who had been sentenced to 25 years' imprisonment in December 2005 for importing 130 kilograms of heroin. Khan conducted conveyancing for properties worth £593,000 for Malik. Khan was sentenced to four years' imprisonment, with a further 12 months to run concurrently. He was struck off by the Solicitors Disciplinary Tribunal on 15 December 2011.

(Sources: SDT, Media, Article)

Case 16: James Thorburn-Muirhead

James Thorburn-Muirhead was convicted in February 2011 of one offence of failure to make a required disclosure of suspicion of money laundering, contrary to POCA 2002 section 330, as well as a number of offences related to the theft of clients' money and false accounting. The money laundering offence was related to Thorburn-Muirhead's involvement in various property transactions for a convicted drug dealer, many of which involved the lodgement of cash deposits. Thorburn-Muirhead was sentenced to 16 months imprisonment, and was struck off by the Solicitors Disciplinary Tribunal at his hearing on 9 December 2011.

(Sources: SDT, Media, Article)

Case 18: Andrew Tidd

Andrew Tidd acted in a number of transactions on behalf of Nevzat Kocabey over a four-year period, including acting as conveyancing solicitor in the purchase of two properties. In August 2007, Kocabey instructed Tidd in the purchase of a £105,000 house and in October 2007 he further instructed Tidd in the purchase of a £72,500 house. The deposits paid on these properties amounted to over £26,000, which was considered to have come from the proceeds of Kocabey's criminal activity. Kocabey had been in custody in 2005 for drug offences.

Tidd was convicted in February 2012 on five counts of failing to report knowledge or suspicion of money laundering, under section 330 of POCA 2002. He was sentenced to four months' imprisonment, suspended for 12 months, concurrent for each of the five counts. On 17 December 2013, he appeared before the Solicitors Disciplinary Tribunal and was fined £2,500, but was not struck off.

(Sources: SDT, Press Release, Media, Article)

(Mis)use of client account

In seven of the 20 cases analysed, passing criminal proceeds through the firm's client account was identified as the primary means of facilitation of money laundering. A client account is a bank account maintained by a legal practice for holding client money. There are two types: general or 'pooled' accounts, which can hold funds from multiple clients, and 'designated' client accounts, which are for money relating to a single client. Client accounts are used to receive fees and deposits, issue or cash cheques, facilitate funds transfers or purchases, and make disbursements to or on behalf of the client. Therefore, in the other categories described, funds may also have been held in, or transferred through, a client account (for example, the deposits used in property purchases), but in this category it is the use of the general client account for passing money from one location to another that is the primary means by which criminal proceeds are managed, and the solicitor's actions in facilitating this that resulted in their conviction.

Case 1: Jonathan Duff

Jonathan Duff was convicted at Manchester Crown Court in July 2002 for failure to disclose knowledge or suspicion of money laundering, under the Drug Trafficking Act (DTA) 1994 section 52. He had been involved in a number of transactions on behalf of businessman Gene Gibson over a three-year period. Gibson was later convicted of drug trafficking offences and the money involved in these transactions was considered to be the proceeds of drug trafficking activity.

In 1998, Gibson had been arrested with a business associate at Birmingham Airport in possession of cocaine valued at about £5 million. Duff acted for Gibson in the criminal proceedings, having become his solicitor five years earlier. Six months after the initial arrest, Gibson and his associate were further charged with conspiracy to import drugs between October 1996 and March 1998, during which time it was alleged they had undertaken more than 30 illicit trips between Dusseldorf and the UK for drug trafficking purposes.

Duff had been involved in a number of transactions on behalf of Gibson during the 1996–1998 period, including: £10,000 paid to Duff by Gibson for costs of ongoing litigation; £50,000 paid to Duff as an investment in a proposed branch office (this was returned to Gibson by cheque a short time later); and £10,000 paid by Gibson into a company set up to solicit personal injury compensation business for Duff's practice. The venture was unsuccessful, and the money was said to have been consumed in advertising and other costs. Following Gibson and his associate's convictions in 1999, Duff took advice from a solicitor in relation to his reporting requirements under section 52 of the DTA 1994; they agreed that there was no duty to report the transactions as they were in the past.

Duff was arrested in October 1999 and convicted in 2002. He was sentenced to six months' imprisonment and was subsequently struck off by the Solicitors Disciplinary Tribunal in May 2003 (he had been disciplined by the Tribunal for other accounting and professional conduct charges and was already on suspension at the time of this hearing).

(Sources: SDT, CoA, Media, Article)

Case 2: Paul Winter-Morris

Paul Winter-Morris was convicted under section 93A of the Criminal Justice Act (CJA) 1988 of three counts of assisting another to retain or control the benefit of criminal conduct.

The convictions related to the laundering of £8 million from a large-scale VAT fraud committed by Raymond Woolley. Just over £5 million had been transferred by Woolley to a bank account in the name of Viltern, a Dublin-based company, and just under £3 million to a bank account in the name of Hocus SL, a Spanish company. The funds were then transferred to the client account of the solicitor's firm where Morris was a partner. Morris arranged these transfers in the names of six different clients. Individual disbursements were then made from the client account, disguised as ordinary solicitor-client transactions. Over £4.5 million was transferred to a company called Thornbush Entertainment Inc. (USA), and other amounts were used for the purchase of a yacht and a number of cars.

Morris was sentenced to five years' imprisonment for each of the three counts, to run concurrently. He was struck off by the Solicitors Disciplinary Tribunal at his hearing on 24 February 2007. He was recalled to prison in February 2011 for failing to pay all of a £410,000 confiscation order, for which he was sentenced to a further three years.

(Sources: SDT, CoA, Media, Article)

Case 3: Andrew Young

Andrew Young was a solicitor in the firm he had set up and ran alone in Manchester. In September 2004, he was convicted of two counts of assisting another to retain the benefit of criminal conduct, contrary to section 93A of the CJA 1988.

Young allowed the proceeds of a number of mortgage frauds carried out by John Fitzpatrick (a solicitor at another firm), Noel Ward (a mortgage broker) and others, to be transferred into his firm's client account. The frauds, which generated over £1 million, involved applications for mortgage advances being made with artificially inflated property prices. The proceeds of the frauds were transferred from Fitzpatrick's legal firm to the client account of Young's firm, where he held the funds before disbursing them as required by Fitzpatrick and Ward. Young was sentenced to 27 months' imprisonment for each count, to run consecutively to a sentence he was already serving for theft.

(Sources: CoA, Press Release, Media, Article)

Case 7: Gerard Hyde

Gerard Hyde was a commercial property solicitor who allowed his firm's client account, and a bank account he controlled in the Isle of Man, to be used to launder the proceeds of a VAT fraud involving the importation of mobile phones. It was estimated that the fraud operated for 16 months and generated around £30 million in criminal proceeds. Hyde was believed to have laundered £2 million of these proceeds, over an eight-month period. He was convicted of concealing or disguising the proceeds of criminal conduct contrary to section 93C of the CJA 1988 in March 2007, and sentenced to 42 months' imprisonment. He was struck off by the Solicitors Disciplinary Tribunal on 9 December 2008.

(Sources: SDT, Media, Article)

Case 8: Jonathan Krestin

Jonathan Krestin was convicted in November 2008 of one charge of facilitating the acquisition, retention, use or control of criminal property by or on behalf of another person, contrary to section 328 of POCA 2002. He was cleared on three other counts. His conviction related to a transaction involving the proceeds of a large scale missing trader intra-community fraud (MTIC, or carousel, fraud; a form of VAT fraud) conducted by Michel Namer. Between 2003 and 2005, Krestin undertook small amounts of commercial work for Namer. The transaction for which he was convicted was the receipt into his firm's client account of €14,000 from a company called Kilmeston Ltd (on the instructions of Namer), and its subsequent disbursement to the bank account of Namer's partner. This payment had been made just a few days after Krestin had received a production order setting out a criminal case against Namer and warning him about the offence of 'tipping off' Namer. The jury found Krestin not guilty of three other counts in relation to transactions that had taken place before receipt of the production order.

Krestin was sentenced to a fine of £5,000 and ordered to pay £9,517 (the sterling equivalent of €14,000) under a POCA confiscation order. Krestin was 'severely reprimanded' by the Solicitors Disciplinary Tribunal on 27 October 2010, but was not struck off the roll of solicitors.

(Sources: SDT, Press Release, Article)

Case 15: Bhadresh Gohil

Bhadresh Gohil was convicted in 2010 on a number of counts relating to the laundering of $37 million, stolen from the state of Delta in Nigeria by James Ibori, then governor of the state. Ibori is believed to have defrauded $250 million from the Nigerian people over a period of eight years. The $37 million related to Gohil's conviction represented the proceeds from the sale of Delta state's share in a mobile phone company to a neighbouring state.

Gohil was convicted for allowing the use of his firm's client account for the money to pass through, opening other bank accounts to be used in the same way, and creating a series of complex financial transactions. He was also found to have assisted in the purchase of a Challenger jet from Bombardier at a cost of $20 million, and kept Ibori's ownership of this jet a secret, by developing a scheme to ensure that the ownership of the jet was made as complicated and obscure as possible, using bank accounts and companies registered in various countries.

Gohil was sentenced to 10 years' imprisonment for the various offences, including money laundering and conspiracy to defraud offences. He was struck off by the Solicitors Disciplinary Tribunal on 8 October 2012.[5]

(Sources: SDT, CoA, Media, Article)

Case 19: Richard Housley

Richard Housley was convicted in January 2013 for laundering money totalling £1.8 million, the proceeds of a VAT fraud scheme run by Michael Voudouri. As well as being the director of a clothing firm owned by Voudouri, which was considered to have been used as a 'front' for money laundering, Housley was found to have allowed proceeds of the frauds to be moved through his firm's client account. Funds were transferred into the client account of Housley's firm from a number of bank accounts outside the UK, and subsequently disbursed on the instruction of Voudouri and others.

Housley was convicted on one charge of entering into or becoming concerned in an arrangement facilitating the acquisition, retention, use or control of criminal property, under POCA 2002 section 328 and one charge of failure to report suspicious transactions, under POCA 2002 section 330. He was also convicted of income tax fraud. He was sentenced to four years' imprisonment, and was struck off the roll of solicitors by the Scottish Solicitors' Discipline Tribunal (SSDT) in June 2015. Housley was subsequently given a confiscation order for nearly £100,000.

(Sources: SSDT, Sentencing Statement, Press Release, Media, Article)

Corporate vehicles and offshore accounts

Concern about the role of legal professionals in the facilitation of money laundering often focuses on the assistance they can provide through the creation and management of companies and other corporate vehicles, such as trusts and foundations, and the use of bank accounts in off-shore locations. Corporate vehicles can be used as a means of confusing or disguising the links between offenders and the proceeds of their crimes, and off-shore bank accounts provide a level of secrecy that can be used to hide illicit funds (i.e. the proceeds of crime, money on which tax is being evaded, or funds being used in the commission of crime). Of course, such financial constructions are not illegal in themselves and are used for legitimate reasons; for example, for the purposes of privacy, security and financial planning. However, there are increasing concerns over the use of

---

5 Gohil later appealed his conviction based on allegations of corruption in relation to the Metropolitan Police Service and a firm of private investigators. The appeal was rejected and Gohil was charged with perverting the course of justice by making the allegations of police corruption. The prosecution against him collapsed, after the Crown Prosecution Service withdrew the charge.

corporate vehicles such as 'shell companies' to hide their 'beneficial owners' (i.e. the person[s] who ultimately owns, controls or benefits from the company or other asset) for illegitimate reasons. The 2017 UK *National Risk Assessment of Money Laundering and Terrorist Financing* assessed the risk of criminals using UK and overseas corporate structures to launder money as 'high', stating that 'corporate structures and trusts are used in almost all high-end money laundering cases, including to launder the proceeds of corruption' (HM Treasury/Home Office 2017: 58), though it goes on to admit that there 'is insufficient evidence to quantify the exact extent of money laundering through corporate structures and trusts (both UK registered and overseas)' and that 'the vast majority of UK trusts, companies and partnerships are assessed to be used for legitimate purposes' (HM Treasury/Home Office 2017: 58). The case of the law firm, Mossack Fonseca, which was revealed by the 'Panama Papers' to have registered more than 200,000 shell companies in secrecy haven locations, raised the profile of – and concern about – the misuse of corporate vehicles to move and conceal illicit funds, and the role that law firms play in this.[6] The subsequent 'Russian Laundromat' and 'Azerbaijani Laundromat' investigations further highlighted the use of corporate vehicles in complex, large-scale money laundering schemes.[7]

However, in the cases of solicitors convicted of money laundering offences analysed in this research, there was little indication of the use of corporate vehicles or off-shore accounts as a means of facilitation, with only two of the cases categorised in this way:

Case 14: Martin Wilcock

Martin Wilcock was convicted in September 2010 of one offence under section 330 of POCA 2002, for failing to disclose knowledge or suspicion of money laundering. Wilcock represented Michael Nevin, who was convicted for housing undocumented migrants in three hotels. He failed to disclose knowledge or suspicion that the money Nevin earned through the hotels was the proceeds of crime. In addition, he transferred ownership of the hotels to an offshore company owned by Nevin while Nevin was under a criminal investigation. Following his conviction, Wilcock was fined £2,500. He was

---

6 The 'Panama Papers' refers to 11.5 million files leaked from the database of Mossack Fonseca, then the world's biggest off-shore law firm. The records were obtained by the German newspaper *Süddeutsche Zeitung* from an anonymous source in 2015, and were shared with the International Consortium of Investigative Journalists (ICIJ) and international partners. See www.icij.org/investigations/panama-papers/ [Accessed 29 July 2019].

7 The so-called Russian Laundromat is a complex scheme involving numerous bank accounts and shell companies used to move large sums of money (estimated at more than $20 billion) out of Russia, exposed by journalists at the Organized Crime and Corruption Reporting Project (OCCRP) in 2014 www.occrp.org/en/laundromat/the-russian-laundromat-exposed/ [Accessed 29 July 2019]. In 2017, the group reported details of a similar scheme related to Azerbaijani government officials, along with a network of politicians, businessmen and others www.occrp.org/en/azerbaijanilaundromat/ [Accessed 29 July 2019].

suspended from practice for three months by the Solicitors Disciplinary Tribunal on 30 May 2012.

(Sources: SDT, Media, Article)

Case 15: Bhadresh Gohil

Bhadresh Gohil has been included in this category as well as the previous '(Mis)use of client account' category, because of the range of actions undertaken on behalf of James Ibori. As well as the use of his firm's client account to transfer some of the money defrauded by Ibori, Gohil's convictions also related to the movement of funds into off-shore trusts and shell companies, and use of such companies to conceal Ibori's ownership of a jet.

(Sources: SDT, CoA, Media, Article)

The lack of involvement of corporate vehicles and offshore accounts in the cases examined might suggest that they are not commonly used by legal professionals to facilitate money laundering, despite the concern in this area and recent high-profile cases. On the other hand, it may actually tell us something about the types of cases that are prosecuted. This research focused on cases of lawyers who had received a criminal conviction for their involvement in money laundering. There will be other cases where legal professionals or firms are found to have breached money laundering regulations but are dealt with through regulatory processes only. For example, in the case of Mossack Fonseca, no criminal charges were brought against the firm (to date) in relation to the transactions highlighted by the Panama Papers, but it was fined $440,000 by the British Virgin Islands Financial Services Commission for breaches of anti-money laundering and other regulations. This raises questions about whether more complex cases, involving corporate vehicles and off-shore accounts, for example, are less likely to result in criminal prosecution or conviction and, if so, why this is the case. Is it simply due to their complexity and the challenges of investigating transactions hidden behind financial constructions whose purpose is to provide secrecy and conceal ownership? Or is the nature of the predicate offence also a factor? If professionals involved in facilitating money laundering are primarily identified through investigation and/or prosecution related to the initial proceeds-generating criminal activity, does the nature of the cases of facilitation that have led to a conviction tell us something about the types of predicate offence or offender that are more likely to be investigated and prosecuted?

Other legal or financial services

The remaining six cases are less easily categorised, but can be considered to fall broadly within the provision of legal and/or financial services. Within the cases in this section are a solicitor who paid bail for a client using what was considered to be the proceeds of illegal activity (ANTHONY BLOK; Case 11); a solicitor who wrote to a bank to try and have an account unfrozen on behalf of his clients

(ANDREW WORMSTONE; Case 20); a solicitor who had written a series of figures on the back of a letter purporting to be the income, expenses and profit of a non-existent motor trading business (RACHEL TAYLOR; Case 10); and a trainee solicitor who had witnessed an email, allowed the use of his headed stationery and provided legal advice for his brother, who was involved in mortgage fraud (MOHAMMED JAHANGIR FARID; Case 9). They underscore the heterogeneity of this sample of cases, demonstrating the variety of behaviours which can be considered as the facilitation of money laundering, and for which legal professionals can be convicted of money laundering offences. They also demonstrate the varying levels of complexity of the transactions or services provided, and highlight the different relationships involved.

Case 4: Peter Obidi

Peter Obidi was associated with a number of solicitors' firms in London, as well as running his own unregistered practice from his home address between 2001 and 2005. Obidi met Mr I in a social setting; Mr I told Obidi that he raised money for charitable projects around the world and requested his help with some financial matters. At some point during this (unofficial) arrangement, Mr I requested that Obidi accept an £18,000 cheque from an associate, Mr M. Subsequently, Obidi paid the cheque into his account and, once it had cleared, went with Mr I to withdraw it by way of a banker's draft and cash. Mr I was later convicted of conspiracy to defraud the £18,000 from Mr M.

In October 2004, Obidi was convicted of assisting another to retain or control benefit of criminal conduct, under the CJA 1988 section 93, and sentenced to six months' imprisonment. He was struck off by the Solicitors Disciplinary Tribunal on 8 November 2005, as a result of this conviction and a number of other actions including failing to register his own practice, practising without insurance, and practising without a certificate.

(Sources: SDT)

Case 9: Mohammed Jahangir Farid

Mohammed Jahangir Farid used his position as a solicitor to assist his brother, Rashid Farid, to manage the proceeds of a series of mortgage fraud offences. Rashid Farid, a qualified accountant and financial advisor, was jailed for 11 years in 2009 for masterminding a large-scale mortgage fraud that defrauded mortgage companies of approximately £800,000. The money was transferred into various bank accounts and eventually sent to Pakistan. A number of others were convicted of involvement in the fraud and/or money laundering.

Mohammed Jahangir Farid was convicted in April 2009 of entering into or becoming concerned in an arrangement facilitating the acquisition, retention, use or control of criminal property under section 328 of POCA 2002, in relation to the proceeds of the mortgage frauds. While it was accepted that his role fell short of a conspirator, he had given advice to his brother, witnessed an email about transfer of title, and used his firm's headed notepaper to produce a forged document which was used in relation to the satisfaction of the money transferor. It was for these actions that he was convicted of a money laundering offence.

Jahangir Farid was sentenced to four years' imprisonment. As he was a trainee solicitor, the Solicitors Disciplinary Tribunal ordered that he should not be employed or remunerated as a solicitor or by another solicitor.

(Sources: SDT, CoA, Media, Article)

Case 10: Rachel Taylor

Rachel Taylor was convicted for assistance she had provided to her former partner, Pardeep Bains. Bains was convicted for drug dealing and laundering the proceeds of his criminal activity through family members' bank accounts and properties. When the police began to look into these accounts, he contacted HMRC to say that he wanted to declare income from his motor trading business (which did not actually exist). Bains went to Taylor with blank tax returns and asked for her help. On the back of a letter from HMRC, Taylor wrote out a series of figures purporting to be the income, expenses and profit from Bains' motor trading for the year 2005/2006. Bains took these figures to his accountant, but the accountant did not accept them or act on them. Taylor's conviction was on the basis that she suspected that the money was the product of criminal activity on Bains' part when writing out these figures.

Taylor was convicted in May 2009 on one count of disguising criminal property, contrary to section 327 of POCA 2002. She was sentenced to 39 weeks imprisonment, suspended for 18 months, with requirements to carry out 200 hours community work and pay a fine of £5,015. She was suspended from practice by the Solicitors Disciplinary Tribunal for 12 months on 22 September 2010.

(Sources: SDT, Press Release, Media)

Case 11: Anthony Blok

Anthony Blok was convicted for money laundering offences related to £75,000 he paid in cash to court for the bail of one of his clients, who had been arrested for money laundering. Blok had applied for bail for his client and subsequently called his client's daughter as a witness to provide evidence about the limited funds available to the family to meet the bail requirements. A few days later, Blok deposited £75,000 with the court cashier. When questioned about its origins, Blok said he was given the funds outside the court by a man he did not know, and understood the funds to have been raised by family and friends over the weekend. However, CCTV footage showed Blok meeting the client's daughter and another woman who handed him two bags of money. The court accepted that, in the circumstances, it was not reasonable for that amount of money to have been raised legitimately in such a short space of time, and that the false story provided by Blok demonstrated that he knew or suspected that the funds were from a criminal source.

Blok was convicted in July 2009 of three money laundering offences under POCA 2002, alongside other offences related to his helping a client to sell a stolen painting. He was sentenced to a total of four years for all the offences. By the time of his Solicitors Disciplinary Tribunal hearing in December 2010, he had already removed his name from the roll of solicitors. Therefore, the Tribunal ordered that he be prohibited from having his name restored to the roll.

(Sources: SDT, Press Release, Media, Article)

Case 17: Nicholas Heywood

Nicholas Heywood was convicted in December 2011 on two counts of prejudicing a money laundering investigation, one count of perverting the course of justice, and one count of concealing, disguising, transferring or removing criminal property, contrary to section 327 of POCA 2002. Heywood represented a lottery winner who was targeted by a fraudster, who took out a fraudulent loan in the lottery winner's name. Heywood transferred £13,750 of this loan to himself. He was sentenced to six months' imprisonment following his conviction, and was struck off by the Solicitors Disciplinary Tribunal on 16 October 2012.

(Sources: SDT, Media, Article)

Case 20: Andrew Wormstone

Andrew Wormstone used his position as a solicitor to attempt to have the proceeds of a fraud released to those who had committed it. A group of individuals led by Gurdip Singh had defrauded £2 million from Sussex University. The money was obtained when officials at Sussex University thought that they were dealing with a legitimate construction firm chosen to carry out redevelopment of student accommodation, on the basis of a forged invoice. The forged invoice instructed the University to pay the money into an account controlled by Singh, under the name Balecourt Ltd. The theft was discovered a few days after payment had been made, and the Balecourt account was immediately frozen. Singh and his associates tried unsuccessfully to persuade the bank to release the funds. Having failed to convince the bank that the funds were obtained legitimately, Wormstone sent documents to the bank purporting to show that Singh and associates were clients of his and that he was acting on their behalf in high-value land deals. None of the deals existed.

Wormstone was convicted in February 2013 on one count of entering into or becoming concerned in an arrangement facilitating the acquisition, retention, use or control of criminal property, contrary to POCA 2002 section 328. He was sentenced to two-and-a-half years' imprisonment, and was struck off by the Solicitors Disciplinary Tribunal on 24 October 2013.

(Sources: SDT, Press Release, Media)

Nature of the predicate offence

For the 20 cases analysed, the offences that generated the proceeds that the solicitors were found to have been involved in laundering can be categorised as in Table 4.3.

Drug trafficking and various forms of fraudulent activity, therefore, made up the clear majority of the predicate crimes. It is notable that none of the cases involved what would be considered as 'traditional' white-collar or corporate crimes (other than fraud), such as anti-trust activities, insider trading, bribery, or offences by corporations or financial institutions. It seems unlikely that there is no involvement of legal professionals in the management of the proceeds of these types of offences, especially with the amounts that may be involved. This raises questions, therefore, about their lack of representation in the cases of convicted solicitors. Are lawyers and other facilitators in corporate or white-collar crimes less likely to be detected, prosecuted or convicted of money laundering offences? If so, why is this the case? Are they more likely to be dealt with in other ways, or are they able to 'slip through the net' completely? There are also questions about the perceptions of money laundering, and whether it is primarily associated with what would be considered as 'organised crime' or activities related to traditional illicit markets. There has been a clear shift in recent years to an increasing focus on 'high-end' money laundering and the proceeds of high-level economic crime, such as corruption and tax evasion (and a greater focus on offending within financial markets following the financial crisis of 2008). Therefore, it may be the case that if this research was repeated, there would be a greater representation of such offending.

Table 4.3 Predicate offences involved in the cases

Predicate offence	Number of cases
Drug trafficking	6
MTIC/VAT fraud	4
Mortgage fraud	2
Other fraud	5
Political corruption	1
Immigration crime	1
Unknown	1

Heterogeneity

The cases analysed demonstrate the multiplicity of actions (or non-action) that can be considered to facilitate money laundering. There is no legal definition or specific criminal offence of 'facilitating money laundering' in the UK; instead, we have to identify this by reference to the various relevant money laundering offences laid out in the Proceeds of Crime Act 2002 (detailed in Chapter 2), and where the individual(s) involved did not also commit the predicate offence (i.e. 'self-laundering'). Cases of 'facilitation of money laundering', therefore, are shaped by the nature of the legislation and what is deemed a criminal offence. This means, for example, that they include instances of not reporting suspicions of money laundering, and do not only include those who were complicit or *actively involved* in the laundering; the legislation allows for prosecution with varying levels of knowingness, intent and complicity (this will be discussed further in Chapters 6 and 7). There are a number of ways that this research could have chosen to identify cases of 'facilitation of money laundering' by lawyers; for example, it could have broadened the scope to include those who had been disciplined by the regulator for involvement in 'transactions that bore the hallmarks of money laundering',[8] or it could have used an alternative starting point by examining cases of 'money laundering' and identifying where lawyers had (or could have) played a role. By choosing to focus on cases of lawyers convicted of money laundering offences in the UK, where the offences committed were related to their professional position and the criminal proceeds involved were generated by others, the *nature of the facilitation* seen is shaped by the nature of money laundering legislation in the UK, which in turn is shaped by the wider anti-money laundering regime and regulatory environment. For this reason, it is important to take into account the context of the global regime, and the legislative and regulatory environments that have emerged from that, when trying to understand the facilitation of money laundering, and how these act to *label*

---

8 For example, Gavin Wilcock, the sole practitioner of a law firm in Great Yarmouth, Norfolk, appeared before the Solicitors Disciplinary Tribunal in August 2016 accused of having 'involved himself in transactions that bore the hallmarks of money laundering'. This followed an investigation into the firm by the Solicitors Regulation Authority which identified payments made into and out of the firm's client accounts where 'there were no underlying transactions'. Wilcock was suspended from practice as a solicitor for 12 months, with a number of conditions imposed following the end of his suspension. He had not been convicted of a criminal offence in relation to this (Solicitors Disciplinary Tribunal Case No. 11474–2016). Two of the partners in the law firm involved in the mortgage fraud whose proceeds ANDREW YOUNG (Case 3) was convicted for laundering were found by the SDT to have 'acted in transactions for which there was no underlying legal nature and which had the hallmarks of money laundering'. However, they noted that 'although the allegations concern transactions where there might well have been mortgage fraud and money laundering perpetrated the Tribunal has not been made aware whether or not those transactions did involve those serious criminal offences' (Solicitors Disciplinary Tribunal Case No. 8382–2001).

certain actions or non-actions as breaches of professional or regulatory norms or even criminal offences.

As the cases summarised in this chapter are cases of *convicted* solicitors, they represent only those for whom a criminal prosecution was brought and a conviction secured. They do not include those who were not detected, detected but not prosecuted (for example, those who were dealt with through regulatory processes only), or prosecuted without being convicted. The 20 cases, therefore, provide a snapshot only; they do not show the full range by which legal professionals could be involved in laundering criminal proceeds, and so should not be seen as an exhaustive account of such. Yet, despite the restrictions on the sample, there is still considerable variation in the actions and behaviours of the solicitor and their client(s), the transactions and processes involved, the purpose of the transactions, the nature and form of the criminal proceeds, and the relationships involved (including personal as well as solicitor-client relationships; this will be discussed in the following chapter).

Complexity of the transactions

The transactions involved are also of varying levels of complexity. Official discourse suggests that legal and financial professionals are playing a greater role in money laundering activity because of the increasingly complex nature of financial transactions used to manage criminal proceeds, which require the specialist skills and services that such professionals can provide (e.g. FATF 2010, 2013; NCA 2016). Likewise, there is a tendency within the money laundering literature and related policy to stress the complexity and sophistication of money laundering arrangements and processes. However, much of what is seen in the data is more mundane, with many transactions that appear to be unsophisticated and lacking in complexity. While some of the solicitors were involved in relatively complex financial arrangements – such as BHADRESH GOHIL (Case 15), who created a number of complex financial transactions to move significant criminal funds around, or RICHARD HOUSELY (Case 19), who allowed funds from several bank accounts outside the UK to be moved via his firm's client account to other bank accounts and individuals – many other cases involved more straightforward transactions. For example, JONATHAN KRESTIN (Case 8) was convicted for his involvement in a simple transfer of money from one account to another, via his firm's client account; ANDREW YOUNG (Case 3) received the proceeds of mortgage fraud from one source, and made smaller disbursements back out of the client account; and PETER OBIDI (Case 4) paid a cheque into his bank account and subsequently regained the funds by way of cash and a banker's draft. These are not complex financial transactions. Many of the conveyancing cases involved the purchase or sale of one or a small number of residential properties, and the figures involved in these transactions were not particularly high. RACHEL TAYLOR (Case 10) wrote out a series of figures on the back of a letter; these figures were not accepted by the accountant they were supposed to convince, and so were not able ultimately to provide cover for laundering. This case demonstrates the lack of sophistication in the means by which the 'facilitation' of money laundering can occur.

Of course, the transaction(s) for which the solicitor was convicted in these cases may not have been the only transaction(s) they conducted with criminal proceeds; other, more complex, transactions may not have been detected or proven. Furthermore, it is likely that there are more complex financial transactions being conducted with criminal money in the UK, involving the assistance of legal professionals, for which there is no conviction or the offence is not detected. Again, this raises questions about whether legal professionals involved in more complex money laundering are less likely to be prosecuted, or successful convictions less likely to be achieved, and about the challenges of investigating or proving involvement in complex laundering transactions. The lack of availability of – or access to – relevant data makes this more difficult to analyse; examining complex money laundering cases for evidence of the involvement of professionals would be one approach, and would certainly be an area for further research. What is clear from the data available for this research is the relative simplicity of many of the transactions involving criminal proceeds that appear in the cases examined.

Purpose

Finally, it is important to note that categorising the cases in terms of the *means of facilitation*, as in this chapter and much of the existing academic and official literature, does not take into account the underlying purpose of the transaction – that is, what the predicate offender is trying to achieve through the transaction. For example, ANTHONY BLOK (Case 11) used criminal proceeds, given to him by a client's family, to pay bail on behalf of his client. For this, he was considered to have been involved in money laundering and convicted of money laundering offences. In this case, the transaction that Blok was involved in was not being carried out *as a means of legitimising* criminal proceeds – that was not its primary objective; it was criminal money *being used for a purpose*, in this case to pay bail. On the other hand, ANDREW WORMSTONE (Case 20) used his position as a legal professional to try to convince a bank that the proceeds of a fraud had been earned through *legitimate means*, and was therefore seeking to conceal the origins of criminal proceeds and provide them with a *false appearance of legitimacy*.

For all the cases that involve the buying or selling of property, we do not know whether the predicate offender was investing in property or buying somewhere for them or family members to live (as is regularly done with 'clean' money), or was using the transaction as a means of 'laundering' their criminal proceeds in the traditional sense: putting 'dirty' money into property in order to be able to take it out again 'clean': in other words, whether the purchasing of property was the end point itself or a means to an end. The involvement of lawyers in the management of criminal proceeds, therefore, may be due to criminals *choosing* to use them to provide the appearance of legitimacy to criminal proceeds ('money laundering' in the strict sense of the term), but it may also simply be that what they are using the proceeds of crime for involves legal professionals. This highlights one of the problems of categorising the facilitation of money laundering in this way: it acts to *decontextualise* the actions of the lawyers involved, grouping together those, for example, whole role relates to involvement in property transactions or who enable financial transactions using their client account, while losing sight of the individual circumstances and situational contexts in which these transactions take place.

Conclusion

This chapter has provided details of 20 cases of solicitors convicted of money laundering offences in the UK between 2002 and 2013, where the offences committed were related to their professional position and involved the facilitation of the laundering of criminal proceeds generated by others. The cases have been grouped into four categories, based on the nature of the 'facilitation' involved, with the purchase or sale of residential property and the (mis)use of the firm's client account being the most common means of facilitation seen. However, the data available on these cases demonstrate the variation within as well as between these groupings, in relation to the ways in which legal professionals can be involved in the management of criminal proceeds, the nature and purpose of the transactions they conduct or services they provide which involve criminal proceeds, the source and form of these proceeds, and the nature of their relationships with those who committed the predicate offence.

We should avoid the temptation, therefore, to see 'the facilitation of money laundering' as a singular phenomenon and ask what 'it' looks like, or 'lump together' all the ways in which professionals are involved in the management of the proceeds of crimes committed by others. Terms such as 'gatekeepers' or 'professional enablers' suggest a homogeneity of actors, actions and relations that does not exist. We should also be wary of relying on simple categorisations to describe and delineate different methods of 'facilitation', as I have done in the first part of this chapter and is seen in much of the existing literature. While this is useful for identifying services provided by professionals that are – or can be – used by those in possession of criminal proceeds, and highlighting areas of vulnerability for certain professions, it tends to decontextualise the behaviours and decision-making involved. Many of the cases identified in this research involve individual, possibly one-off actions that emerge out of particular circumstances at a particular point in time, and cannot be easily grouped with others. We need to move beyond *descriptions* of actions and processes, therefore, to understand the *contexts* of these actions and the decisions they involve, and the factors that shape individual lawyers' roles in the facilitation of money laundering. The following chapter considers some of these factors. First, it focuses on how the occupational context and organisational setting of the legal profession can provide opportunities for those wishing to assist others in the laundering of their criminal proceeds and can make the profession vulnerable to exploitation for the purposes of laundering. It then considers how the nature of a legal professional's relationship with the predicate offender, and the potential financial or commercial benefit, could influence his/her involvement in the facilitation of money laundering.

5 Opportunity and vulnerability

Factors influencing lawyers' involvement in money laundering

Introduction

The nature of the legal profession, and the legitimate business activities and processes that it encompasses, can provide opportunities for those working within the profession to facilitate the laundering of criminal proceeds. The essential similarity of transactions which involve criminal proceeds to the 'normal' transactions that legal professionals carry out for legitimate clients provides them with the superficial appearance of legitimacy required to hide them from the view of the authorities and other 'capable guardians'. Furthermore, as with other offences committed by legitimate occupational actors, the 'invisibility' of transactions involving criminal proceeds is increased because the lawyer is 'legitimately present at the scene' (Croall 2001: 8). Principles of confidentiality and legal professional privilege that are a key function of the lawyer-client relationship in most jurisdictions may further shield interactions between lawyers and their clients that act to facilitate money laundering from external scrutiny. As well as the broader occupational characteristics – relevant for all those within the profession – that may influence lawyers' involvement in the facilitation of money laundering, firm-specific factors may create conditions that are more or less conducive to such involvement (as well as to other forms of misconduct). The structure and dynamics of particular legal practices (or particular *types* of practice) can create opportunities for those working within to provide assistance with laundering, or shape the availability of such opportunities, and organisational cultures and processes have been shown to influence individual behaviour and decision-making (e.g. Vaughan 1992, 2002; see Chapter 3 for discussion). However, the involvement of legal professionals in the facilitation of money laundering cannot only be seen through the lens of 'opportunity'. This would imply an active, knowing choice to assist the predicate offender in the laundering of their criminal proceeds, and a decision to take advantage of an available opportunity to do so, which, as will be discussed in the following chapter, is not evident in all cases of professional facilitation of money laundering. Therefore, the same factors that can provide *opportunities* for legal professionals to facilitate money laundering can also be considered as creating *vulnerabilities* for those working in the profession.

This chapter discusses a range of factors which may play a role in legal professionals' involvement in money laundering on behalf of others. It begins by considering how the occupational and organisational contexts in which legal professionals are situated may encourage such involvement, by providing opportunities and/or creating vulnerabilities for money laundering. The chapter highlights the relationship between transactions that serve to launder criminal proceeds and transactions that legal professionals carry out as part of their normal occupational role, the legitimate and specialised 'access' they have to functions and processes that enable the facilitation of money laundering, and thus the ability of transactions involving non-legitimate funds to be 'hidden' amongst legitimate activity. It also considers whether the size and complexity of the organisations in which legal professionals work could influence the likelihood of their becoming involved in money laundering; the implications of autonomy and a lack of internal oversight on misconduct by legal professionals; and the potential risks associated with new forms of organisation providing legal services. The chapter then examines two other factors which may influence legal professionals' involvement in the facilitation of money laundering: the financial benefit they receive from doing so, and the nature of their relationship with the predicate offender. The chapter argues that the structures, processes and transactions of the legal profession *provide opportunities* for individuals within the profession to assist others in the management of their criminal proceeds, and also *create vulnerabilities* for members of the profession because of the potential proximity of their occupational role to illegally derived funds. It suggests that actions taken by legal professionals which in some way 'facilitate money laundering', and the decisions they take which result in these actions, will be shaped by the situational contexts in which they occur, including both the occupational and organisational contexts and the nature of the relationship with the individual(s) in possession of the criminal proceeds.

'Normal' transactions

Most of the transactions that served to launder criminal proceeds in the cases examined in this research were 'normal' transactions; that is, they were the same transactions that legal professionals would carry out or facilitate on behalf of clients, for legitimate reasons, as part of their normal occupational role. For example, acting as conveyancer in the purchase or sale of property, passing money through the client account or using the client account in business transactions, and transferring ownership of assets, are all services that legal professionals will provide to legitimate clients on a regular basis. With 'clean' money these would be considered as routine business transactions, but with 'dirty' money, originating from illegal activity, these same transactions constitute money laundering. This means that non-legitimate transactions (or, transactions with non-legitimate funds) will be hidden amongst the legitimate transactions that make up the majority of lawyers' professional activity. As such, transactions conducted by lawyers involving criminal proceeds can be seen as being 'parasitical' on the legitimate transactions they carry out as a function of their regular occupational role (Benson, Madensen and Eck 2009: 185; Benson and Simpson 2018). This provides *opportunities* for money laundering, as legal professionals can hide non-legitimate transactions amongst their legitimate transactions, but it also creates *vulnerabilities* for those working in the profession, as transactions involving criminal funds can be hidden *from* them.

Property

The purchase of property using the proceeds of crime was one of the most common transactions seen in the cases analysed (Cases 5, 6, 12, 13, 16, 18), and solicitors interviewed during the research highlighted conveyancing as the area of business that was of most concern to them in relation to money laundering risk (interviewees S1; S2; S3). Interviewee S1, for example, suggested that it provided an "easy way" to move illicit funds through a law firm:

> [Conveyancing] is probably the biggest area, I would have thought, that there's most risk. Because it's an easy way to get money into the firm isn't it, and then out again.
>
> [S1]

The Solicitors Regulation Authority (SRA) *Risk Assessment on Anti-Money Laundering and Terrorist Financing* (March 2018) considers conveyancing as one of the services provided by solicitors that pose the highest risk for money laundering, along with client account services and trust and company formation (SRA 2018b). It reports that approximately half of the Suspicious Activity Reports (SARs) that are submitted by the legal sector in the UK relate to property transactions, suggesting that purchasing property is an attractive means of money laundering 'because of the large amounts of money that can be laundered through a single transaction, and the fact that property will tend to appreciate, or can be used to generate rental income' (SRA 2018b).

The purchase of commercial or residential property provides an ideal method of laundering criminal funds, offering two points at which the funds can be legitimised: firstly, as deposits are moved through a law firm's client account and, secondly, as the funds are exchanged for the ownership of the property. Furthermore, as the SRA points out, rental income or profit made by the sale of the property also provide legitimate income from initially illegitimate funds. There is growing concern about high-value real estate in major global cities being used to hide, store or transfer the proceeds of corruption or other major crimes. For example, investigations by Transparency International (2016) and Global Witness (2015a, 2015b) have highlighted the role of London property as a destination for corrupt wealth from overseas, and the 2018 UK *National Strategic Assessment of Serious and Organised Crime* highlighted the purchase of property within the 'London super-prime property market' as a continuing threat in relation to 'high-end money laundering' (NCA 2018: 39). Unger and Ferwerda (2011) suggest that the real estate sector is particularly vulnerable to infiltration from illicit funds, due to a range of factors including the high value of property and fluctuations in the market. It is worth noting that, as well as using property as a means of legitimising criminal funds (laundering in the strict sense), those involved in criminal activity may purchase property as a home or investment in the same way that those with legitimate incomes do. The cases examined in this research involved relatively small-scale property transactions, involving the purchase or sale of single or multiple residential properties, but it is not possible to ascertain the underlying purpose or strategy behind these transactions (see Chapter 4). The likelihood of those involved in profit-making criminal activity choosing to buy or invest in property, and the necessary role of legal professionals in such transactions, makes it inevitable that legal professionals will come into contact with the proceeds of crime in this way (see also Schneider 2005; Cummings and Stepnowsky 2011). This also has implications for other occupational actors who typically play a role in property transactions, at various stages, including mortgage brokers and real estate agents.

Client account

Law firms' client accounts (sometimes called 'trust accounts' outside the UK) can play an important role for those wanting to launder criminal proceeds. They provide a "façade of legitimacy" [SA2] to funds that pass through them, and transactions that originate from them. As well as funds being used as the deposit in a property purchase, this includes money that is being transferred to other bank accounts or being used to make large-scale purchases (Cases 1, 2, 3, 7, 8, 15, 19). Client accounts can be used as a way of 'moving money from one individual to another through a legitimate third party under the guise of a legal transaction without attracting the attention of law enforcement agencies' (SRA 2018b). Furthermore, because of the principle of lawyer-client confidentiality, banks are unaware of the identity of the client whose funds are being moved through the client account, and so their use can help to circumvent banks' anti-money laundering procedures (Middleton 2008).

The cases analysed in this research show client accounts being used as a conduit for money being transferred from bank accounts in the names of companies (including another law firm) to individuals' personal accounts or other company accounts (Cases 2, 3, 8, 19); money being transferred from individuals' personal accounts to company bank accounts (Case 1); and money being transferred to the convicted solicitor's firm itself as an investment (Case 1). They also show money that has been transferred into a client account being used to purchase cars, yachts or jets, thus obscuring the owner of the funds/purchaser of the assets (Cases 2, 15), and a client account being used as one part of a complex series of accounts for money to pass through (Case 15). Client accounts are also known to have been used to facilitate other types of financial crime, as well as being used as a means of transferring or concealing the origins of the criminal proceeds *following* a predicate offence, as in these cases. For example, Middleton (2004) highlights the use of client accounts for the transfer of funds in connection with high-yield investment frauds, and discusses cases involving the movement of significant amounts of money through client accounts for the purposes of facilitating corruption and VAT fraud, amongst others (Middleton 2008). The line between funds being transferred through client accounts for the purposes of committing particular financial crimes or to launder the proceeds of such crimes is not always a clear one.

The potential for client accounts to be misused, therefore, poses a wider problem than just the opportunities they provide for money laundering, and concern about such accounts being used inappropriately has led to changes in the SRA Accounts Rules to try to prevent this. The *SRA Handbook* sets out the standards and requirements that those they regulate are expected to uphold, and includes, alongside a set of Principles and a Code of Conduct, a number of Accounts Rules intended both to protect client money and ensure client accounts are used for appropriate purposes only (SRA 2017).[1] Since 2011, following recognition of the potential for misuse of client accounts and growing concern within the SRA about the risks associated with the amount of money that can pass through solicitors' hands, a rule has been included in the Handbook which states that legal professionals

> must not provide banking facilities through a client account. Payments into, and transfers or withdrawals from, a client account must be in respect of instructions relating to an underlying transaction (and the funds arising therefrom) or to a service forming part of your normal regulated activities.
>
> (SRA 2017: Accounts Rules 2011, Rule 14.5)

The focus of this rule is that money should not be passed through a client account (or, indeed, any other office or related account) without there being *an underlying transaction upon which they are providing legal advice*. This makes sense, as legal professionals should *only* need to handle client money 'when it is necessary to facilitate the services they are providing' (Law Society response to Treasury consultation February 2003, cited in Middleton 2008). However, being able to identify the presence of funds in client accounts where there is no legitimate underlying transaction is another matter, and it is difficult to see how regulators would be able to do this without constant monitoring of all firms' accounts – *prohibiting* such actions does not necessarily *prevent* them. It is interesting to note that Accounts Rule 14.5 refers to transactions through a client account being acceptable if they relate to 'a service forming part of your *normal regulated activities*' (SRA 2017: Accounts Rules 2011; Rule 14.5; emphasis added). As we have seen, funds transfers through client accounts that act to facilitate money laundering are often linked to transactions or processes that form part of solicitors' 'normal' activities.

---

1 The *SRA Handbook* is due to be replaced in November 2019 with the *SRA Standards and Regulations*; see Chapter 8.

Implications for identification and prevention

The ability to hide transactions involving criminal proceeds, and their essential similarity to normal, legitimate transactions, has implications for their identification and prevention. It becomes much harder to identify non-legitimate transactions if they are hidden amongst legitimate transactions, and if the behaviours of those carrying them out are essentially the same. It may be the case, therefore, that identification of lawyers' involvement in the management of criminal proceeds would be more likely to begin with the predicate offender and their funds or assets. Much of the data on the cases analysed in this research makes reference to the predicate offender and the offence they committed, suggesting that the discovery of the solicitor's role in the money laundering – and their ultimate conviction – began with the prosecution of, or investigation into, the predicate offender (although this cannot be concluded definitively from the data available). In relation to preventing lawyers from becoming involved with transactions involving criminal proceeds in the first place, opportunity theories of white-collar crime would suggest 'making adjustments to the legitimate process that thwart the ability of individuals to act parasitically in relation to the legitimate process' (Benson, Madensen and Eck 2009: 185). This reflects the principle of situational crime prevention and can be seen in many of the measures that have been implemented, or suggested, for preventing professional involvement in money laundering: for example, the obligation for those in regulated sectors to check clients' identities, keep appropriate records and report suspicions of money laundering, and the requirement in the SRA Accounts Rules stipulating that money should not be passed through client accounts without there being an underlying transaction. Middleton and Levi (2015: 659–660) suggest other (current and potential) approaches to preventing lawyers' involvement in money laundering, using a framework of situational crime prevention based on one by Crawford (2007: 874). They identify techniques aimed at: increasing the perceived risk to lawyers from their involvement in money laundering; reducing the anticipated reward from such involvement; reducing 'provocations', or more accurately, conditions that may encourage or be conducive to lawyers' involvement in laundering; and 'removing excuses'.[2] However, it would be difficult, if not impossible, to prevent all opportunities for facilitating money laundering without stopping lawyers having any involvement in financial transactions – or dealing with money in any way – which would clearly impede their legitimate professional activity.

---

2 Soudijn (2012) also argued for use of the 'removing excuses' technique to prevent 'financial facilitators' from acting for criminals – given that the goal of ensuring those in a position to facilitate money laundering 'do not find themselves in situations where their services are required' is 'impossible' (Soudijn 2012: 162). Such a technique would involve four components: setting rules, alerting conscience, controlling disinhibitors, and assisting compliance. Middleton and Levi (2015: 660) include information campaigns and warnings, simplification of laws and rules to enhance their legitimacy, and publication of regulatory action against offenders, as techniques to 'remove excuses'.

Legitimate and specialised access

Opportunities for crimes within an occupational context arise in part because the offender 'has legitimate access to the location in which the crime is committed', helping to provide their actions with 'a superficial appearance of legitimacy' (Benson and Simpson 2018: 85). They have access to the 'target', or situations that can be taken advantage of for personal (or organisational) gain, and are more likely to encounter or become aware of these situations as they 'move through familiar places' (Madensen 2016: 396; see Brantingham and Brantingham 1993, 2011). Where money laundering is facilitated by legal professionals, this access may also need to be *specialised*, requiring certain skills and expertise that are available to legal professionals and allow them to take advantage of opportunities they encounter. For example, lawyers who play a role in the purchase or sale of property bought with the proceeds of crime have legitimate 'access' to the conveyancing process which acts to launder the criminal proceeds, and also have the expertise and necessary qualifications to facilitate this process. Their access to a client account allows them to move funds from illicit sources as required and give the funds the necessary veneer of legitimacy. The setting up, structuring and management of complex financial transactions and corporate vehicles requires specialist knowledge and expertise that is available to those in certain occupational roles, such as lawyers, accountants, and trust and company service providers. It is this legitimate and specialised access to certain services that can be used to move or conceal criminal proceeds that makes professionals who provide such services of use to those in possession of the proceeds of crime. Those who have committed the predicate offence are unlikely to have such access, meaning they require the assistance of those who do; this makes legal professionals targets for those who require these services, and therefore vulnerable to exploitation.

Lawyers' positions as 'respected' professionals, and the status that this confers, may also enhance their ability to take advantage of situations that can facilitate money laundering. For example, the data show that MOHAMMED JAHANGIR FARID (Case 9) helped his brother manage the proceeds of mortgage frauds by witnessing an email related to a transfer of title and using headed paper to forge a document to support a funds transfer (amongst other actions), thereby making use of his position as a solicitor, and the trust and status that this imparts. ANDREW WORMSTONE (Case 20) used his position as a solicitor to try to convince a bank that funds obtained through fraud had been earned legitimately, in order that they would release the funds from a frozen account.

Confidentiality and privilege

A central feature of the relationship between the legal professional and the predicate offender is that it is a lawyer-client relationship, which confers principles of confidentiality and legal professional privilege (LPP). The nature and scope of these principles and their application in relation to money laundering vary between countries and depend on the legal and constitutional framework within a country (and, in some federal systems, within each state) (FATF 2013). Legal professionals are required, both professionally and legally, to keep the affairs of present or former clients confidential, 'unless otherwise allowed or required by law and/or applicable rules of professional conduct' (IBA 2011: 6). LPP protects the client against disclosure; it recognises the right of individuals to be open and candid with their lawyer, without fear that their communications will later be disclosed to their prejudice. LPP does not apply to all communications between lawyer and client, and is therefore not as broad in its coverage as the principle of confidentiality. Within the UK, for example, it covers only confidential communications that fall under the categories of 'advice privilege' and 'litigation privilege'. Advice privilege covers communications between lawyers and their clients for the purpose of giving or receiving legal advice. Litigation privilege protects confidential communications between clients or their lawyers and third parties made in relation to litigation that has commenced or is in reasonable prospect (see Thanki et al. 2018).

However, there are limits to the protections provided by LPP. In the UK, the 'crime/fraud exception' to the principle states that LPP 'does not extend to documents which themselves form part of a criminal or fraudulent act, or communications which take place in order to obtain advice with the intention of carrying out an offence' (LSAG 2018: 103). In relation to (anti-)money laundering specifically, POCA 2002 requires the reporting of suspicions of money laundering and disclosure of information on the client(s) involved to the relevant authorities, as discussed in Chapter 2, and this can override the duty of confidentiality. However, exemptions from certain provisions of POCA 2002, and a defence to the associated reporting requirements, are provided when certain communications are received by legal professionals in 'privileged circumstances' (POCA 2002, ss.330[6][b] and [10]). However, again, an exception applies when the communication was given with a view to furthering a criminal purpose. 'Privileged circumstances' under this part of POCA 2002 are not the same as provided by the principle of LPP, although in many cases communication that falls under 'privileged circumstances' will also be covered by LPP.

The scope and application of principles of confidentiality and privilege in relation to money laundering, therefore, are complex. It is suggested that this complexity, and the lack of uniformity across jurisdictions, makes them open to misunderstanding and divergent interpretations by legal professionals and law enforcement (FATF 2013). The need to ensure that privilege is respected can increase the time and resources required in criminal investigations, and claims of LPP can cause delays to investigations and impede the gathering of evidence (FATF 2013; Middleton 2008). Furthermore, the UK's *National Risk Assessment of Money Laundering and Terrorist Financing* states that there have been instances of lawyers falsely or incorrectly claiming LPP to prevent the disclosure of certain documents (HM Treasury/Home Office 2017), and the FATF suggests that individuals involved in criminal activity may believe that they are protected by LPP, without understanding the limitations of this protection (FATF 2013).

Therefore, despite the exceptions detailed above, the protections provided by the duty of confidentiality and LPP may create challenges for investigations that require access to documents or details of discussions, and for surveillance or monitoring of legal professionals' actions, and may provide a *perception* of protection that makes lawyers attractive to individuals with criminal proceeds to launder. Lawyer-client confidentiality has 'shielded interactions between lawyers and their clients from external view' (Loughrey 2011: 2) and, as discussed earlier in the chapter, means that banks are unaware of the identity of clients whose funds are being moved through a client account, adding to the veneer of legitimacy provided by these accounts. It is argued that these principles, unique to and a fundamental part of the legal profession and the lawyer-client relationship, may provide an explanation for the lack of prosecutions of lawyers for money laundering offences (Middleton 2008; Middleton and Levi 2015).

Organisational structure and culture

The nature and characteristics of the organisation in which lawyers work may provide opportunities for them to assist with money laundering or create vulnerabilities which could be exploited by those in possession of criminal proceeds. Moreover, the culture of particular legal practices (or *types of* practice) may produce environments that are more or less conducive to the involvement of their employees in money laundering (as well as other forms of misconduct). Research and theory on misconduct within and by organisations (i.e. activity that breaks criminal, civil or administrative laws, or fails to comply with regulations or codes of conduct) shows the various ways that organisational characteristics and dynamics can shape offending behaviour.[3] The 'particularities of organizations' can shape the availability and distribution of opportunities for misconduct within them (Huisman 2016: 438), and the nature of the organisational setting can influence individuals' decisions to take such opportunities (Vaughan 1992, 2002). The role of organisational culture in illegal or unethical behaviour is less easy to demonstrate empirically, but it is argued that the underlying assumptions, values and norms of behaviour which make up the organisational culture (Schein 1992) will affect the behaviour of employees of the organisation (Campbell and Göritz 2014), as (often tacit and informal) shared standards of conduct and norms 'are a powerful influence on individual behaviour' (Tomlinson and Pozzuto 2016: 367). The structure of a law firm could refer to its size and complexity; the way

3 See Chapter 3 of this book for a discussion on the significance of the organisational context in the commission of 'white-collar crime'. See also, for example, Huisman (2016) for an overview of the criminogenic properties and dynamics of organisations; Campbell and Göritz (2014) for a summary of research on the role of organisational culture in misconduct by employees; Linstead, Maréchal and Griffin (2014) for consideration of 'the dark side of organization'; and Palmer (2013) and Palmer, Smith-Crowe and Greenwood (2016) for discussion of theories on misconduct in organisational settings and arguments for the normalcy of organisational wrongdoing.

that authority, accountability, roles, responsibilities, information flows and decision-making processes are structured or allocated; the organisation of compliance processes and management; the levels of autonomy of different members; and the extent and nature of oversight processes and procedures (Huisman 2016). This section considers the potential role of the nature of law firms – including size, levels of autonomy and internal oversight, and new forms of organisations providing legal services – in creating opportunities or vulnerabilities for money laundering.

Size and complexity

The size and structure of law firms within the UK vary widely, from large international City firms to small 'high street' practices with much lower turnovers and fewer employees. In addition, many solicitors in the UK work as 'sole practitioners', providing legal services from practices in which they are the only lawyer (though which may also include other non-lawyer personnel). The 2017 UK *National Risk Assessment of Money Laundering and Terrorist Financing* reported that there were more than 14,000 firms providing legal services in the UK in 2016, with 72% of those employing fewer than 10 employees (Office for National Statistics 2016 cited in HM Treasury/Home Office 2017: 49). Sole practitioners made up 23% of legal practices in the UK in 2019 (IRN Research 2019).

There was consensus amongst interviewees working in financial investigation units involved in investigating organised crime groups that those looking to launder the proceeds of their crimes would be more likely to use small "high street" legal practices than larger firms. The reasons for this included the desire to stay "local" – within the area that they knew and were familiar with – and the lower costs associated with using small practices:

> It's the same with solicitors, isn't it? They don't use the big practices; it's going to be a one- or two- person practice on the high street, local to where they are.
>
> [LE4]

> Plus the larger firms charge more as well. And although criminals have got a lot of money, they still don't want to pay too much, because it's hard earned money for them.
>
> [LE3]

Smaller practices may also be considered a lower-risk option for those with criminal proceeds to launder, with sole practitioners being seen as particularly attractive due to the lack of oversight from others in the practice:

> I'd say in the main that they're sole practitioners, where there's no other solicitor – you know, they're not having meetings and all that, why are you dealing with him? You know, it tends not to be a large company.
>
> [LE2]

From the data used in this research, it is difficult to ascertain the size or structure of the firms involved in all the cases analysed, or the convicted solicitor's role in the firm, and so it is impossible to come to conclusions about whether size is correlated either positively or negatively with compliance with anti-money laundering requirements or involvement in money laundering. Evidence from research on organisational crime provides no consensus on the relationship between size or complexity and illegal behaviour or compliance with laws or regulations. Some suggest that large firms are more likely to engage in illegal behaviour, often on multiple occasions, due in part to more complex business processes and management structures (e.g. Simpson 1986; Dalton and Kesner 1988; Simpson and Rorie 2011). However, large firms also have the resources to invest in training, preventative systems and compliance programmes, may put a greater emphasis on compliance, and may be more visible to regulatory agencies (see Huisman 2016: 448). Complex organisations, with several layers of management or consisting of multiple sub-divisions, may create more opportunities for misconduct or regulatory noncompliance (Huisman 2016: 447). On the other hand, smaller firms might lack the ability or expertise to comply with required standards. For example, sole practitioners and small legal practices may find it much more difficult than larger firms to keep up with anti-money laundering regulations and guidance provided by their supervisors or professional bodies, due, for example, to lower exposure to guidance documents and necessary expertise or a lack of resources to enable staff to attend training sessions.

Autonomy and (lack of) oversight

A certain level of autonomy, and lack of internal oversight in relation to particular activities or transactions, may allow legal professionals to take advantage of opportunities to facilitate money laundering if they choose to do so. The degree (and effectiveness) of oversight *within* law firms will vary, influenced by the size, structure, organisational strategy and culture of the firm. For example, the autonomy enjoyed by sole practitioners may allow them to conduct transactions or act for clients without scrutiny from partners or other colleagues. In Case 3 above, ANDREW YOUNG was a sole practitioner, and so was in a position to accept the proceeds of mortgage fraud into his client account and redistribute them with impunity. However, a lack of effective oversight can also exist in larger organisations, especially those with more decentralised structures (Huisman 2016), and the case data highlight a certain level of autonomy and possible lack of oversight in a number of those cases where passing money through the firm's client account was the means of facilitation, even though the solicitors involved were not sole practitioners:

- PAUL WINTER MORRIS (Case 2) was one of four partners in his firm. However, it was noted that Morris "had in fact sole operational control over the [client] account" [CoA – Morris] through which he transferred £8 million of criminal proceeds.

- JONATHAN DUFF (Case 1) was the sole principal partner in his firm, though it is unclear what size and structure the firm had; he may therefore have been in a position to avoid scrutiny.
- JONATHAN KRESTIN (Case 8) and RICHARD HOUSLEY (Case 19) held the positions of managing and senior partner respectively, but were also the designated Money Laundering Reporting Officer (MLRO) for their firms, which may have meant they were not subject to the same degree of oversight or scrutiny as they might otherwise have been.

This suggests that if solicitors' client accounts are considered to be a site of vulnerability for money laundering, further consideration should be given to the oversight of these accounts and how they are managed within firms. For example, no single practitioner within a firm should have 'sole operational control' of the client account, and there may be an argument for someone within each firm, who is not a legal professional and who will not use the client account, to be responsible for monitoring the account and transactions involved (of course, this is more difficult for sole practitioner practices and the risk of client accounts being used for transactions involving criminal proceeds could not be completely eliminated). Misconduct within organisations is more likely to take place at the 'edges' of commonly trodden 'paths' (Benson, Madensen and Eck 2009); that is, at the less regulated, less visible or less transparent parts of the processes or transactions involved in an organisation's day-to-day business. This suggests that the more transparent the 'normal' transactions that can provide opportunities for money laundering (such as those which utilise the client account or involve the sale or purchase of property), and the more effectively they are regulated or overseen, the more difficult it would be for them to be misused.

Of course, this discussion has referred only to the limits of *internal* oversight, and one of the features of professions such as the legal profession is the presence of *external* oversight, in the form of regulatory bodies. The role of those tasked with the regulatory oversight of the legal profession (in relation to money laundering and more broadly) will be discussed in Chapter 8. However, clearly such external actors would not be able to monitor all financial transactions or activities within all law firms in their jurisdiction, and so the role of internal oversight becomes critical.

'Conveyancing factories' and alternative business structures

A number of the solicitors interviewed raised the issue of what they called "conveyancing farms" or "conveyancing factories". One solicitor, who specialised in conveyancing work, suggested that this was the "main problem" in relation to the risk of money laundering through the purchase of property:

S1: Because I think that the main problem is that . . . we've gone to 'conveyancing farms' now, so there are big companies that just do really cheap conveyancing. And there are solicitors and partners who deal with teams of 20–30 people . . . these huge 'conveyancing factories', as I call them. How one partner or solicitor could possibly know what everybody is doing, all these 20 members of staff. . .

. . .

So . . . as a paralegal you can walk in having no legal experience and without the training. So I think that's where the main problems lie, in these sort of low cost operations.

RESEARCHER: So they wouldn't be solicitors then?

S1: No, it'd be paralegals or, it's the sort of low-level staff who are doing it, dealing with these huge amounts of files. But then you've got a stressed solicitor trying to deal with 20 different people or whatever.

. . .

You know, paralegals are obviously cheap, so it's cost-effective to do that. But whether you're getting a good service or not is a different matter, isn't it? Conveyancing by numbers!

A second solicitor also voiced concern about firms that processed large numbers of conveyancing transactions, by using teams of paralegals rather than qualified solicitors:

They're factory firms, and they just churn things out. And they, they are okay because they have, like, a pyramid system. So, say, 20 paralegals are then supervised by one lawyer, one qualified person. And every case gets signed off by the qualified person before it goes through. But that's much more risk. Because if someone is literally just checking that certain things are in before it gets signed off, then they're much more at risk.

[S3]

This solicitor highlighted the potential problems for carrying out effective due diligence with the quantities of work that such firms were processing:

I've got, I think, about 50, 60 cases at the moment, off the top of my head. These firms expect each person to have at least 60 or 100. And then they've got to complete, say, eight a week. And if you're dealing with that volume then it's very difficult to even make sure you've seen all the proper bank statements, never mind had a chance to read them properly and check them

. . .

I think those types of firm are at much, much higher risk of money laundering.

[S3]

The significance of property transactions for the facilitation of money laundering is widely accepted, as discussed previously in this chapter, and so the rise of such 'conveyancing factories' should be seen as an area of concern. It can also be seen as a reflection of the changing nature of the market for legal services in the UK, which has been opened up in recent years to encourage greater competition and more choice for users of legal services. The most notable manifestation of this has been the introduction of new forms of law firm, known as Alternative Business Structures (ABSs). ABSs were introduced through the Legal Services Act 2007, and the first ABSs were licensed by the SRA in 2012. The purpose of their introduction was to increase competition, variety and flexibility within the legal services market and allow new forms of capital into regulated law firms to improve market efficiency (Legal Services Board 2017). Traditionally, only lawyers could own, invest in and become partners in law firms. ABSs allow much greater flexibility: their management and control can be shared by lawyers and non-lawyers; they can be owned and invested in by individuals and organisations external to the legal profession; and they can act as 'multidisciplinary practices', offering multiple services to clients (including but not limited to legal services).[4]

The 2019 *UK Legal Services Market Trends Report* states that, at the time of the report in February 2019, there were almost 1,300 ABSs operating in England and Wales in a field of more than 10,000 law firms in total (IRN Research 2019). Approximately 60% of these are regulated by the SRA (Langdon-Down 2018), which means that they provide reserved legal activities. A report by the Legal Services Board (2017) showed that only a minority of the ABSs licensed since their introduction were new firms, with the majority being existing legal services providers that had converted to ABSs. The 2019 *Market Trends Report* also highlighted the broader changes in the law firm business model in the UK, with almost half of law firms now being incorporated companies and the traditional partnership model having 'declined dramatically' at just 17% of firms (IRN Research 2019).

The growth of alternative providers of legal services, as well as other emerging and predicted changes in the legal services market, such as a growing online legal services provision, increased use of technology within firms, and the rise of 'freelance' solicitors (able to offer unreserved legal services only) and qualified solicitors working in unregulated practices (SRA 2016; Langdon-Down 2018; IRN Research 2019), raises questions about the potential impact on the conduct of those working in the profession. More open, competitive market systems can create pressures on organisations and individuals to strive for competitive advantage and financial success, which may lead to the violation of laws or regulatory norms in the pursuit of certain goals (see e.g. Vaughan 1983, 1992), and instil a 'fear of falling' (Coleman 1995) that may lead to rule-breaking behaviour (Huisman and Vande Walle 2010; see Chapter 3 for further discussion). For example, concerns have been raised about the conflicts created for solicitors in a firm that has external, non-lawyer investors: is their primary duty to their clients or shareholders? (Langdon-Down 2018). The 2017 UK *National Risk Assessment*

---

4 See, for example, SRA (2016) and Legal Services Board (2017) for analysis of the changing legal services market in the UK, including the effect of the introduction of ABSs.

of Money Laundering and Terrorist Financing suggested that innovation within the legal services market presents challenges for those responsible for supervising the profession for anti-money laundering purposes, as opportunities for accessing legal services without engaging a supervised firm are created (HM Treasury/ Home Office 2017: 52). It may take some time before the impact of the changes to the legal services market can be fully assessed.

Financial benefit

A number of the interviewees from law enforcement and supervisory backgrounds talked about the advantage gained by professionals who helped others to launder criminal proceeds, as a means of explaining why they might become involved. In relation to one who was suspected to be providing advice and services to a number of organised crime groups, Interviewee LE1 highlighted the "competitive advantage" gained through the "steady" and "predictable" nature of the income:

> [T]he competitive advantage that he has is access to a client base which is going to provide him with a steady stream of fees, and the behaviour of that income is more predictable than it would be if it was entirely legitimate.
>
> [LE1]

It was suggested that, for some professionals, becoming involved with criminals needing to launder money was about "greed" and "making a bit of money":

> Sometimes it's just greed, because of the amount of work that they can get off them, and that can give them a particular lifestyle that they wouldn't otherwise have if they just did legitimate business. . . . And it's, there's vast amounts of money to be made out of it.
>
> [LE2]

> I think there comes a point where they think "Hm, you know, I could actually make a bit of money out of this".
>
> [LE9]

Whereas, for others, it was felt that it was more about 'need':

> I would say that, from our experience of it, it tends to be motivated by them falling on hard times, . . . It tends to be, they were performing this well ten years ago, [and now] they're not performing anywhere near there.
>
> [SA2]

> They're in it because they've come up with some financial adversity or some personal problem, which has basically drawn them into that side of life in order to survive.
>
> [LE1]

And I don't think there's much doubt that in the majority of cases where people do something quite serious, it's because they've got into a desperate financial position, and that's what's really going on

[SA3]

From the data available, it is difficult to determine with any certainty or precision the degree of financial benefit received by the solicitors (or their organisation) in the cases examined. However, an indication can be obtained in some of the cases, and while it is clear that the way in which lawyers benefit from their involvement in money laundering varies, there was little evidence of significant financial gain in most of the cases examined. The data also highlight some of the challenges for understanding the level of financial benefit received by the professional in such cases, where they facilitate the laundering of criminal proceeds generated by others.

PAUL WINTER MORRIS (Case 2) was found to have been involved in the laundering of approximately £8 million, a proportion of the proceeds from VAT fraud committed by Raymond Woolley. The total loss to the revenue due to the fraud was estimated at over £38 million. During confiscation proceedings that followed Morris' conviction, it was argued on behalf of Morris that he had not obtained any financial benefit from his involvement in the money laundering:

He was merely a trustee of funds for Woolley, and he received no personal benefit, direct or indirect, from the funds in his firm's client account.

[CoA – Morris]

However, the trial judge rejected this argument, saying that Morris' connection with the relevant monies was "far more than that" of a trustee. This conclusion was primarily based on a series of transfers totalling £4.5 million made by Morris from his firm's client account to a company called Thornbush Entertainment Inc. (USA), an organisation with which Morris "had a considerable pre-existing connection but with which Mr Woolley had none". These particular transfers did not appear to be based on instructions from Woolley, as other transactions involving the funds were. The judge in the confiscation hearing concluded that "the true nature of the receipt of the relevant funds by Morris was such as to amount to an obtaining of them" within the meaning of the relevant legislation, and he "assessed the amount obtained by Morris as £7,928,682.47". Following a further hearing to consider the amount of Morris' realisable assets, a confiscation order was made in the sum of £410, 077.20 [CoA – Morris].

This case raises interesting questions about asset confiscation in relation to professionals who facilitate money laundering. If monies are held in accounts which the professional controls – such as the client account – they may technically be considered to have 'obtained' these monies under the asset recovery legislation. Morris was considered to have 'obtained' the amount of £7,928,682.47 because this was the amount that had passed through a bank account under his control, and so this was considered to be his 'benefit' for confiscation purposes, even though he had not actually acquired these funds for his personal use.[5] Morris argued that he had received no personal benefit from his involvement in the money laundering and continued to appeal the confiscation order. Indeed, he did not pay the confiscation order and consequently received a further custodial sentence of just more than two years.

Similarly, BRIAN DOUGAN (Case 5), who acted in a number of property transactions for someone involved in organised fuel fraud, was ordered to pay a sum of £86,500 at a confiscation hearing following his conviction. This was based on the £66,500 that constituted the deposits paid for the properties, plus £20,000 court costs [HMRC – Dougan]. JONATHAN KRESTIN (Case 8) received a confiscation order for £9,517, representing the €14,000 he received into his firm's client account and subsequently disbursed on behalf of fraudster Michel Namer, even though

> [i]t was clear that [Krestin] had not been aware of, actively involved in, or *had made any profit from* the money laundering.
>
> (emphasis added) [SDT – Krestin]

Therefore, because these funds had passed through accounts controlled by the solicitors – either as deposits or money transfers – they were considered to have 'obtained' these amounts for the purposes of confiscation, even if they had not actually received direct personal gain from them. In the case of Morris, the role of Thornbush Entertainment Inc. described during the confiscation hearing suggests that he may have received some degree of financial benefit from his involvement in the laundering scheme, but there is no indication that Dougan or Krestin received any direct financial gain from the role they played (except for their standard fees).

Other cases indicated that the professional received some direct financial benefit from the laundering, though it is difficult to say how much. AMINAT AFOLABI (Case 12) received a payment of £15,000 from the proceeds of sale of the property she was involved in the conveyancing of – a property bought and sold by her husband using funds derived from his criminal activity. It was argued by the SRA's representative at Afolabi's Solicitors Disciplinary Tribunal (SDT) hearing that as she

> had benefitted considerably [from her involvement in laundering]; this made the offences proportionately more serious.
>
> [SDT – Afolabi]

---

5 This book will not address such questions, or the intricacies of asset confiscation legislation. For further detail on confiscation proceedings against Morris, and the explanation for him being considered to have the benefit of the full amount that had passed through his firm's client account, see the Court of Appeal case *R v Allpress & Others* [2009] EWCA Crim 8, which addresses the issue of benefit in relation to money laundering by considering appeals against confiscation orders in relation to five cases.

She may also have had indirect benefit from the money laundered by her husband; the nature of the relationship between professional and predicate offender in this case affecting what could be conceived as the benefit of her involvement.

ANDREW YOUNG (Case 3) was considered to have "extracted some financial benefit" for himself during the process of receiving the proceeds of mortgage frauds into his firm's client account and redistributing it "for the benefit of others" [CoA – Young]. GERARD HYDE (Case 7) was adjudged to have received a "relatively small" [SDT – Hyde] profit from allowing his firm's client account and a bank account he controlled in the Isle of Man to hold and move approximately £2 million generated through a VAT fraud. The data available give no indication, however, of the actual level of financial benefit received.

On the other hand, data from several of the cases suggest that the professional received no direct financial benefit from the actions for which they were convicted. RACHEL TAYLOR (Case 10) does not appear to have benefitted financially from writing down a series of figures on the back of a letter for Pardeep Bains; there is no indication that ANTHONY BLOK (Case 11) received personal gain from the proceeds of crime used to pay his client's bail; and PETER OBIDI (Case 4) appears to have received no financial benefit from the funds he paid into a bank account and later withdrew and returned to the same individual. At the SDT hearing for ANDREW WORMSTONE (Case 20), who unsuccessfully tried to have a bank account unfrozen in order to release the proceeds of a fraud to those who committed it, it was stated that

> [i]t did not appear that [Wormstone] had had any financial gain from his actions.
>
> [SDT – Wormstone]

For those whose involvement centred around their role in the purchase or sale of property, there appears to be no direct financial benefit received from the funds being laundered (apart from Aminat Afolabi, as discussed above). What they – or their firm – will have received, of course, is the fee for carrying out the conveyancing:

> [Tidd] had not received any gain; his firm had received a normal level of fees for the transaction in which [Tidd] had acted for Mr K.
>
> [SDT – Tidd]

> [Griffiths] had received no more than his normal conveyancing fee of £399.
>
> [CoA – Griffiths]

So, while there may be no *direct* financial benefit in such cases, there is a degree of *indirect* benefit in terms of the business provided and the fees paid. The quotes above highlight that what the solicitors received was the *normal* conveyancing fee; this means that they were acquiring no greater benefit from a transaction involving criminal funds than they would have for the same transaction involving non-criminal funds.

The data suggest that there was no significant personal financial benefit gained by the professional in most of the cases. While the available data may provide only a partial picture of the financial benefit to the solicitors in these cases, and receiving no financial *gain* is not the same as having no financial *motive* (they may have expected more), it seems that a purely economic explanation for professionals' involvement in money laundering is insufficient. A range of factors will play a role in their decisions to take actions which facilitate money laundering in some way (or are considered to do so under relevant legislation), including the nature of the relationship between them and the predicate offender.

Relationship with the predicate offender

The most obvious relationship in the cases examined, and in the facilitation of money laundering by lawyers on behalf of others in general, is that of solicitor and client. This relationship is central to the framing of the problem, primarily in relation to the issues of lawyer-client confidentiality and legal professional privilege discussed earlier, and the need for criminals to use the services provided by such professionals to launder their criminal proceeds (see e.g. Bell 2002; Di Nicola and Zoffi 2004; Middleton 2008; Soudijn 2012). Within the cases, this relationship is central to the activity involved in a number of ways; for example, if the solicitor's involvement is based on them conducting transactions for their client – such as conveyancing (Cases 5, 6, 12, 13, 16, 18) – as a function of their professional role, or the predicate offender's position as client of the solicitor allows their illegal funds to be passed through the solicitor's client account (Cases 1, 2, 3, 7, 8, 15, 19). In addition, the solicitor-client relationship can provide a cover for the solicitor to carry out transactions on behalf of the predicate offender, such as making purchases or transferring ownership of assets, and can provide a superficial appearance of legitimacy to their actions. An example of this is the case of ANDREW WORMSTONE (Case 20), where he (ultimately unsuccessfully) attempted to have a bank account unfrozen by making a point of his professional relationship with the predicate offenders, to try to persuade the bank that he was aware of their business dealings and knew them to be legitimate.

However, little is known about the social relations between legal professionals and those whose criminal proceeds they help to launder beyond their status as lawyer and client. No existing literature or previous empirical research in this area has fully examined the nature of the relationship, its duration, or how the different actors came into contact, for example, and the scope of this research and the data available did not allow analysis of this in any detail. (This would be a very worthwhile area for future research, although there would be challenges with finding data that would enable it.) However, for some of the cases a degree of detail about the relationship beyond that of solicitor and client could be established.

Personal relationship

In a small number of the cases there was a personal relationship of some form between the professional and the predicate offender. For example:

MOHAMMED JAHANGIR FARID (Case 9) was convicted of money laundering offences for the role he played in a number of mortgage fraud offences orchestrated by his older brother, Rashid Farid. A number of other family members and associates were involved in the frauds or subsequent matters involving the proceeds of the frauds, and it was judged that Rashid Farid was the "mastermind" behind the scams, whose "influence on others played a critical role in leading them astray" [CoA – Farid]. The offences of Mohammed Jahangir Farid were said to have been "committed under the malign influence of his older brother", and the judge in the case concluded that Rashid Farid "was responsible not only for the destruction of his own brother and some of his friends, but also for having brought down his father who was 'a man of high standing'" [CoA – Farid].

AMINAT AFOLABI (Case 12) was convicted for her involvement in the conveyancing of a property bought, and subsequently sold, by a company controlled by her husband. This property was bought using money that had been obtained by fraud, carried out by Mr Afolabi, who had a number of fraud convictions over a period of five years. There had also been movement of sums of money between bank accounts belonging to the Afolabis. It was concluded at her trial that Aminat Afolabi must have been aware of her husband's fraudulent activities – even though she argued that she now believed him to be "going straight" – and therefore that properties he was buying and selling constituted criminal proceeds [CoA – Afolabi].

RACHEL TAYLOR's (Case 10) conviction related to assistance she provided to her former partner, Pardeep Bains. While Taylor and Bains were no longer in a relationship at this point, they had remained friends. The judge in Taylor's case referred to her as "a 'misguided fool', misguided by her feelings for [Bains]" [SDT – Taylor].[6]

In these cases, therefore, it is not just about a professional, solicitor-client relationship. There is a further dimension to the relationship, which would provide a different dynamic to the interactions between those involved. The existence

---

6 Taylor and Afolabi were the only female solicitors in the cases examined. One aspect that has not been considered in this book, but which may provide an interesting area for further analysis, is the gender of solicitors involved in the facilitation of money laundering, and whether there is a gendered dimension to the nature of their involvement and/or to the response to this involvement. The available research on gender differences in white-collar offending more broadly is limited and somewhat contradictory (see Dodge 2009, 2016 for an overview of gender constructions and the gendered nature of white-collar crime). It has been noted that women are more likely to commit white-collar offences 'for their families or for others with whom they have a close personal relationship' (Goldstraw-White 2012: 163), which fits with the cases of Taylor and Afolabi, but it would be unwise to draw conclusions from such a small number of cases.

of a personal relationship could have created a pressure to act in a certain way, or affected the judgement of the professionals, and may have been the driving force for them to become involved in the laundering. For example, in the case of Mohammed Jahangir Farid, it was suggested that his brother influenced his actions, and so he may not have become involved in criminal activity without this influence. Similarly, the actions of Afolabi and Taylor may have been influenced by the relationships they had with their husband and ex-partner, respectively. In Afolabi's case, this relationship led her to be seen by the court as more culpable because it was assumed that she must have known about her husband's fraudulent activity because of their relationship. However, in Taylor's case the judge appeared to show sympathy for the solicitor, as he accepted that their relationship and her feelings for Bains had clouded her judgement, commenting that "he hoped that she would not lose forever the benefits of her qualifications and hard work" [SDT – Taylor]. Therefore, a personal relationship between professional and predicate offender may not only affect the actions of the professionals, but also the way that they are subsequently judged in a criminal court.

Presence of a 'broker'

A number of the cases indicate the presence of what could be described as a 'broker' to the relationship. For example:

PHILLIP GRIFFITHS' (Case 6) involvement in the sale of a property from convicted drug traffickers to an estate agent, Leslie Pattison, appears to have been driven by Griffiths' relationship with Pattison, who was a close associate:

> In May 2004, Peter Davis approached Mr Pattison and offered to sell him Bryn Arden for the value of the outstanding mortgage, the £43,000. The case for the Crown was that this was an attempt to frustrate the confiscation proceedings. Mr Pattison approached Mr Griffiths with a view to effect conveyance. . . . Mr Griffiths said that Mr Pattison had told him that some friends of his were in financial trouble and that he, Mr Pattison, was buying out the mortgage to help them.
>
> [CoA – Griffiths]

In sentencing, the judge in the trial stated that Griffiths had become involved in the sale, and had not considered carefully enough the risk that the sale was being conducted as a means of preventing asset recovery proceedings, because of his relationship with Pattison:

> As far as I could see, you were unable to say no to Mr Pattison, with whom you had had a close relationship on and off for a number of years. . . . I take the view that because of your connection with Pattison, you closed your eyes to what would otherwise have been the clearest of evidence staring you in the face.
>
> [SDT – Griffiths]

JONATHAN KRESTIN (Case 8) was convicted of a money laundering offence in relation to a transaction he carried out on behalf of Michel Namer, involving the proceeds of a large-scale VAT fraud perpetrated by Namer. Namer had been introduced to Krestin by a tax partner at Baker Tilly (an accountancy firm), as "a client of theirs needing a solicitor to undertake some commercial work". Therefore, Krestin argued, he "had relied on the due diligence checks of Baker Tilly" [SDT – Krestin], as well as his awareness that Namer held accounts at major banks, to satisfy himself about Namer's legitimacy.

ANDREW TIDD (Case 18) acted as conveyancer in the purchase of residential properties for Nevzat Kocabey. Kocabey had been introduced to Tidd as a client by Kocabey's brother, for whom Tidd had acted for a number of years and who he believed to be "a proper and upstanding businessman" [SDT – Tidd]. In addition, Tidd had

> received a reference for [Kocabey] from a high street bank, in connection with a proposed transaction, which stated that he had been a customer of the bank for two–five years; this appeared to provide evidence that the client was a bona fide businessman.
>
> [SDT – Tidd]

In all these cases, there is someone acting as a 'broker' to the relationship between the professional and the predicate offender. These are persons that the professional trusts, knowing them either in a personal or professional capacity, and so their presence is likely to affect the decision-making of the solicitors and the choices they make. These cases, and the ones involving a personal relationship between the professional and the predicate offender, highlight the relevance of the social relations between actors involved in the facilitation of money laundering, and the bearing they have on the actions of the professionals. They draw attention to the interaction between actors from legitimate and criminal settings (Passas 2002; Morselli and Giguere 2006) and the 'social circumstances' of individual action (Suchman 2007: 70).

Conclusion

For legal professionals who seek to facilitate money laundering, the occupational context of the legal profession and the characteristics of particular organisational settings can provide opportunities to do so. Many of the transactions carried out by legal professionals and services they provide, as part of their normal occupational role, can also be used by those wishing to use, move or conceal the proceeds of crime. Transactions with illegally derived funds can be hidden amongst the legitimate transactions also being conducted, making them harder to prevent or identify and creating challenges for those tasked with oversight of the profession. Legal professionals therefore have legitimate access to processes which can be used to manage criminal proceeds, and have the skills, expertise and professional status to take advantage of this access. Furthermore, the principles of confidentiality and legal professional privilege which are fundamental to the lawyer-client relationship may provide a degree of protection for those wishing to launder criminal proceeds, by making the effective oversight necessary to prevent illicit transactions and investigations into suspected illicit transactions more difficult (though there are limits to this protection). A lack of internal oversight within legal practices over lawyers' actions, the services they provide to clients and transactions they carry out, and their ability to act autonomously within the structure of their firm, may allow legal professionals to more easily take advantage of the opportunities provided by the nature of their occupational role. The levels of oversight and autonomy that exist will vary between law firms, influenced by their structure, culture and the size and complexity of the organisation. Recent developments in the characteristics of organisations that provide legal services in the UK – driven by changes in the market environment for legal services provision – may create greater opportunity for the facilitation of money laundering, by decreasing oversight and increasing workload, and may promote a culture of competition that could foster misconduct.

Focusing on 'opportunity', and using it as the sole lens for examining lawyers' involvement in money laundering, however, does not provide a complete picture. Opportunity theories of crime are predicated on there being a *motivated offender*:

> The opportunity perspective assumes that rationality lies behind the *decision to commit* a white-collar crime. It assumes that people *see or recognize criminal opportunities and choose to take advantage of them* for their own benefit (or, in the case of some people in organizations, for the benefit of their organizations).
>
> (Benson and Simpson 2018: 175–176; emphases added)

However, the involvement of legal professionals in the facilitation of money laundering may not always be the result of an active, knowing choice to assist the predicate offender (as will be discussed in the following chapter). Therefore, it cannot simply be viewed as lawyers *choosing to take advantage of* the opportunities presented by their occupational and organisational context, or *deciding to commit* a crime.

The motivation to 'take advantage of' available opportunities for offending is said to come from the 'benefit' individuals will receive – either for themselves or their organisation as a whole (Benson and Simpson 2018: 175–176). Professionals who choose to facilitate money laundering on behalf of others are often framed as rational actors making the decision to become involved in money laundering for economic reasons of personal or business profit or competitive advantage (e.g. Chevrier 2004; Di Nicola and Zoffi 2004; Sikka 2008; FATF 2010). For example, the Financial Action Task Force suggests that, as professionals who provide services to criminals have access to a source of income unavailable to those who practise legitimately, they gain an advantage over their competitors and generate profit that they might not otherwise have been able to (FATF 2010). While no definitive conclusions can be drawn from the data analysed in this research about the motivations – financial or otherwise – involved in shaping the solicitors' actions, it seems clear that a purely economic explanation for professionals' participation in money laundering, based on actual or expected financial gain, is insufficient. The choices taken by legal professionals to proceed with actions which serve to facilitate money laundering in some way (or are considered to do so under relevant legislation) will be shaped by a range of situational contexts and the particular circumstances leading up to and surrounding these choices. One such context is the nature of the relationship between the legal professional and the client with criminal proceeds to launder. This relationship will involve various facets, and may take different forms, but will have a bearing on the actions and decisions of the legal professional, reinforcing the need to consider the social circumstances and situational contexts of individual action.

If we accept that not all legal professionals who become involved in the facilitation of money laundering are 'motivated offenders', making an active choice to take advantage of opportunities to commit money laundering offences, for personal or organisational material benefit, the 'opportunity structures' (Benson, Madensen and Eck 2009) described above could therefore also be seen as 'vulnerability structures'. The proximity of legal professionals' occupational structures, processes and transactions to money of criminal origin, as well as to that of legitimate origin, means that there are inherent risks for those within the profession. The essential similarity of transactions used to launder criminal funds to 'normal' transactions carried out by legal professionals as part of their day-to-day work allows them to be hidden *from* the professionals, as well as hidden *by* them. In addition, the access legal professionals have to processes and transactions required to use, move or conceal criminal proceeds, the specialist skills and expertise they possess which facilitate this access, and the professional status and protections of confidentiality and privilege that being a lawyer confer, make legal professionals targets for those with proceeds of crime to launder. The following chapter demonstrates the different degrees of knowledge and intent apparent in legal professionals' facilitation of money laundering, and shows that not all are complicit, active participants. These vulnerability structures, therefore, may play a role in less intentional or knowing involvement in laundering, and the occupational contexts and organisational settings of the profession may shape decisions taken by legal professionals which result in actions that serve to launder criminal proceeds. Following that, Chapter 7 will show how the legislative framework itself may pose a 'risk' to legal professionals, due to the far-reaching nature of anti-money laundering legislation in the UK, which allows for the prosecution and conviction of regulated professionals who had no intent to launder criminal proceeds and were not actively engaged in the laundering.

6 On the 'borders of knowingness'

Understanding complicity, knowledge and intent

Introduction

Much of the academic and official literature on the role of legal professionals in the facilitation of money laundering makes reference to the level of 'knowingness' or complicity of the professional. This is often presented as a simple dichotomy, with their involvement described as being either 'knowing' or 'unwitting', but it is clearly more complex than that. This chapter explores concepts of knowledge and intent, and how they relate to the complicity and culpability of legal professionals involved in facilitating money laundering. It demonstrates the difficulties of trying to understand and describe the extent of professionals' knowledge, intent and complicity in an accurate or meaningful way. Ultimately, therefore, the chapter suggests that attention should be turned to consideration of the points of decision-making of legal professionals when dealing with clients or conducting financial or commercial transactions, and to the situational contexts that shape these decisions. Decisions to proceed with transactions requested by a client, to agree to act in the purchase or sale of property, to accept funds into the client account, or to provide legal or financial advice or services to a client, friend or family member, for example, will be taken in the course of a legal professional's routine, everyday work, and will be influenced by their occupational and organisational context, relationship with the other actors involved, particular circumstances leading up to and surrounding the decisions, and the wider environment in which they are located.

The chapter begins by discussing the various ways that the nature of legal professionals' involvement in the facilitation of money laundering has been conceptualised and categorised in relevant academic literature and official reports. It considers different terms used to describe this involvement, including 'corrupt', 'complicit', 'culpable', 'not culpable', 'unwitting', 'unwilling', 'wilfully blind', 'coerced', 'negligent' and 'innocent', and considers the meaning and degrees of 'knowledge' and 'intent' in relation to these terms. It draws attention to the 'borders of knowingness' on which legal professionals' involvement in money laundering often exists, and examines the way that the complicity, knowledge and intent of solicitors convicted for money laundering were characterised by the courts and disciplinary tribunals that heard their cases. While some of the solicitors appeared to be complicit, active participants in the laundering, or had chosen 'deliberately to turn a blind eye' to suspicions about the origins of their clients' funds, others were described as being 'unwittingly drawn into' the money laundering offence, not 'aware of' or 'actively involved' in the laundering, or as having 'not known or, indeed, suspected' that their client was involved in laundering. Despite this apparent lack of knowledge or intentional engagement in the money laundering, these solicitors were nonetheless convicted of criminal offences which hold a maximum penalty of 14 years' imprisonment.

Conceptualising complicity, knowledge and intent

Within academic literature and official reports, the level of 'knowingness' or complicity of legal professionals who facilitate money laundering is primarily presented dichotomously, with their involvement described as being either 'knowing' or 'unwitting'. For example:

> Legal professionals . . . have the ability to furnish access (*knowingly* or *unwittingly*) to the various functions that might help a criminal with funds that need to be moved or concealed.
>
> (Di Nicola and Zoffi 2004: 213; emphases added)

> Although lawyers like to deny it, there is no doubt that they assist criminals and money launderers, sometimes with *full knowledge* of what they are doing but also *unwittingly*.
>
> (Middleton 2008: 34; emphases added)

Attempting to develop a systematic way of organising the 'financial facilitators' in his study, Soudijn (2012: 150) focuses on their *willingness* to be involved. He suggests differentiating between 'willing and unwilling facilitation', describing unwilling facilitation as 'unknowingly providing assistance (through misuse, for example), or involuntarily providing services (through force, for example)', and so groups together unknowing assistance with that which is knowing but not voluntary – for example, involving some kind of coercion. This approach, therefore, incorporates issues of *culpability*, or the extent to which the professional should be considered responsible, or to blame, for their involvement. Lankhorst and Nelen (2004: 184) use the concept of culpability to categorise the actions of professionals who assist organised crime (in various ways, including money laundering), suggesting that 'culpable involvement' includes situations where the professional acts as an accessory or co-perpetrator in the criminal activity ('active' involvement) and where they are negligent or allow the abuse of their office or position ('reactive' involvement). They suggest that 'active' involvement occurs in only a small number of cases, but that 'reactive' involvement still entails a level of culpability because the professional 'has taken insufficient care to avoid the abuse of his practice for criminal purposes' (Lankhorst and Nelen 2004: 184).

Within UK policing and policy documents, 'professional enablers' – involved in enabling money laundering or other aspects of serious criminality – are described variously as 'corrupt', 'complicit', 'criminally complicit', 'negligent', 'witting' and 'unwitting'. Various iterations of the UK's *National Strategic Assessment on Organised Crime* talk about 'criminally complicit' (NCA 2015: 22) or 'complicit, negligent or unwitting professionals' (NCA 2014: 12). The 2018 UK *Serious and Organised Crime Strategy* also uses the phrase 'complicit, negligent or unwitting' in reference to 'professional enablers' (Home Office 2018), whereas an earlier version used similar categories but also introduced the term 'corrupt', discussing the problem of 'corrupt, complicit or negligent professionals' (Home Office 2013: 14). The 2016 *National Strategic Assessment* refers simply to the ability of 'a variety of professionals, such as accountancy service providers (ASP), the legal profession, estate agents, and trust and company service providers (TCSP)' to 'assist, *wittingly or unwittingly*, in creating complexity' in money laundering transactions for the benefit of organised crime groups (NCA 2016: 29; emphasis added). Table 6.1 summarises the various characterisations of professional involvement in money laundering (and other forms of crime) seen in the literature, showing the range of terms that have been used to describe and categorise levels or types of complicity. For example, professionals that are *knowingly* and *willingly* involved could be considered to have made an 'active choice' to facilitate the laundering; terms used to describe such a category in the academic and official literature include *complicit, corrupt* and *willing*. On the other hand, if they were *knowingly* but *not willingly* involved, this implies an element of 'coercion' or force, and Lankhorst and Nelen (2004) would not consider them to be culpable in such cases. The final two columns refer to characterisations that suggest the professional was *unknowing* and (therefore) *unwilling*; this could have involved

Table 6.1 Categorisations of knowingness and complicity in the literature

KNOWING		UNKNOWING	
WILLING	UNWILLING		
'ACTIVE CHOICE'	'COERCION'	'NEGLIGENCE'	'EXPLOITATION'
Culpable: Active (Lankhorst and Nelen 2004)	Not culpable (Lankhorst and Nelen 2004)	Culpable: Reactive (Lankhorst and Nelen 2004)	Not culpable (Lankhorst and Nelen 2004)
Willing (Soudijn 2012)	Unwilling (Soudijn 2012)	Unwilling (Soudijn 2012)	Unwilling (Soudijn 2012)
Complicit (NCA 2014, 2015) (Home Office 2018)		Negligent (NCA 2014) (Home Office 2018)	Unwitting (NCA 2014, 2016) (Home Office 2018)
Criminally Complicit (NCA 2015)			
Corrupt (Home Office 2013)			

the 'exploitation' of non-culpable professionals, or they may have been culpable of 'negligence'.

There are obvious problems with trying to draw discrete categories in this way, with blurred boundaries and ambiguities within and between the categories, and some of the terms used seeming to conflate or confuse notions of 'knowledge' and 'intent'. The concepts of knowledge and intent, in relation to the complicity or culpability of legal professionals involved in money laundering, are also unclear (the focus is not on *legal* concepts here; some of the legal issues related to knowledge, suspicion and intent will be considered in the following chapter). What, for example, does it mean to be 'knowingly involved' in money laundering carried out by a client? What does this actually look like? The professionals could have *actual knowledge* that the actions they were taking were facilitating money laundering, or that the transactions they were conducting involved criminal proceeds. However, beyond that lie different degrees or forms of knowingness: the professionals may know or suspect that their client is involved in criminality, for example, but not know for sure the origin of the funds involved in a particular transaction; or they may have suspicions about the funds involved in transactions they are conducting, or suspicions related to the services they are providing for the client, but no actual or confirmed knowledge about either. It would be possible, therefore, for the professional to have a certain amount of *knowledge* but not have actual *intent* to launder. If intent refers to the professional *intending to facilitate laundering*, or *intending to commit an offence* (or do something unethical), they could have a degree of knowledge or suspicion without intent, but could not have intent without knowledge.

In a key report on the vulnerability of the legal profession to money laundering and terrorist financing, the FATF (2013) recognised the problems with a simple dichotomous distinction between types of involvement. The report initially tried to distinguish between 'complicit' and 'unknowing' involvement in its case analysis, but felt that 'such a stark distinction' was not appropriate (FATF 2013: 34). Instead, it suggested that legal professionals' roles in money laundering or terrorist financing could be more accurately depicted on a continuum, incorporating the following categories: Innocent involvement; Unwitting; Wilfully blind; Being corrupted; Complicit (Figure 6.1).

This model (Figure 6.1) more effectively reflects the complexity of legal professionals' involvement in the management of criminal proceeds, with various categories between completely innocent involvement and actual knowledge of the criminality in which they are involved. It also, importantly, begins to highlight the numerous *points of decision-making* for the professional, and differentiates between 'isolated' and 'repeat' actions or transactions. The model refers to the appearance or otherwise of 'red flags', and uses the identification of such as the marker separating 'innocent' or 'unwitting' involvement from more complicit forms. Reference to 'red flags' has become common language in guidance, risk assessment and policy documents related to the prevention of money laundering by lawyers and other regulated professionals. The term denotes certain 'warning signs that money laundering could be taking place' (SRA 2014: 12), identified

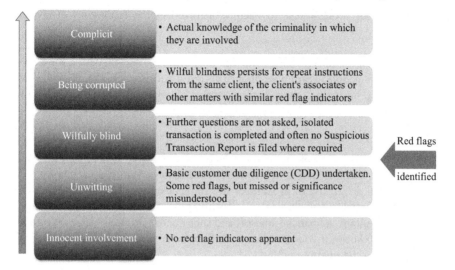

Figure 6.1 Involvement of legal professionals in money laundering and terrorist financing

Source: Adapted from FATF 2013: 35

by bodies such as the FATF and the professions themselves. The FATF identified 42 red flags in its report on the vulnerability of the legal profession to money laundering and terrorist financing, relating to the client, the source of funds, the type of legal professional, and the nature of the retainer (FATF 2013: 77–82). Guidance produced by the Legal Sector Affinity Group, which comprises the anti-money laundering supervisors for the UK legal sector, provides details of a range of 'warning signs' which should give legal professionals 'cause for concern' (LSAG 2018: 132–144), including secretive clients, unusual instructions, use of cash, unclear source of funds, links to particular 'high risk' jurisdictions, and certain methods of funding for property, amongst others. The concept of 'red flags' is related to the move towards a 'risk-based approach' to preventing money laundering which has become increasingly prevalent in recent years (see FATF 2008; Bello and Harvey 2017; van Duyne, Harvey and Gelemerova 2018; Sinha 2020).

Coercion

The FATF continuum does not include a category for *coerced* or *forced* involvement, where legal professionals are made to involuntarily provide services through force (Soudijn 2012) or are 'coerced with threats of violence or by the criminals exerting familial and cultural pressure' (NCA 2014: 7). This might follow initial complicity, where '[o]nce the professional is recruited, physical and other threats may be employed to stretch the boundaries within which the complicit professional is willing to act' (FATF 2010: 46). Interviews with law enforcement personnel working in financial investigation units highlighted the issue of coercion as a reason for professionals to become involved in the facilitation of money laundering:

> Organised crime is no different from anybody else, and they look for weaknesses in people. You know, if they've got a solicitor who they maybe sell drugs to, find in a compromising position or whatever, then they'll exploit that if they can.
>
> [LE3]

> Undoubtedly a lot of the reason they become involved is because they have been compromised, through their private lifestyles. Which does involve recreational drugs, use of prostitutes and things like that. Organised crime are obviously behind all that, [they] identify: hold on here, I've got a solicitor, an accountant, a financial advisor, and then there's no doubt that they go in and, you know, if you don't start working for us we've got pictures or we'll be telling the missus.
>
> [LE2]

The second quote suggests that coercion is a common reason for professionals to become involved in money laundering, but the interviewees provided little evidence to support such an assertion, mentioning just a single case of a solicitor who had been pressured to provide assistance to a criminal group in this way. There is no suggestion in any of the cases of solicitors prosecuted for money laundering offences analysed for this research that coercion was involved, or that the solicitor was forced in some way to agree to provide assistance to the predicate offender. It seems likely that if the use of force or other means of coercion were involved, this would have been used in mitigation during criminal trials or disciplinary proceedings, but the data show no evidence of this argument being made in any of the cases examined. There are inherent risks in the use of coercion, as it would create a relationship with the professional based on antagonism, tension and a lack of trust. Unless it was absolutely necessary, therefore, an approach that made use of 'negligent' or 'corrupt' professionals, or that found a way of exploiting the vulnerabilities identified in the previous chapter without the need for coercion or force, seems more likely.

Wilful blindness

The category of 'wilfully blind' appears on the FATF continuum following the identification of 'red flags', indicating that something about the transaction or client has raised suspicions but these suspicions have been ignored, or further questions which could have confirmed or allayed the suspicions have not been asked, and the transaction has been completed. The *presence* of red flags does not in itself indicate 'wilful blindness' as, according to the model, they could be missed or their 'significance misunderstood'; this would be considered as 'unwitting' involvement. The FATF (2013) model suggests that if the wilful blindness persists beyond 'isolated transactions', for 'repeat instructions from the same client, the client's associates or other matters with similar red flag indicators', the professional should be considered as having been 'corrupted' (it is interesting that they refer to 'being corrupted' rather than 'being *corrupt*' – suggesting a process that has occurred rather than an innate characteristic of the individual). Wilful blindness involves 'conscious avoidance of the truth' and is defined as the 'deliberate failure to make a reasonable inquiry of wrongdoing, despite suspicion or an awareness of the high probability of its existence'.[1] Other terms are used to describe the same behaviour, such as deliberate or wilful ignorance, conscious avoidance, or deliberate indifference; all of which are based on the notion that 'there is an opportunity for knowledge, and a responsibility to be informed, but it is shirked' (Heffernan 2011: 3).

In two of the cases of solicitors convicted of money laundering analysed in this research, reference was made to the solicitors 'turning a blind eye' to suspicions of money laundering or 'closing their eyes' to information that would have indicated the possibility that laundering was taking place (these cases will be considered in the following section). In her book exploring the phenomenon of wilful blindness, Margaret Heffernan (2011) suggests that individuals in certain settings (especially organisational contexts) do not see what they should, or ignore certain indications or information, for a variety of psychological, social, structural and cultural reasons. It was suggested by a number of the interviewees that professionals may ignore their suspicions about a client or the transactions they are involved in, or not ask the right questions or pay sufficient attention to their anti-money laundering obligations to confirm the legitimacy of the client or their funds, because of "commercial considerations", or needing the business that they provided. For example:

> They sort of turn a blind eye to it, influenced no doubt by commercial considerations.
>
> [LE1]

> [F]irms at the lower end of the market who didn't have much work would sort of turn a blind eye or not really think it through.
>
> [SA3]

These quotes suggest that the need to take business opportunities and make a profit may lead legal professionals to agree to act on behalf of clients or in

---

1 Definition from Merriam-Webster's Dictionary of Law (2011). The legal concept of 'wilful blindness' originated in the UK in the case of *R v Sleep* (1861), where the court ruled that the defendant accused of possession of government property could only be convicted if the jury found that he either knew the goods came from government stores or had 'wilfully shut his eyes to the fact' (*R v Sleep* [1861] CCR All ER). For analysis of the legal concept of 'wilful blindness', see, for example, Charlow (1992); Alexander and Furzan (2009: 33–35); Badar (2013: 60–63).

transactions that were not legitimate, without acknowledging suspicions about the client or their funds or asking the questions required to confirm or allay these suspicions. This may happen more often during periods of economic downturn – if firms are struggling to get sufficient work – or other economic pressures are being experienced, and an individual may 'turn a blind eye' during a period of stress or economic difficulty, having acted properly at all other times (Sikka 2008; Huisman and Vande Walle 2010).

The challenge of categorisation

Categorising the nature of legal professionals' involvement in money laundering in terms of their complicity, knowledge and intent, therefore, becomes a significant challenge. It is far more complex and ambiguous than a simple binary distinction allows, and the boundaries between different degrees of intent or 'knowingness' are blurred. As one of the interviewees involved in law enforcement in this area put it, legal professionals' involvement in money laundering often exists "on the sort of borders of knowingness" [LE1]. Interviews with those involved in regulating solicitors, or investigating and/or prosecuting them for money laundering offences, showed an appreciation of these ambiguities and drew attention to the contexts in which legal professionals' actions exist:

> I mean, facilitating is a strange thing. . . . [I]t's not always easy to make the differentiation, I think, between wilful assistance and just ignorance of what they're supposed to do or what's going on in the background. . . .
>
>   You've got people who are not clued up or, or not wilfully assisting. I think you've got those who wilfully assist, and you've got those who, who don't: who do it just because they don't understand the . . . legislation. Someone's coming in and paying in cash, and they're not putting in a suspicious activity report. Not necessarily because they are in collusion with the criminals, but because they just don't really understand that . . . the goal posts have moved. . . . The requirement to report has not really got through their front door yet, they haven't quite got it.'
>
> [CPS1]

> Sometimes it's quite hard to believe that they weren't aware, you know, the situation was so obvious. But at the same time you have to remember that . . . we're dealing with that isolated case when we're assessing it. . . . They probably had any number of different transactions and spent maybe an hour on it in that particular week. The information was drip-fed to them by often very credible, very plausible, very charismatic individuals. And the stories, when we hear them, well if it wasn't for the fact that we have the background and know who these individuals are, you could see how a solicitor could believe them. Whether they accepted that, whether they were duped

and were as much a victim as anybody else, or whether they've got involved in it, it's very difficult to ascertain.

[SA2]

[I]t should be really obvious [that money laundering is involved]. . . . [W]ith hindsight, it's very difficult to see how it wasn't, but to be fair that's often because it's been properly investigated.

[SA3]

In the first quote, the interviewee makes reference to "wilful assistance" – a term that suggests actual knowledge and complicity on behalf of the professional – but struggles to articulate the nature of involvement for those who do not fit this description. The second and third quote highlight that, while it may seem "obvious" that money laundering was taking place with the benefit of hindsight (during or after an investigation), at the time the professional will have been dealing with a number of transactions, may have had little time to spend making checks or taking precautions, and little knowledge of the client's background. The second quote also highlights the difficulty in ascertaining the level of knowledge or intent of the professional after the fact.

The following section considers cases of solicitors convicted for money laundering in relation to the way that their complicity in the laundering, and levels of knowledge or intent, were characterised by those responsible for hearing the cases and making judgments on them. This is based primarily on statements made by judges in sentencing the solicitors during criminal trials and/or by members of the Solicitors Disciplinary Tribunal in subsequent disciplinary hearings. The categorisations, therefore, are based on *assessments* of knowledge, intent or complicity made by those who have heard the cases, rather than *actual* levels of knowledge, intent or complicity. It is not possible to make assertions about the *actual* levels of knowledge or intent involved based on the data that were available, and, as the research did not involve talking to convicted solicitors (for reasons outlined in the 'Research methodology' section of Chapter 1), these issues could not be explored with the solicitors themselves. Interviewing solicitors who had been involved in the facilitation of money laundering, to explore issues of knowledge, intent and complicity, would clearly be a valuable area for future research, but there would still be questions about whether this would allow accurate conclusions to be drawn about their motivations, their intentions when taking actions that served to facilitate money laundering, or the extent of their 'knowingness' in relation to the illicit nature of the funds involved.[2]

---

2 As Levi (2008b: xix) remarks in his study of long-firm fraudsters, '[i]t remains a fascinating problem for psychological and sociological researchers . . . whether and how one can tell when accounts by offenders (and non-offenders) of their motivations (a) are genuinely believed, and (b) represent their 'true' motivations'. Such accounts may be subject to distortion, neutralisation or post hoc rationalisation (see, for example, Benson (1985), Goldstraw-White (2012), Payne (2012: 272–275) and Stadler and Benson (2012) for discussion of the role of denial,

Considering the cases

Transcripts of UK Court of Appeal and Solicitors Disciplinary Tribunal judgments related to some of the 20 cases of solicitors convicted for money laundering offences analysed in this research provide an insight into how issues of knowingness, intent and culpability are considered by those hearing and making decisions on the cases. Three broad categories can be identified:

1   cases where the solicitor is considered to be actively and 'knowingly concerned' in the money laundering; that is, where they know that they are facilitating transactions involving criminal proceeds and intend to do so;
2   cases where reference is made to the solicitor 'turning a blind eye' to knowledge or suspicion of money laundering, or failing to ask appropriate questions to check the legitimacy of transactions;
3   cases where the solicitor's involvement in the money laundering is described as 'unwitting' or 'unknowing'.

This section discusses a few of the cases, incorporating relevant quotes from Court of Appeal and Solicitors Disciplinary Tribunal transcripts. These cases were summarised in Chapter 4; this section includes details of the cases that are relevant for the present discussion. As before, the details of the cases have been compiled by amalgamating a range of data from publicly available sources including Court of Appeal transcripts; Solicitors Disciplinary Tribunal transcripts; media reports; law enforcement, regulator and prosecuting authority press releases; reports, articles and other legal professional publications.

'Knowingly concerned'

PAUL WINTER MORRIS (Case 2) was convicted for involvement in the laundering of £8 million, the proceeds of a large-scale VAT fraud carried out by Raymond Woolley. The criminal funds were diverted to a number of bank accounts controlled by Woolley, and then transferred to Morris' firm's client account. Morris subsequently made individual disbursements from the client account, including to a US-based entertainment company, to Woolley himself, and to make purchases of yachts and cars. As was highlighted in the previous chapter, Morris was judged to have made a degree of financial gain from his involvement in these transactions and was considered to be "far more than" simply a trustee of the funds derived from Woolley's criminal activity [CoA – Morris]. This suggests

---

justification, excuse and 'techniques of neutralisation' (Sykes and Matza 1957) in the accounts of white-collar offenders). Furthermore, this would represent their after-the-fact account of the events only; it would not be possible to understand levels of knowledge and intent or whether processes of neutralisation were used *prior to or at the time* that the specific actions and decisions which led to their involvement in money laundering were taken (see Maruna and Copes 2005).

that Morris was complicit in the laundering activity, and the judge in his trial concluded from the evidence of the case that Morris had been fully aware of his involvement in the laundering of criminal proceeds, telling Morris:

> [You] allowed yourself to play an important role in the laundering of a very large sum of money and did so, in my judgement, and I have sat through this case and heard all the evidence and heard your explanation, you did so in my judgement knowing that it represented the proceeds of criminal conduct.
>
> [SDT – Morris]

GERARD HYDE (Case 7) was a commercial property solicitor who was found to have allowed his firm's client account and a bank account he controlled in the Isle of Man to be used in the movement of the proceeds of a VAT fraud that operated for over a year and was estimated to have defrauded the public revenue by approximately £30 million. Hyde was believed to have laundered £2 million of these proceeds, over an eight-month period. In his sentencing remarks, the trial judge stated that Hyde "for eight months or thereabouts continued to deal in what you knew was very very large money laundering" [SDT – Hyde]. He acknowledged that the personal profit Hyde received from his involvement "was relatively small", but suggested that this was outweighed by Hyde's complicity in the laundering:

> You used your firm's account thereby giving credibility and reputation to the money, that was a very important part of the laundering and you must have known it. You allowed an offshore company of your own to be used. That again had the same consequences, and perhaps most important of all you used the reputation of your firm and the reputation of your profession to persuade others that they were dealing in honest commercial transactions. As you must have known, without that money laundering of the size which we are dealing with here becomes virtually impossible. That is the gravamen of it.
>
> [SDT – Hyde]

BHADRESH GOHIL (Case 15) was convicted in 2010 on a number of counts related to the laundering of $37 million defrauded from the people of Delta State in Nigeria by James Ibori, then governor of the state. Gohil was found to have created a series of complex financial transactions to move and conceal the origins of funds on behalf of Ibori, involving off-shore trusts and shell companies, and allowed his firm's client account to be used for the transfer of criminal proceeds. He was also found to have facilitated the purchase of a $20 million Challenger jet on behalf of Ibori, concealing Ibori's ownership of the jet by devising "a sophisticated money laundering scheme to ensure that the ownership of the jet was made as complicated and as obscure as possible" [CoA – Gohil]. As well as the money laundering offences under POCA 2002, Gohil was convicted of conspiracy to defraud and conspiracy to make false instruments; these convictions related to his long-standing professional relationship with Ibori. During the SDT hearing that followed Gohil's conviction, it was noted that the trial judge's sentencing remarks and the severity of the sentence imposed "left no doubt that the convictions were for offences of dishonesty" [SDT – Gohil].

RICHARD HOUSLEY (Case 19) was convicted of laundering funds totalling £1.8 million, also the proceeds of VAT fraud. Housley was the director of a clothing firm owned by Michael Voudouri, who carried out the frauds with others, and also allowed money from the frauds to be moved through his firm's client accounts. The sentencing statement from Housley's trial concluded that he had been "knowingly concerned in the facilitation of money laundering", and stated that it was "clear [. . .] that the jury did regard you as having actual knowledge or suspicion" [Sentencing Statement – Housley]. The sentencing statement makes it clear, therefore, that Housley was judged to be actively involved in the laundering: he knew that Michael Voudouri was involved in criminal activity, and so knew that the funds that he was moving through his firm's client account on instruction from Voudouri represented the proceeds of crime.

The sentencing statements in these cases suggest that the solicitors were aware that the funds they were passing through their firm's client account, or using to make purchases or other transactions, were of illicit origin (and do not refer to coercion). It is notable that all the cases discussed in this category involve the use of the solicitor's client account as a means of laundering, and that the funds involved are relatively substantial and represent the proceeds of large-scale frauds, such as VAT fraud. This may indicate that a complicit professional is required in such situations – when large amounts are involved and the client account can be used as a means of providing legitimacy and as a conduit for transferring funds (not cash-based; for example, the unpaid tax in VAT fraud) from one or multiple accounts to others. In addition, the laundering in which the solicitor was involved appears to have occurred over a period of time (for example, Gerard Hyde was believed to have been moving criminal funds over an eight-month period). The actions of these professionals, therefore, were not isolated, one-off incidences. The FATF (2013) continuum outlined earlier differentiates between 'isolated' and 'repeat' transactions when distinguishing between legal professionals who are 'wilfully blind' and those they consider to have been 'corrupted'.

'Turning a blind eye'

ANDREW WORMSTONE's (Case 20) conviction for entering into or becoming concerned in an arrangement facilitating the acquisition, retention, use or control of criminal property was related to £2 million that had been defrauded from Sussex University by a group of fraudsters who used a forged invoice for construction work that had been carried out at the University. When the University realised it had made payment into an account that did not belong to the real construction firm, the account was immediately frozen. Wormstone sent documents to the bank in an attempt to provide authenticity to the group who had stolen the funds and persuade the bank to unfreeze the account. Wormstone's conviction was based on the finding that he had "suspected that the funds were criminal property, rather than actual knowledge that this was the case", and he was considered to have "[a]t the very least" turned "a blind eye" to these suspicions [SDT – Wormstone]. The sentencing judge in his trial remarked that

> the jury's verdict means that you suspected that you were being involved with criminal property and being used to cast a cloak of respectability over attempts to free up those funds. At the very least the verdict means that you chose deliberately to turn a blind eye to what you suspected.
>
> [SDT – Wormstone]

PHILIP GRIFFITHS (Case 6) acted as conveyancer in the sale of a property for a couple who had been convicted of involvement in a drug trafficking conspiracy. The property was sold for significantly less than its market value to an estate agent, Leslie Pattison, whom Griffiths had known for a number of years. In his sentencing remarks, the judge in the trial suggested that Griffiths would have seen clearly that money laundering was occurring had he not "closed [his] eyes", and suggested that he did this due to his relationship with Leslie Pattison:

> I take the view that because of your connection with Pattison, you closed your eyes to what would otherwise have been the clearest of evidence staring you in the face.
>
> [SDT – Griffiths]

So, in this case, it was suggested that Griffiths did not consider carefully enough the circumstances of the transaction and its legitimacy, and therefore was unable to see that illegal activity was occurring. He failed to ask appropriate questions or consider the possibility of laundering because of his relationship with Pattison (who acted as a trusted 'broker' in the transaction, as discussed in the previous chapter).

'Unwitting' or 'unknowing'

JONATHAN DUFF (Case 1) was convicted in 2002 for failing to disclose knowledge or suspicion of money laundering. In 1998, a client of Duff's, Gene Gibson, was arrested along with a business associate at Birmingham Airport in possession of cocaine valued at approximately £5 million. They denied all knowledge of the drugs and Duff acted for Gibson in the subsequent criminal proceedings. Six months after the initial arrest, the two men were further charged with conspiracy to import drugs between the years of 1996 and 1998. During this two-year period, Duff had been involved in a number of transactions on behalf of Gibson, involving upwards of £70,000. Following Gibson's arrest on conspiracy charges, Duff claimed, he became aware that he might have been used for the purposes of money laundering. He consulted Law Society literature on the matter and concluded that, as the transactions were in the past and because of his duties to

Gibson as a client, he was under no duty of disclosure. At that stage, he took no further advice on the matter. Following Gibson's and an associate's convictions in 1999, Duff took advice from a solicitor who advised him that his conclusion that he had been under no duty to report was correct.

The judgment from Duff's (failed) appeal against his sentence states that he "had been drawn, albeit unwittingly" [CoA – Duff] into the money laundering offence, and in the transcript from the Solicitors Disciplinary Tribunal (SDT) hearing, Duff is described as having "been unwittingly used for the purpose of drug money laundering" [SDT – Duff]. This suggests that Duff's involvement in the facilitation of money laundering was unintentional; that he did not purposefully provide assistance to his client in the laundering of criminal proceeds. The transactions that Duff carried out on behalf of Gibson had occurred prior to Gibson's initial arrest at Birmingham Airport. It is not possible to ascertain from the information available what Duff knew or suspected about Gibson's business activities, illicit or otherwise, prior to his arrest, but it is clear that the judge in his case and subsequent appeal, and the members of the SDT present at his hearing, were satisfied that he had been 'unwittingly used' to facilitate money laundering. Duff was sentenced to six months' imprisonment following his conviction for failing to disclose knowledge or suspicion of money laundering. Therefore, this case demonstrates that it is possible to be convicted and receive a custodial sentence even if it is concluded that there was no criminal intent involved, and that the professional had been 'unwittingly used' in the money laundering activity. This is due to the broad scope of money laundering legislation in the UK, which allows for conviction without criminal intent; this will be discussed in the following chapter.

JONATHAN KRESTIN (Case 8) was convicted under section 328 of POCA 2002, in relation to the movement of the proceeds of a large-scale VAT fraud conducted by Michel Namer. Between 2003 and 2005, Krestin undertook small amounts of commercial work for Namer, who had been introduced to Krestin by a tax advisor at a large accountancy firm, as a client of the tax advisor who required a solicitor to undertake this work. The transaction for which Krestin was convicted was the receipt and subsequent disbursement (on Namer's instructions) of €14,000 to a bank account controlled by an acquaintance of Namer's.

In sentencing Krestin, the judge remarked that

> I do not think for one moment that Mr Krestin given his excellent character, his long experience as a lawyer working his way up to become the senior and managing partner of his firm, was in any sense guilty of knowing assistance
>
> [SDT – Krestin]

and that Krestin

> was certainly not knowingly trying to break the law.
>
> [SDT – Krestin]

The SDT agreed with this conclusion, stating in its final decision:

> It was clear that [Krestin] had not been aware of, actively involved in or had made any profit from the money laundering activities of his client.
>
> [SDT – Krestin]

Therefore, as with Jonathan Duff, those involved in hearing Krestin's case in the criminal courts and disciplinary tribunal concluded that he had not been actively involved in the money laundering, had not knowingly assisted Namer to manage his criminal proceeds, and had received no profit from the laundering. However, reports on the case and the transcript from his SDT hearing highlight that prior to Krestin transferring the €14,000, he had received a court order cataloguing the criminal offences that Namer was suspected of:

> The payment had been made following a draft production order to [Krestin], dated 21st September 2005, that had set out the criminal case against Mr Namer, had named the companies and entities in whom the customs had been interested and had warned [Krestin] about the offence of tipping-off Mr Namer.
>
> Leading Counsel explained that in the circumstances [Krestin] had believed that he had no choice but to make the payment as instructed by Mr Namer, but the jury had found the offence proved. [Krestin] now fully accepted that he should have taken legal advice at the time about whether or not to make the payment requested after the date of the production order because that order had put him on notice.
>
> [SDT – Krestin]

This indicates that Krestin would have suspected that any money belonging to Namer could have been the proceeds of criminal activity, but would not have known for certain that this was the case. It therefore highlights the *decision taken* by Krestin in choosing to go ahead with the transfer of funds, a decision he made without first taking legal advice. Krestin argued that he "had believed that he had no choice but to make the payment as instructed by Mr Namer" [SDT – Krestin], and the tribunal accepted that this "had been [. . .] a very difficult decision" [SDT – Krestin].

ANDREW TIDD (Case 18) acted as conveyancing solicitor for a client, Nevzat Kocabey, in the purchase of two properties. The transactions occurred while, or shortly after, Kocabey was in custody for drug offences. Tidd maintained that he had been aware that Kocabey was in custody, but believed it to be related to a dispute with a former business partner. He said that he was not aware until much later, when he was questioned by the police, that it was related to drug offences, and said that he had never had any suspicions that Kocabey was involved in drugs or that the transactions were in any way tainted. The data on the Tidd case show that the court and disciplinary tribunal accepted that he had not known or suspected that Kocabey was engaged in money laundering, but that he had reasonable grounds to suspect he was:

> It was clear that the Respondent had not known or, indeed, suspected that Mr K was involved in money laundering. Rather, the Respondent had had information which he received in the course of his legal practice which gave reasonable grounds for knowing or suspecting that Mr K was involved in money laundering but he had not made the required disclosure.
>
> [SDT – Tidd]

> [T]his showed a degree of culpability considerably below that of a person who had actually suspected money laundering. The offences were ones of failing to report, not of involvement in money laundering.
>
> [SDT – Tidd]

These quotes highlight that Tidd was convicted under section 330 of POCA 2002, the offence of 'Failure to Report: Regulated Sector', for failing to disclose to the authorities knowledge or suspicion that his client was involved in money laundering. Under this part of the legislation, regulated professionals can be convicted even if they did not have actual knowledge or suspicion that someone was engaged in money laundering, but they had reasonable grounds to suspect this (the offence of 'Failure to Report', and its implications for regulated professionals, will be discussed in the following chapter). As shown in the second quote, different money laundering offences are associated with different levels of culpability. Solicitors such as Tidd, convicted under section 330 of POCA 2002, are considered to have a lower "degree of culpability" than those who had 'actual knowledge or suspicion'. During Tidd's trial, the judge had underlined that this was "the lowest level of criminal responsibility under the Scheme of the 2002 Act" [SDT – Tidd]. The assessment that Tidd's actions entailed a lower personal culpability and level of criminal responsibility was related to a lack of intention to cause harm, the absence of dishonesty, and Tidd being guilty of 'misjudgement' rather than deliberate, knowing involvement in the laundering:

> [T]he degree of personal culpability on the part of the Respondent in this particular case was minimal; he had misjudged his client and the situation and had not intended any harm.
>
> [SDT – Tidd]

Decision-making and context

Examination of the case data highlights the various *points of decision-making* of legal professionals when dealing with clients and transactions that may be used to facilitate money laundering, and the role of the situational context in shaping the decisions or choices that are made. These are not necessarily decisions *to facilitate money laundering* or *to commit an offence*. Instead, for example, there are decisions to proceed with a transaction requested by a client; to agree to act as conveyancer in a particular property purchase or sale; to accept certain funds into client account; to transfer the ownership of assets; to provide legal or financial advice when requested; to help a friend or family member; to make a phone call or send a letter; to not ask certain questions or look for further information; or to not make a disclosure under the money laundering regulations.

For example, JONATHAN KRESTIN (Case 8) chose to conduct a transaction requested by Michel Namer, which involved the receipt of funds into client account and their subsequent disbursement to another account. This transaction involved the same processes and behaviours as a legitimate transaction – that is, it was a 'normal' transaction, as described in the previous chapter. The difference between this transaction and a legitimate transaction is not in the *action* taken but in the *origins of the funds* involved, and so Krestin's decision on whether to proceed in this context was not based on a question of the nature of the *transaction* but of the licit or illicit nature of the *funds*. Looking back at the Krestin case, and considering that the transaction had been conducted following his receipt of a production order setting out a criminal case against Namer, it may seem obvious that Krestin should have had suspicions about the illicit nature of the funds. However, this isolates his decision-making, failing to take account of the particular circumstances surrounding the decision which may have influenced it – for example, the other decisions he was making or other business that he was involved in at that particular point in time, or the nature of his relationship with Namer. Krestin's decision may also have been influenced by the warning he had received alongside the production order about 'tipping off' Namer. 'Tipping off' is an offence under section 333 of POCA 2002; it refers to the act of making a disclosure likely to prejudice a money laundering investigation. If Krestin had told Namer that he was subject to a criminal investigation relating to money laundering, he would have been committing an offence under this part of the legislation. Therefore, had Krestin decided not to proceed with the transaction, he would have had to do this without letting Namer know that he was under suspicion.

Similarly, ANDREW TIDD (Case 18) made the decision to proceed with a transaction – or series of transactions – that, in themselves, were no different to other transactions that he would regularly conduct (Tidd was a conveyancing solicitor, and so the focus of his work was acting as conveyancer in the purchase and sale of property; he would therefore have acted for many clients in the same way that he acted for Kocabey). The decision on whether to proceed with this conveyancing was, again, not based on the nature of the *transaction* but on the nature of *funds* or the *client* involved. Therefore, like Krestin, Tidd's decision to proceed with these transactions was grounded in the context of his regular work and in the specific circumstances surrounding the decision-making. The Tribunal in Tidd's case, having heard the facts of the case, concluded that while Tidd

> should have been on notice that there were circumstances which required further enquiry, [. . .] all of the circumstances had given him comfort. The transactions on which he had been instructed by Mr K were entirely normal

for a businessman engaged, as Mr K was, in the fast food business. [. . .] Whilst [Tidd] should have been alert to the reasons for Mr K's detention the Tribunal accepted that he had accepted the explanation given by Mr K's wife, which in turn tied in with other information held by [Tidd]. [Tidd] may have been naïve, but he had not acted with any malice.

[SDT – Tidd]

In addition, Tidd had

received a reference for Mr K from a high street bank, in connection with a proposed transaction, which stated that he had been a customer of the bank for 2–5 years; this appeared to provide evidence that the client was a bona fide businessman.

[SDT – Tidd]

These statements recognise the circumstances in which Tidd made the decisions to proceed with property purchases on behalf of Kocabey, including the fact that, as Kocabey was involved in legitimate businesses, the transactions in which he instructed Tidd were "entirely normal". Kocabey's position as a businessman granted him a level of legitimacy that impacted on Tidd's decision. In addition, as was discussed in the previous chapter, there was a 'broker' involved in the relationship between the solicitor and his client, as they had been introduced by Kocabey's brother, who was a long-standing client of Tidd's and himself a 'respected businessman'. These factors could have contributed to the perception of Kocabey as trustworthy and legitimate, and therefore may have affected Tidd's decision to proceed with the transactions. During his SDT hearing, Tidd suggested that the error he made was not to find out what Kocabey was in custody for; had he done this, "none of the events leading to his conviction would have happened" [SDT – Tidd]. Therefore, the five counts on which he had been convicted "all flowed from one error of judgement, which he made in the first instance" [SDT – Tidd].

The presence of a 'broker' was also identified in the case of PHILLIP GRIF-FITHS (Case 6), who acted as conveyancer in the sale of a property from convicted drug traffickers to an estate agent, Leslie Pattison, who was a close associate. Griffiths' relationship with Pattison provided a degree of legitimacy to the transaction, and the decision he made to be involved in the transaction can be seen in the context of this relationship. Griffiths was considered to have made an error of "professional judgement" in deciding to proceed with the transaction, not consistent with the "high standards expected" of someone in his professional position:

He was well acquainted with his client and the legitimacy of the source of the funds used to finance the transaction. The jury found that he had been wrong in his professional judgement as to the reason for and legitimacy of the transaction.

[SDT – Griffiths]

[T]his offence is the product of a lapse in the high standards expected of a solicitor.

[CoA – Griffiths]

As discussed in the previous chapter, the cases of MOHAMMED JAHANGIR FARID (Case 9), RACHEL TAYLOR (Case 10) and AMINAT AFOLABI (Case 12) highlight how a personal relationship between the professional and the individual whose criminal proceeds they are involved in laundering may impact on their decisions. For example, Jahangir Farid's actions were said to have been "committed under the malign influence of his older brother" [CoA – Farid], and Taylor's conviction related to assistance she had provided to her former partner, Pardeep Bains, with whom she remained on close terms. Bains asked Taylor for help completing tax returns for a fake motor trading business that he used to account for the income from his criminal activity. Taylor's actions in this case, which amounted to little more than writing out a series of figures purporting to be income, expenses and profit from the motor trading business, but which nonetheless were enough to result in a conviction for money laundering, were surely a direct result of her relationship with Bains, and the decision she took to help Bains based on this relationship.

The point of highlighting the decisions taken by those who have become involved in money laundering, and the factors that might have shaped them, is not to excuse the choices that were made, to imply that no wrongdoing occurred, or to suggest that no blame should be attached. It is simply to draw attention to the idea that actions (or non-actions) that serve to facilitate money laundering may not be the result of a 'motivated offender' who has made a deliberate choice to assist in the laundering of criminal proceeds. Instead, they may be a consequence of errors of judgement or 'bad' decisions in relation to specific transactions or clients; decisions that will be taken in the course of legal professionals' routine, everyday work, and will be shaped by their occupational and organisational context, the relationship(s) between actors involved, the particular circumstances leading up and surrounding the decisions, and the wider environment in which they are located. The rationality of these decisions, therefore, is 'bounded' by personal and situational factors, including the personal characteristics, perceptions, emotions and biases of those making the decisions; the limits of the information they possess and how they process it; and the situational contexts in which the decisions are being made (e.g. Simon 1957, 1996; Nee and Meenaghan 2006; Van Gelder 2013).

Conclusion

Undoubtedly, there are legal professionals who are fully complicit, active participants in money laundering, who *know* that they are facilitating transactions involving criminal proceeds and *intend* to do so (and have not been coerced or forced into doing so). A small number of the cases of convicted solicitors analysed in this research could be considered to fall within this category, and their actions may be described as 'knowing involvement' or 'wilful assistance'. It is for this group that understanding how and where the *opportunities* for facilitating money laundering arise, and how these opportunities could be impeded, is particularly important. In line with 'opportunity theories' of white-collar crime, such complicit professionals could be seen as motivated offenders, making a rational choice to take advantage of opportunities to facilitate money laundering for the (financial or competitive) benefit of themselves or their organisation (e.g. Benson and Simpson 2018). For this group of actors, therefore, there are a number of further research or policy questions that should be considered, for example: What are the opportunities for the facilitation of money laundering and how, where and why are they created? What can be done to reduce or impede these opportunities? How do these actors facilitate money laundering? What are the mechanisms or 'crime commission' processes (Cornish 1994; Levi and Maguire 2004) involved? ('Why' matters less than 'how' in this question.) How do the professional and predicate offender come together (at 'the points at which criminals and conventional society meet' [Passas 2002: 31])? What is the basis of this relationship, and who finds or seeks out whom? Some of these questions have been addressed in this book, but they should also form the basis for future research and analysis.

However, for many legal professionals whose actions (or non-actions) have in some way facilitated money laundering, their role will *not* have involved complicit, intentional participation. For some there may have been a *complete* lack of knowledge and intent, as described in the FATF model as 'innocent involvement', where no warning signs or 'red flags' were apparent and so there was no opportunity for suspicions to be raised. An absence of intent (i.e. intending to facilitate money laundering) may be more likely than a complete lack of knowledge, however, and for many legal professionals who facilitate laundering, their involvement will sit on the 'borders of knowingness'. This 'border region' could include professionals that suspect that a transaction is not completely legitimate, or involves funds that may come from criminal activity, but do not know for sure. They may choose not to act on these suspicions, perhaps due to commercial reasons or a lack of understanding of their obligations, or not ask the questions that would confirm or refute their suspicions, or look too closely at the transactions. It could also include those that had no suspicions of money laundering, but did not carry out sufficient checks or failed to undertake correct procedures. In these cases, there will be no real intent to launder, or actual dishonesty on the part of the professional; their actions will not represent a *deliberate choice to offend* and they are not *taking opportunities* to facilitate money laundering, for reasons of financial gain or otherwise.

Attention should be focused, therefore, on consideration of the *points of decision-making* of legal professionals when dealing with clients or conducting financial or commercial transactions, and the situational contexts that shape these decisions. Decisions made by professionals to proceed with certain transactions, or not report a suspicion of money laundering, may be shaped by the nature of their occupational role, their organisational setting, relationships with other actors involved, and the particular circumstances leading up to and surrounding the point at which the decision is made. Their occupational role involves carrying out transactions on a regular basis that do not differ essentially from transactions which can serve to facilitate money laundering, apart from the licit or illicit nature of the funds involved. Due to the nature of their work environment, professionals may be making a number of decisions at the same time, be carrying out multiple transactions, or conducting other business. Decisions they make to proceed with transactions will be encouraged by the perceived legitimacy of a client, which may be influenced by the presence of a trusted 'broker' of some kind in the relationship. In addition, these choices will be made within certain organisational contexts (with associated structural and cultural features) and within the context of a profit-making business in a competitive market, with the commercial considerations that this entails.

Even if they are not fully complicit, active participants in money laundering, professionals whose actions serve to launder criminal proceeds are still *making choices*, even if they are not *choosing to offend*, and are *taking decisions*, even if they are not *taking opportunities*. The decisions and choices they make which act to facilitate money laundering are rational within their situational context; that is, their actions are 'made rational' by their situated nature (Vaughan 1998: 25). So, for this group, rather than considering opportunities for the facilitation of money laundering and questions about the nature of these opportunities and how they could be impeded, consideration should be given to how they could be encouraged to make the 'right' decisions and who is responsible for that. (This also raises questions about what is meant by the 'right' decision and who gets to decide that, and how encouragement to make the 'right' decision is balanced with legal professionals' responsibilities towards their clients and other professional and legal obligations.)

Complicit professionals, who were actively and knowingly engaged in money laundering on behalf of their clients, appeared to comprise only a small number of the cases analysed in this research (i.e. Cases 2, 7, 15, 19). Many fell within a 'grey area', where the degree of knowledge and intent was less clear, and for some of the solicitors there appeared to have been no criminal intent or active, knowing involvement in the laundering.[3] Despite this, these professionals were prosecuted and received criminal convictions. The following chapter examines in more detail the legislative framework under which these professionals were convicted, which was outlined in Chapter 2. It focuses particularly on the concepts of knowledge and suspicion within the legislation, and the wide scope of the legislation, which allows for conviction without criminal intent or active, knowing involvement.

---

3 It is not possible, however, to conclude from the available data that 'complicit' involvement is less common than other less knowing or intentional forms. As the data were based on *convicted* solicitors, it is possible that cases of complicit professional involvement were missed, if they were not prosecuted or a conviction was not secured (reasons for failure to prosecute or secure a conviction in such cases will be considered in Chapter 8).

7 Knowledge and suspicion in the legislative framework

Introduction

The cases analysed in this research include solicitors who had been convicted of money laundering offences even though they were adjudged to have had no intention to launder criminal proceeds, nor active engagement in the laundering. JONATHAN DUFF (Case 1) was considered to have "been drawn, albeit unwittingly" [CoA – Duff] into the money laundering offence, and "unwittingly used for the purpose of drug money laundering" [SDT – Duff]. In sentencing JONATHAN KRESTIN (Case 8), the judge stated that he believed Krestin was not "in any sense guilty of knowing assistance" or "knowingly trying to break the law" [SDT – Krestin]. The Solicitors Disciplinary Tribunal panel concluded that Krestin "had not been aware of, actively involved in or had made any profit from the money laundering activities of his client" [SDT – Krestin]. In the case of ANDREW TIDD (Case 18), it was found that he "had not known or, indeed, suspected that [his client] was involved in money laundering" [SDT – Tidd]. Instead, Tidd "had information which he received in the course of his legal practice which gave *reasonable grounds for knowing or suspecting* that [his client] was involved in money laundering" [SDT – Tidd; emphasis added]. As the previous chapter highlighted, it is difficult (and may be impossible) to know the actual level of knowledge or intent involved when a legal professional facilitates money laundering. What this research has highlighted, however, is that lawyers (and other regulated professionals) can be convicted of money laundering offences even if they are not considered to have been actively or knowingly involved in the laundering. This is possible because of the wide scope of the legislation used to prosecute such activity in the UK, which allows for conviction without criminal intent or even, in certain circumstances, actual knowledge or suspicion that laundering was taking place. This chapter explores relevant sections of the Proceeds of Crime Act 2002 – specifically provisions relating to *knowledge* and *suspicion* – to demonstrate how the UK legislative framework goes beyond the requirements and recommendations of international standards. It then presents arguments by individuals involved in the investigation and prosecution of professionals suspected of facilitating money laundering, in support of the inclusion of aspects of the legislation that allow for conviction without actual knowledge of the laundering or criminal intent, and considers the views of legal professionals themselves on their obligations under anti-money laundering laws.

Proceeds of Crime Act 2002: sections 327, 328 and 329

As detailed in Chapter 2, the three principal money laundering offences in UK legislation are contained in sections 327, 328 and 329 of Part 7 of the Proceeds of Crime Act (POCA) 2002. Section 327 covers the offence of concealing, disguising, converting or transferring criminal property, or removing criminal property from England and Wales, Scotland or Northern Ireland (POCA 2002, s.327[1]). Section 328 focuses on involvement in arrangements known or suspected to facilitate money laundering, stating that a person commits an offence if he

> enters into or becomes concerned in an arrangement which he *knows or suspects* facilitates (by whatever means) the acquisition, retention, use or control of criminal property by or on behalf of another person.
>
> (POCA 2002, s.328[1]; emphasis added)

Section 329 relates to the acquisition, possession or use of criminal property (POCA 2002, s.329[1]). Within all three offences, the proceeds of crime to which the offences relate are referred to as 'criminal property', defined as property that:

> constitutes a person's benefit from criminal conduct or it represents such a benefit (in whole or part or whether directly or indirectly), and the alleged offender *knows or suspects* that it constitutes or represents such benefit.
>
> (POCA 2002, s.340; emphasis added)

These offences, therefore, have a *mens rea* at the level of 'suspicion'; actual knowledge is not required for a conviction. Sections 327 and 329 do not stipulate *mens rea* in themselves; that is taken from the definition of 'criminal property' in section 340. However, under section 328, there is a double *mens rea* requirement: this offence covers situations where a third party becomes involved in an arrangement they *know or suspect* facilitates the acquisition, retention, use or control of what they *know or suspect* to represent direct or indirect 'benefit' from criminal conduct. Kebbell (2017: 742) highlights the broad scope of the definition of criminal property, which is 'so widely cast that it encompasses all crimes, and extends to any direct or indirect "benefit" derived from criminal conduct'.[1] This means that minor offences and regulatory breaches with crimi-

---

1 The precise meaning of 'benefit' is also unclear. Reference is made in POCA 2002 to 'property' and 'pecuniary advantage' ('property' is defined in s.340[9] as[a] money; [b] all forms of property, real or personal, heritable or moveable; [c] things in action and other intangible or incorporeal property; 'pecuniary advantage' is not defined but is referenced in s.340[6] and [7]). However, the concept of 'benefit' also 'includes any notional saving made pursuant to criminal conduct' (Kebbell 2017: 742).

nal sanctions attached can constitute a predicate offence, and as soon as a legal professional has a suspicion that a client has benefitted in any way from such an offence they are at risk of committing an offence under POCA 2002 if they facilitate a transaction on his or her behalf (Kebbell 2017; Law Commission 2019: Chapter 5).

The concept of suspicion in these provisions is ambiguous, and there is no objective definition provided. The case of *R v Da Silva* [2007] 1 WLR 303 provided some direction on how it should be interpreted, stating:

> It seems to us that the essential element in the word 'suspect' and its affiliates, in this context, is that the defendant must think that there is a possibility, which is more than fanciful, that the relevant facts exist. A vague feeling of unease would not suffice.

Guidance on the meaning of 'suspicion' is provided for the legal profession by the anti-money laundering guidance document produced by the legal sector anti-money laundering supervisors in the UK (LSAG 2018: 88), which advises its members:

> There is no requirement for the suspicion to be clearly or firmly grounded on specific facts, but there must be a degree of satisfaction, not necessarily amounting to belief, but at least extending beyond speculation.
>
> The test for whether you hold a suspicion is a subjective one.
>
> If you think a transaction is suspicious, you are not expected to know the exact nature of the criminal offence or that particular funds were definitely those arising from the crime. You may have noticed something unusual or unexpected and after making enquiries, the facts do not seem normal or make commercial sense. You do not have to have evidence that money laundering is taking place to have suspicion.

Therefore, although suspicion requires a level of satisfaction greater than mere speculation, it does not require a clear factual basis. Legal professionals could be considered to have suspicion of money laundering without specific facts or evidence, and without knowing the nature of the predicate offence or that the funds they were dealing with were definitely the proceeds of crime.[2]

---

2 A 2018 Law Commission consultation on the UK's Suspicious Activity Reporting regime found that 'the concept of suspicion itself remains ill-defined, unclear and inconsistently applied' by those with an obligation to report suspicions of money laundering (Law Commission 2018: para 4.16). The subsequent report considered whether this lack of definitional clarity meant that a statutory definition of suspicion should be included in POCA 2002, but concluded that 'a definition of suspicion is unwarranted and likely to be unworkable in practice' (Law Commission 2019: para 5.49). Instead they suggested that a single authoritative source of guidance on the suspicion threshold would be a better approach, recommending that 'POCA is amended to require the Secretary of State to issue guidance on suspicion' (Law Commission 2019: para 5.83).

The *mens rea* requirements for these offences differ markedly from the international frameworks from which POCA 2002 derived. The FATF 40 Recommendations, related UN conventions and successive Money Laundering Directives have a much greater focus on intent and knowledge, and are directed more towards those deliberately laundering criminal proceeds. The use of 'suspicion' as the basis for criminal liability cannot be found in money laundering provisions in either the 1998 United Nations Convention Against Illicit Traffic in Narcotic Drugs and Psychotropic Substances (the Vienna Convention) or the 2005 Council of Europe Convention on Laundering, Search, Seizure and Confiscation of the Proceeds from Crime and on the Financing of Terrorism (the Warsaw Convention). In addition, both Conventions require states to create criminal offences related to money laundering under domestic law only 'when committed intentionally'.[3] EU Money Laundering Directives have consistently defined money laundering as conduct that is 'committed intentionally'. For example, Article 1 of the Fourth Money Laundering Directive, introduced in May 2015, states:

1   This Directive aims to prevent the use of the Union's financial system for the purposes of money laundering and terrorist financing.
2   Member States shall ensure that money laundering and terrorist financing are prohibited.
3   For the purposes of this Directive, the following conduct, *when committed intentionally*, shall be regarded as money laundering:

   (a) the conversion or transfer of property, *knowing* that such property is derived from criminal activity or from an act of participation in such activity, for the purpose of concealing or disguising the illicit origin of the property or of assisting any person who is involved in the commission of such an activity to evade the legal consequences of that person's action;
   (b) the concealment or disguise of the true nature, source, location, disposition, movement, rights with respect to, or ownership of property, *knowing* that such property is derived from criminal activity or from an act of participation in such activity;
   (c) the acquisition, possession or use of property, *knowing*, at the time of receipt, that such property was derived from criminal activity or from an act of participation in such activity;
   (d) participation in, association to commit, attempts to commit and aiding, abetting, facilitating and counselling the commission of any of the actions referred to in points (a), (b) and (c).[4]

---

3 Council of Europe Convention on Laundering, Search, Seizure and Confiscation of the Proceeds from Crime and on the Financing of Terrorism CETS 198 (2005), Article 9, para. 1; United Nations Convention Against Illicit Traffic in Narcotic Drugs and Psychotropic Substances (1998), Article 3, para. 1.
4 Directive 2015/849/EU of the European Parliament and of the Council of 20 May 2015 on the prevention of the use of the financial system for the purposes of money laundering or terrorist financing [2015] (Fourth Money Laundering Directive) (emphases added).

The wording in this Article echoes that of the previous three Directives. The most recent (at time of writing) Directive states that it 'aims to criminalise money laundering when it is committed intentionally and with the knowledge that the property was derived from criminal activity' (Sixth Money Laundering Directive,[5] para. 13). It is clear, therefore, that the primary money laundering offences in UK law go well beyond what is required by international standards, with no requirement for criminal intent and the mental element being satisfied by suspicion. In other words, the legislation is not aimed solely at those deliberately laundering criminal proceeds; its scope is much broader, allowing for the inclusion of a wider range of acts (and omissions) and for those who are less directly – and unintentionally – involved in money laundering.

'Failure to Disclose: Regulated Sector' (section 330)

The section 330 offence of Failure to Disclose: Regulated Sector, which creates the obligation to inform the authorities of suspicions of money laundering, goes even further. In this offence, the mental element of knowledge and suspicion is extended to include the objective test of '*having reasonable grounds*' for such knowledge or suspicion. Section 330 states that persons commits an offence if:

- they know or suspect, *or have reasonable grounds to know or suspect*, that another person is engaged in money laundering; and
- the information or other matter on which their knowledge or suspicion is based, *or which gives reasonable grounds for such knowledge or suspicion*, comes to them in the course of a business in the regulated sector; and
- the person does not make the required disclosure as soon as is practicable after the information or other matter comes to him.

(POCA 2002, s.330[1–4]; emphases added)

The objective test therefore asks whether there were

> factual circumstances from which an honest and reasonable person, engaged in a business in the regulated sector, should have inferred knowledge or formed the suspicion that another was engaged in money laundering.
>
> (LSAG 2018: 88).

This means that those working in the regulated sector can be found guilty of a 'failure to disclose' offence under section 330 if they *should have* known or suspected another person was engaged in money laundering, even if they lacked *actual* knowledge of such conduct. As such, a failure to disclose knowledge or suspicion of money laundering is treated as a criminal offence in the same way

---

5 Directive (EU) 2018/1673 of the European Parliament and of the Council of 23 October 2018 on combating money laundering by criminal law [2018].

as deliberate money laundering, albeit with a lesser sentence attached for conviction.[6] This was reflected in the cases examined in this research, with criminal convictions for solicitors such as PHILLIP GRIFFITHS (Case 6) and ANDREW TIDD (Case 18), who the court accepted "had not known or, indeed, suspected that [the client] was involved in money laundering", but had received information "which gave reasonable grounds for knowing or suspecting that [the client] was involved in money laundering" [SDT – Tidd].

Within the cases, those who were convicted only of 'failure to disclose' offences under section 330 (or, in the case of Jonathan Duff, section 52 of the Drug Trafficking Act 1994, which preceded POCA 2002) received sentences at the lower end of the spectrum. There was considerable variation in the sentences received by the solicitors in the cases examined, ranging from a fine of £2,515 to custodial sentences of up to five years for money laundering offences alone (BHADRESH GOHIL (Case 15) received a sentence of seven years' imprisonment, but he was convicted of multiple offences including conspiracy to defraud and conspiracy to make false instruments).[7] Four solicitors were convicted solely of 'failure to disclose' offences: JONATHAN DUFF (Case 1), PHILLIP GRIFFITHS (Case 6), ANDREW TIDD (Case 18) and MARTIN WILCOCK (Case 14). They received sentences ranging from a fine of £2,515 (Wilcock), to a suspended sentence of 4 months' imprisonment (Tidd), to six-month custodial sentences (Duff and Griffiths). Therefore, while these sentences are at the lower end of the range, they show that it is still possible to receive custodial sentences for 'failing to disclose' suspicions of money laundering. This has significant implications for individuals and organisations in the regulated sector, and places considerable responsibility on them to be alert to possible money laundering. The rationale for the inclusion of the 'reasonable grounds' test was that

> persons who are carrying out activities in the regulated sector should be expected to exercise a higher level of diligence in handling transactions than those employed in other businesses.[8]

This reflects the characterisation of professionals in the regulated sector as 'gatekeepers', and their obligations to prevent money laundering in line with their role in the global 'fight' against money laundering. However, once again, UK legislation goes further than international requirements, with the Moscow

6 Under sections 327, 328 and 329, maximum sentence is six months' imprisonment or a fine on summary conviction, and 14 years' imprisonment and/or a fine on indictment. Under section 330, maximum sentence is six months' imprisonment or a fine on summary conviction, and five years' imprisonment and/or a fine on indictment.
7 See Appendix for details of sentences received in all the cases.
8 POCA 2002: Explanatory Notes. Available at: www.legislation.gov.uk/ukpga/2002/29/notes/contents [Accessed 29 July 2019].

Communiqué referring only to 'making the *intentional* failure to file [suspicious transaction] reports a punishable offence'.[9]

Scope of the legislation: justifications and risks

Money laundering legislation in the UK, therefore, has an extremely broad scope, allowing for conviction without criminal intent; incorporating a *mens rea* of suspicion, which does not require a clear factual basis, knowledge of the nature of the predicate offence, or certain knowledge of the criminal origins of the funds involved; and, for regulated professionals specifically, allowing for conviction if there were 'reasonable grounds' to suspect that someone was engaged in money laundering and not reporting this, even if they did not actually have such suspicions. This represents a notable departure from the international frameworks from which UK money laundering legislation derived, which focus on those who have *deliberately* laundered criminal proceeds. The breadth of the legislation means that what is considered as the 'facilitation of money laundering' by legal professionals in legal terms is wide ranging, incorporating different degrees of intent and knowingness. This was demonstrated in the cases discussed in the previous chapter, which included not only those who were actively, knowingly engaged in laundering, but also those who were considered to have been unwittingly involved or to have had no actual knowledge or suspicion that laundering was taking place.

It was argued by representatives of law enforcement and the Crown Prosecution Service (CPS) interviewed during this research that the 'Failure to Disclose' offence was a necessary and beneficial element of the legislation, due to the difficulties of proving actual knowledge or suspicion, and the possibility that those who 'turn a blind eye' to money laundering could avoid prosecution. Interviewees from a financial investigation unit stated that the section 330 offence offered them a better route for prosecution of professionals involved in money laundering, by avoiding the difficulties they had previously experienced with proving active involvement:

> We've discussed recently . . . that, in the cases we currently have going, that do have a number of solicitors involved, is that we'd look at the 'Failing to Disclose' element of it. Lower burden of proof for us, there's a reasonable person test in there, isn't there? And we perhaps pursue that instead of trying

9 Ministerial Conference of the G-8 Countries on Combating Transnational Organized Crime (Moscow, October 19th–20 1999) Communiqué, para. 32 (emphasis added) Available at: www.justice.gov/sites/default/files/ag/legacy/2004/06/09/99MoscowCommunique.pdf [Accessed 29 July 2019]. The Moscow Communiqué was published following a meeting of G8 interior and justice ministers in 1999, at which concerns about the involvement of financial intermediaries in money laundering schemes were highlighted, and which led to the FATF Recommendations on money laundering being revised to extend due diligence and reporting requirements to those identified as 'gatekeeper professionals' (see Chapter 1).

to prove these guys were involved in money laundering. So that's our, certainly a live discussion we're having. And that's how we're going to pursue currently to see if we have a different outcome.

[LE4]

So, you know, they can't hide behind the fact that they're a professional, you know, they made their enquiries about knowing who the customer was. You know, how would they know that [D]'s a drug dealer? But when you ask them, well [D]'s buying a house but £20,000 is coming from a third party – who is that third party and why would they be giving you £20,000 when you've asked them, on your file, where did the money come from? Or, the other side of the sale's asked where did the money come from for the deposit? And they don't ask, there's nothing captured anywhere. Well, surely a reasonable person would have said "where's your money coming from?" . . . We're going to rely on that.

[LE4]

It is notable that some of the cases analysed that resulted in convictions under section 330 had originated as prosecutions for other offences, or had included other offences alongside the section 330 offence. In these cases, the solicitor had either been acquitted of the other charges but found guilty of a 'failure to disclose' (e.g. PHILLIP GRIFFITHS (Case 6), who was also charged with section 328 and section 329 offences but found not guilty of these), or had agreed to plead guilty to the section 330 offence on the agreement that the other charges would be dropped (e.g. ANDREW TIDD (Case 18)). This supports Interviewee LE4's suggestion that the section 330 offence offers a better chance of achieving a successful conviction.

The CPS prosecutor interviewed considered the lower burden of proof required by the section 330 offence to be

a concession to the recognition that [regulated professionals] are the weak point in terms of . . . facilitating, or the strong point for criminals. So we need to make it, not easier to prosecute, but we need to put a more onerous burden on them to ensure they are not complicit . . . in money laundering.

[CPS1]

He did not consider the 'reasonable grounds' test to be problematic, and argued that there were safeguards in place:

I recognise that it's a low *mens rea* suspicion, but in the context of the regulated sector, with all the support, input they have from their own professional bodies, I don't think it's outrageously low.

. . .

And I think, when we looked at it, making the charging decision, we would look at the level of suspicion. You know, if it's someone who's . . .

had a failing because of their lack of training or whatever, then . . . you can look at the people higher in the firm, et cetera. But I don't think we just go around prosecuting people who . . . we think suspected, on the lowest level of suspicion, and didn't do something. I think we'd . . . look at it a bit more in depth.

[CPS1]

These quotes raise a number of interesting points. The prosecutor highlights the support that legal professionals receive from their professional bodies in relation to money laundering, suggesting that this should allow them to avoid becoming unwittingly caught up in money laundering. In return, he argues for "a more onerous burden" to be put on them to ensure that this does not happen. His assertion that they do not "just go around prosecuting people" who had "the lowest level of suspicion" is slightly contradicted by some of the cases identified during this research, although prosecutions may have originated with the belief that a higher level of knowledge or suspicion was involved. The financial investigator's suggestion that they were "going to rely on" the section 330 offence more often seems likely to improve their chances of achieving successful prosecutions because of the lower burden of proof, but may also increase the possibility of professionals being convicted of money laundering offences as a result of errors of judgement and individual 'bad' decisions.

Views of legal professionals

Finally, it is important to consider what legal professionals themselves think about their money laundering obligations and the risks that this involves. This was not a primary focus of the research, and so was not explored in any depth. Interviews with practising solicitors demonstrated mixed views, with one solicitor conveying a feeling of vulnerability due to the nature of their anti-money laundering obligations, and suggesting that they imposed an unfair and inappropriate burden:

[I]t is scary, as a professional, that, you know, you could misinterpret something or just, or not intentionally facilitate, but just miss something. The amount of transactions that we deal with, it is a scary thought, to be honest that you could have your whole life ruined, if there were proceedings, just for making the mistake. It's different if you're intentionally doing it, and you know what's happening, and you still go ahead with it. But it's scary that you can get caught by just simple, not omission, but just failing to pick up on something.

I think it is too, it's too much. You know, we're not forensic accountants, and so we're having to do part of that job, that's got nothing to do with the legal aspects of the transaction, but it's extra things that we've got to be aware of.

[S3]

However, another solicitor interviewed stated that the responsibility that solicitors had to prevent money laundering "doesn't really" concern them, as

> [i]t comes with the territory. It's one of the most responsible positions you can have in society, isn't it? . . . So no, I don't think it bothers me at all. It's a privilege isn't it, to have a practising certificate.
>
> [S2]

> I mean we all know don't we? Everybody knows what the rules are; everybody knows that you have to check these things nowadays. I don't know whether being particularly dozy is a really good excuse for it, to be honest! Morally, perhaps not, but whether you should be legally any less culpable, I'm not entirely sure about.
>
> . . .
>
> Yes, you should really [be able to see when money laundering might be occurring]. And if you're not sure, if you're ever in doubt, . . . [i]f you've been deliberately hoodwinked and there's no way that you could have found out that was what was happening, then that's fair enough. You know, I think that's one thing. If you've not been alert to something that you should have been alert to, you know, you can always ring the SRA, you can always ask people within your firm.
>
> [S2]

Reference to the "responsibility" that goes along with having the position of solicitor shows an acceptance of the duty they have to be aware of the risks of money laundering, and the comments from Interviewee S2 show an awareness of the support and advice available to help avoid these risks. However, the interviews also made clear the pressure felt by solicitors, highlighting the fear of being "caught by . . . just failing to pick up on something". Interviewee S3 also draws attention to the "amount of transactions" that they deal with, and the "scary thought" that "you could have your whole life ruined . . . for making a mistake".

There has been limited empirical research on legal professionals' views on their role in anti-money laundering. Of note is Kebbell's (2017) study of transactional and compliance professionals at Top 50 UK law firms, and Helgesson and Mörth's (2016, 2018, 2019) research, which involved conducting interviews with lawyers in Sweden, France and the UK. Helgesson and Mörth's (2018) Swedish research found reluctance from lawyers in large- and medium-sized firms to take on the responsibilities of 'policing' money laundering (and terrorism financing). The lawyers saw their role as being in conflict with anti-money laundering reporting requirements, and aimed to protect client relationships and business interests, and uphold their professional ethics and norms, while 'being compliant enough' (Helgesson and Mörth 2018: 230). UK lawyers considered their anti-money laundering obligations 'as a threat to their independence' (Helgesson and Mörth 2019: 266) and differentiated themselves from state anti-money laundering actors (i.e. the police), as they had 'obligations in society, including obligations to provide professional services and advice to clients' alongside their anti-money laundering (and counter-terrorism financing) obligations (Helgesson and Mörth 2019: 266). Lawyers in France, in particular, highlighted the issue of client privilege, and articulated 'explicit resentment towards the state treating them like any "other" reporting entity' (Helgesson and Mörth 2019: 266). Many of Helgesson and Mörth's interviewees were partners at 'prestigious firms' (2019: 264), compliance lawyers, and/or the designated Money Laundering Reporting Officer (MLRO) – or equivalent – in their firm. Therefore, they will have been steeped in the narratives and discourse around 'anti-money laundering', and their responses will have reflected this. An interesting and valuable area for future research would be to explore the experiences of legal professionals with less direct contact with the anti-money laundering regime, to understand their day-to-day experiences as 'gatekeepers'.

Conclusion

Examination of the anti-money laundering legislation in the UK, alongside the analysis of cases of solicitors convicted for money laundering offences presented in the previous chapter, shows that legal professionals can be convicted for facilitating money laundering on behalf of a client, or in the process of assisting or providing services to a client, without having criminal intent or actual knowledge or suspicion that their client was involved in laundering. This is due to the wide scope of anti-money laundering legislation in the UK, which goes beyond the international frameworks from which it was derived, as these frameworks focus on those who have intentionally laundered criminal proceeds. This means that what can be considered as the facilitation of money laundering by legal professionals from a criminal law perspective incorporates the range of different levels of intent and knowingness that were highlighted in the previous chapter. The characterisation of legal professionals as 'gatekeepers of the financial system', rooted in the global anti-money laundering regime, and imposing on them considerable responsibilities and obligations for the prevention of money laundering, means that legal professionals can be considered to have facilitated money laundering by *failing* to do something (i.e. not fulfilling these obligations), not just for *doing* something. This reflects the regulatory approach to white-collar and corporate crime more broadly, where failure to take certain actions can constitute an offence, described as crimes of omission as opposed to crimes of commission (see e.g. Huisman and van Erp 2013).

The wide scope of the legislation is justified with arguments that proving actual knowledge or suspicion of laundering is extremely difficult, and that those in the regulated sector may choose not to report suspicious transactions because they felt safe from prosecution if actual knowledge was required. In addition, professionals are seen as representing a 'weak point' in the anti-money laundering regime and, as qualified, skilled professionals in a privileged position, as being able to bear the responsibility for money laundering prevention that this requires.

However, this means that the legislation is able to 'catch' legal professionals that are not complicit or actively involved in money laundering, creating a sense of burden and feeling of vulnerability about the risks of unintentional money laundering. The far-reaching nature of the legislation, therefore, has significant implications for those working in the legal profession, whose occupational role means they are likely to come into contact with illicit funds and individuals wishing to launder them, and who face serious potential consequences for failing to fulfil their 'gatekeeper' obligations (see also Benson 2018).

8 Criminal justice and regulatory responses to the facilitation of money laundering

Introduction

In this chapter, attention moves to the response to legal professionals' involvement, or potential involvement, in money laundering in the UK, which involves both criminal justice and regulatory systems and processes. Preventing professionals becoming involved in the facilitation of money laundering, investigating and prosecuting those suspected of such involvement, and sanctioning those who are found guilty of wrongdoing, involves a range of actors with various goals, responsibilities and priorities (both related and *un*related to money laundering). The anti-money laundering role of these actors is shaped by the national legislative framework, which includes the Proceeds of Crime Act (POCA) 2002 and various iterations of the Money Laundering Regulations, which are, in turn, shaped by international standards (e.g. EU Money Laundering Directives and FATF Recommendations) and the global anti-money laundering regime more widely (see Chapters 2 and 7). As 'gatekeepers' to the financial system and potential 'professional enablers' of money laundering, the control of legal professionals in relation to anti-money laundering is aimed at (1) preventing illicit funds entering the legitimate financial system and (2) preventing others from benefiting from criminal activity. As part of the regulated sector under the anti-money laundering framework, legal professionals in the UK must comply with the Money Laundering Regulations. While this applies to all types of legal professional, anti-money laundering regulatory activity is primarily focused on solicitors, due to the nature of their occupational role and the services they provide which are vulnerable to abuse by those with criminal proceeds to launder.

The Solicitors Regulation Authority (SRA) has primary responsibility for the supervision of solicitors in England and Wales in relation to their compliance with the Money Laundering Regulations. The SRA was established in 2007 following the recommendations of a review – by Sir David Clementi – of the regulatory framework for legal services in England and Wales. The Clementi Review was set up in response to criticism of the profession's handling of complaints and a series of competition investigations, to consider what regulatory framework should be adopted in order to best promote innovation and competition and provide the best service for the public (Clementi 2004). At the time, the legal profession followed a model of self-regulation, with its members being regulated by their professional associations: the Bar Council for barristers and the Law Society for solicitors. The Clementi Review raised a number of concerns about the complexity of the self-regulatory regime and its lack of transparency and accountability, and recommended that the representative and regulatory roles held by the professional bodies be separated (Clementi 2004). This led to the introduction of the SRA – through the Legal Services Act 2007 – to act as the regulatory and disciplinary body for solicitors in England and Wales, with the role of representing solicitors remaining with the Law Society. This separation between representation and regulation did not take place in Scotland and Northern Ireland, which are separate legal jurisdictions to England and Wales, and so in these areas of the UK the regulation of solicitors remains as the remit of the professional bodies – the Law Society of Scotland and the Law Society of Northern Ireland – alongside their representative functions. The Law Society, Law Society of Scotland and Law Society of Northern Ireland are the named anti-money laundering supervisors for solicitors across the UK, but in England and Wales this responsibility has been delegated to the SRA.

Legal professionals must also adhere to rules and norms of professional conduct, which govern a wider set of behaviours than just involvement in money laundering. In England and Wales, for example, these standards are laid out in a series of 'Principles', a Code of Conduct, and various other rules, regulations and requirements that together provide a framework for ethical and professional legal practice. The SRA is responsible for setting and enforcing these standards and taking disciplinary action against solicitors or firms that breach them, including by non-compliance with the Money Laundering Regulations, misuse of client accounts or facilitating suspicious or improper transactions, or having been convicted of money laundering offences and thus breaching principles of 'upholding the rule of law' and 'acting with integrity'.[1] Disciplinary action may consist of a warning, fine or reprimand for less serious breaches, or prosecution before the Solicitors Disciplinary Tribunal (SDT) for more serious behaviour. The SDT, which is independent from the SRA, 'adjudicates upon alleged breaches of the rules and regulations applicable to solicitors and their firms' (SDT 2019).

A recent addition to the anti-money laundering regulatory landscape for solicitors in the UK is the Office for Professional Body Anti-Money Laundering Supervision (OPBAS). OPBAS was set up in 2018 to supervise the various 'professional body supervisors' responsible for anti-money laundering supervision in the legal and accountancy sectors in the UK, as designated in the Money Laundering Regulations. Its establishment (within the Financial Conduct Authority [FCA]) was a response to concern about the wide range of professional bodies acting in this capacity, and the lack of consistency and information-sharing between them. Its aim is to improve the consistency of these bodies' supervisory practices in relation

---

1 Principles 1 and 2 of the SRA Principles, contained in the *SRA Handbook* (SRA 2017: Part 1).

to anti-money laundering and facilitate collaboration and the sharing of information between them, other supervisors in the anti-money laundering framework, and law enforcement (FCA 2019; OPBAS 2019).

As has been shown throughout the course of this book, actions (or non-action) which facilitate money laundering in some way may constitute a criminal offence under various sections of POCA 2002. Moreover, they may enable wider criminal activity, especially 'crimes for profit' such as the distribution of illicit commodities, fraud, tax evasion and corruption. Therefore, there are responsibilities for law enforcement (particularly those organisations and departments focusing on 'serious and organised' crimes) and prosecuting authorities to investigate and prosecute legal professionals suspected of facilitating money laundering. The main law enforcement bodies with responsibility for this in England and Wales are the National Crime Agency (NCA), which leads on the policing of serious and organised crime in the UK; the regional network of nine Regional Asset Recovery Teams (RARTs); and the Financial Intelligence Units (FIUs) of police forces. Within Scotland, money laundering investigations are the remit of one central and several divisional Economic Crime and Financial Investigation Units (ECFIU) of Police Scotland. Prosecution of legal professionals suspected of committing an offence under POCA 2002 would fall to the Crown Prosecution Service (CPS) in England and Wales and the Crown Office and Procurator Fiscal Service (COPFS) in Scotland.

This chapter analyses data from interviews with members of relevant professional and regulatory bodies (n = 3), investigators in force FIUs and RARTs and other law enforcement personnel involved in the policing of organised crime (n = 9), and a CPS prosecutor specialising in money laundering investigations and asset recovery, alongside documents relating to the role and responsibilities of the SRA. The chapter begins by analysing the nature of the regulation of legal professionals in relation to their role in the facilitation of money laundering in the UK. It then considers the role of criminal investigation and prosecution in the response to suspected facilitation, and highlights some of the challenges associated with this, including difficulties with proving the guilty knowledge of the legal professional and their connection to the criminal proceeds; wariness on the part of the prosecuting authorities when dealing with such cases; and the complexity and specialist nature of money laundering investigations. While recognising these challenges, the chapter suggests that investigation and prosecution of professionals is often not pursued because investigators see those involved in the primary criminality as a greater priority. Therefore, it suggests that a *shared response* to suspected involvement in the facilitation of money laundering, with criminal justice and regulatory bodies working together on a case-by-case basis, may be the most appropriate and effective. However, a shared response would require a cooperative and collaborative relationship between regulators, police and prosecuting authorities, and this chapter highlights a lack of communication, respect and trust between police and regulators, and a misunderstanding of each other's roles, objectives and modes of working, that would hinder the effectiveness of such an approach. Potential strategies for controlling the facilitation of money laundering, and their challenges and limitations, are discussed further in Chapter 9.

Regulating legal professionals

Within the UK, the regulation of legal professionals in relation to their involvement, or potential involvement, in the facilitation of money laundering occurs in two ways: first, as part of the 'regulated sector' covered by the Money Laundering Regulations, and second, as a member of the legal profession, expected to uphold certain standards, norms and professional ethics. In accordance with the Money Laundering Regulations, members of the legal profession are supervised by a designated supervisory authority to ensure their compliance with the requirements of the Regulations. The Money Laundering Regulations name nine supervisory authorities for the legal profession in the UK,[2] including the Law Society (the professional body for solicitors in England and Wales). However, since its establishment in 2007 to separate the representative and regulatory roles of the Law Society, the SRA has taken the role of supervisory authority for solicitors in this jurisdiction. The role of the Law Society in relation to anti-money laundering is focused on providing education, guidance and training for members of the profession, and also making representation on behalf of solicitors in response to proposals for new or amended anti-money laundering policy. In Scotland and Northern Ireland the regulation of solicitors remains as the remit of the professional bodies – the Law Society of Scotland and the Law Society of Northern Ireland – alongside their representative functions, and so they maintain responsibility for the anti-money laundering supervision of solicitors.

The role of a supervisory authority under the Money Laundering Regulations is to effectively monitor the persons it is responsible for; to take necessary measures to ensure their compliance with the requirements of the Regulations; and to report any suspicions or knowledge that a person it is responsible for is or has engaged in money laundering or terrorist financing to the National Crime Agency (MLR 2017, Reg 46). Furthermore, in line with the risk-based approach to anti-money laundering that has come to the fore in recent years (see Chapter 6), the supervisory authority must adopt a risk-based approach to supervision, by identifying and assessing the international risks of money laundering and terrorist financing to which its sector is subject; ensuring its employees and officers have access to information on money laundering and terrorist financing risks; and basing the operation of its supervisory activities on the risk profiles it has prepared for the sector. It must also review the risk assessments carried out by members of its sector, and assess the adequacy of the policies, controls and procedures that

2 Chartered Institute of Legal Executives; Council for Licensed Conveyancers; Faculty of Advocates; Faculty Office of the Archbishop of Canterbury; General Council of the Bar; General Council of the Bar of Northern Ireland; Law Society; Law Society of Northern Ireland; Law Society of Scotland (MLR 2017, Reg 7).

have been implemented (LSAG 2018: 120). The SRA describes its anti-money laundering supervisory role thus:

> As a professional supervisory body, we have a statutory duty to make those we regulate assess risks and take proactive steps to mitigate and respond to money laundering issues. We must also take "effective, proportionate and dissuasive disciplinary measures" (MLR 2017: Reg 49[d]) where firms do not reach the required standard.
>
> (SRA 2019a: 1)

The broader regulatory role of the SRA comprises authorisation, supervision and enforcement, with the aim of ensuring solicitors uphold certain standards and behaviours, and act honestly and with integrity in all aspects of their work. As well as setting standards for qualification as a solicitor and requirements for continuing professional development, the SRA's role involves: setting the 'standards and requirements' of professional conduct, by way of the SRA Principles, Code of Conduct and other frameworks brought together in the *SRA Handbook* (SRA 2017); monitoring solicitors and law firms to ensure compliance with the standards and requirements set out in the *Handbook*; investigating concerns about compliance with these standards and requirements; and taking enforcement action against anyone caught breaching them (see SRA 2019b). The SRA's approach to regulation is 'outcomes-focused', concentrating on high-level principles and outcomes, avoiding prescriptive rules for behaviour and 'encourag[ing] practitioners to use their professional judgement . . . to decide how to achieve the required outcomes' (Rees 2013: 12). The SRA Principles 'embody the key ethical requirements' for individuals and firms involved in providing legal services, and are considered as the 'starting point when faced with an ethical dilemma' (SRA 2017: section 2.1). They state that individuals and firms involved in providing legal services must:

1 uphold the rule of law and the proper administration of justice;
2 act with integrity;
3 not allow your independence to be compromised;
4 act in the best interests of each client;
5 provide a proper standard of service to your clients;
6 behave in a way that maintains the trust the public places in you and in the provision of legal services;
7 comply with your legal and regulatory obligations and deal with your regulators and ombudsmen in an open, timely and co-operative manner;
8 run your business or carry out your role in the business effectively and in accordance with proper governance and sound financial and risk management principles;
9 run your business or carry out your role in the business in a way that encourages equality of opportunity and respect for diversity; and
10 protect client money and assets.

(SRA 2017: Part 1)

In addition to these general principles, the *SRA Handbook* contains a number of provisions which address specific behaviours, such as the Accounts Rules. The primary objectives of the Accounts Rules are to keep client money safe (and give clients and the public the confidence that client money held by firms will be safe) and to ensure that client accounts are 'used for appropriate purposes only' (SRA 2017; SRA Accounts Rules 2011).

Therefore, the regulatory remit of the SRA is focused more broadly than the prevention of money laundering, but involvement in money laundering would be a clear breach of the expected standards of the profession. While there are no specific rules against money laundering in the SRA Principles or other parts of the *SRA Handbook*, they do address behaviours that would allow the facilitation of laundering and include standards that involvement in laundering would contravene. For example, knowingly assisting a client to launder or otherwise manage the proceeds of criminal activity clearly breaches the principles of 'upholding the rule of law' (Principle 1) and 'acting with integrity' (Principle 2). Similarly, while the main purpose of the Accounts Rules is to keep client money safe, it addresses the prevention of money laundering through the aim that client accounts should be 'used for appropriate purposes only' (SRA 2017) and, in particular, through the rule that '[p]ayments into, and transfers or withdrawals from, a client account must be in respect of instructions relating to an underlying transaction (and the funds arising therefrom) or to a service forming part of your normal regulated activities' (SRA 2017: section 14.5). This rule was introduced because of the potential for client accounts to be misused for illegal purposes, such as facilitating money laundering, corruption and fraud (see Middleton 2008) and concern that such accounts had been used inappropriately, and was discussed in Chapter 5.

In March 2019, the SRA announced the introduction of a new regulatory model, due to come into effect on 25 November 2019. The new *SRA Standards and Regulations* will replace the *SRA Handbook* and are intended to be more targeted than the existing rules; to focus on 'the issues most important to protecting the public and their money'; and to reduce the burden on solicitors and law firms by removing many of the prescriptive rules to 'allow solicitors greater freedom to use their professional judgement in considering how they meet the standards' (SRA 2019c). While there will not be fundamental changes to the key features of the Principles, Codes of Conduct or Accounts Rules, the new *Standards and Regulations* explicitly refer to the SRA's role in relation to the Money Laundering Regulations. This reflects the emphasis that the SRA now places on the anti-money laundering aspect of their role and the increasing pressure they are under to prevent and respond to money laundering in the sector, due to the high priority of the anti-money laundering agenda and assessment of the legal profession as 'high risk' in the UK *National Risk Assessment of Money Laundering and Terrorist Financing* (HM Treasury/Home Office 2015, 2017).

The SRA uses the 'pyramid' approach to enforcement articulated by Ayres and Braithwaite (1992), with a hierarchy of sanctions available depending on the nature of the behaviour and attitude – or 'compliance motive' (Mascini 2016) – of the 'offender'. At the base, supervision and guidance will be provided to firms and individuals willing to comply with the rules, in order to aid them in their compliance (for example, providing guidance and advice on adherence to the Money Laundering Regulations). If a breach of rules occurs that requires disciplinary action, the SRA has a range of options at its disposal, from warnings, fines and reprimands for less serious breaches, to prosecution at the SDT or immediate closure of the practice for more serious offences. Rule breaches related to (suspected) money laundering or the misuse of client accounts, for example, are generally considered to be serious and would be likely to be referred to the SDT, although minor infringements such as failure to undertake proper due diligence measures, have the correct policies and procedures in place, or ensure adequate training for relevant employees, may result in supervision and engagement with the firm to ensure future compliance, rather than more serious sanctions. Being convicted of a money laundering offence in a criminal court would be considered as an act of professional misconduct for solicitors, and so following conviction they would expect to be additionally prosecuted at the SDT, as was the case with the solicitors analysed in this research. This may result in a disciplinary sanction of, for example, a reprimand, fine, suspension, supervision order, or – the ultimate sanction – removal from the roll of solicitors. The level of sanction received by solicitors convicted of money laundering offences in this research varied; while the majority were 'struck off' the roll, others received a suspension, reprimand or fine, depending on the circumstances of their actions (details of the disciplinary sanctions received can be found at the Appendix).

Criminal investigation and prosecution

The cases analysed in this research involved solicitors who had been prosecuted for one or more of a range of offences under POCA 2002, or the relevant parts of legislation that preceded it (Drug Trafficking Act 1994 or Criminal Justice Act 1993). Within much of the case data, reference is made to the individual(s) involved in the proceeds-generating predicate offence and the solicitor's actions are described in relation to the actions of these individuals. In addition, the SDT transcripts indicated that the solicitors appeared before the tribunal following – and as a result of – their convictions for money laundering offences. It is likely, therefore, that the identification of the solicitors and the role they played originated in the initial criminal investigation into the predicate offender(s) or offence(s) (though it is impossible to know this for certain from the available data). This reflects the nature of the facilitation of money laundering as part of the 'organisation of crime for profit', as highlighted in Chapter 3, with the legal professional's role being intrinsically connected to the primary criminality and the actors and relations involved in that. In contrast, lawyers who had stolen client funds or used their position to commit fraud, for example, would also fall under the scope of both a criminal justice and regulatory response, but without that connection to wider offending committed by others. This is important to note, as it adds certain dynamics to the response to legal professionals' involvement in money laundering, which will become apparent over the course of this chapter, and demonstrates the benefit of an integrated framework which sees professionals' role in the facilitation of money laundering as both a form of 'white-collar crime' and part of 'the organisation of crime' (see Chapter 3).

The role of 'legitimate' professionals who provide assistance (of various forms) to 'organised crime groups' and other high-priority criminal actors has become increasingly prominent on the agenda of 'serious and organised crime' policing in the UK over the last decade or so. It began with an awareness of the role that 'corrupt, complicit or negligent professionals, notably lawyers, bankers and accountants' (Home Office 2013: 14) were playing in relation to known organised crime groups, and a realisation that this could provide an alternative avenue for the disruption of such groups (see e.g. Murray 2013, 2015). At this point, the focus was primarily on their involvement in what might be considered as 'traditional' forms of organised crime and illicit markets (e.g. drug trafficking/ markets). More recently, there has been increasing attention on the involvement of 'professional enablers' in 'high-end money laundering', and their facilitative role in serious economic crimes, such as major frauds and overseas corruption (NCA 2014: 1; also NCA 2017, 2018). This is linked to a growing interest in this kind of criminal activity more broadly, with high-profile cases highlighted by investigative and campaigning work by, for example, Global Witness, Transparency International, and the Organized Crime and Corruption Reporting Project (occrp.org), and increased political rhetoric about the need to address global corruption (e.g. the Anti-Corruption Summit hosted by the then Prime Minister, David Cameron, in 2016).

The focus on 'high-end' money laundering and economic crime in the UK is driven by the National Crime Agency (NCA), which leads on the policing of serious and organised crime at a national and international level. The NCA also contains the National Financial Intelligence Unit (UKFIU), which has responsibility for collecting, analysing and disseminating intelligence submitted through the Suspicious Activity Report (SAR) regime. At a regional level in England and Wales, the investigation and prosecution of money laundering is conducted via a network of nine Regional Asset Recovery Teams (RARTs). The RARTs were initially established to focus on asset recovery and conduct confiscation investigations, but their remit was soon expanded to include proactive investigation of money laundering activity linked to organised crime and provision of specialist financial investigation expertise, alongside the confiscation work. These teams contain a mixture of police, Crown Prosecution Service (CPS) and HM Revenue and Customs (HMRC) personnel, and sit within the Regional Organised Crime Unit (ROCU) network. Money laundering investigations are also carried out at force level, usually by the force Financial Intelligence Unit (FIU), and cases can be referred by forces to the RARTs for specialist support. Within Scotland, money laundering investigations are the remit of one central and several divisional Economic Crime and Financial Investigation Units (ECFIU) of Police Scotland.

The challenges of investigation and prosecution

Attention is often drawn to the lack of convictions of 'professional enablers' for facilitating money laundering, and the reasons that few prosecutions are pursued or secured. While some (primarily within the relevant professions) argue that this suggests less involvement by professionals than the official rhetoric indicates, others highlight the challenges faced by those trying to investigate and prosecute this group of actors (see e.g. Middleton and Levi 2004, 2015; Nelen and Lankhorst 2008). Lankhorst and Nelen (2004: 172) suggested that the lack of prosecutions can be partly explained by the reluctance of law enforcement and prosecuting authorities to commence investigations into legal professionals, due to their status and 'special position' in society, meaning that a number of cases are never even investigated. Even when they are, the complexity of money laundering transactions and a concomitant lack of financial expertise and the skills to unravel these transactions within investigating bodies make investigations difficult, time-consuming and resource intensive. Middleton (2008) highlighted the difficulties imposed by the principles of lawyer-client confidentiality and legal professional privilege on the investigation of lawyer misconduct (see Chapter 5), suggesting that this made a low prosecution rate for involvement in laundering almost inevitable.

This research identified only 20 cases of solicitors convicted of money laundering offences from 2002 to 2013. Even taking account of the challenges of identifying such cases (see 'Research methodology' section in Chapter 1), this is not a very high number when considering the concern that surrounds this issue. The low number may simply be because there have been few solicitors who *could* have been prosecuted for such offences. However, as has been shown in previous chapters, legal professionals' likely proximity to criminal proceeds – due to the structures, processes and transactions involved in their occupational role, and the opportunities or vulnerabilities that these create – makes it highly possible for them to be involved in activity that would be considered as the facilitation of money laundering, and the legislation is broad enough to allow for prosecutions even if there is no criminal intent or actual knowledge of laundering. The introduction of POCA 2002 (followed by the first Money Laundering Regulations in 2003) replaced what was considered to be 'inadequate' prior money laundering legislation (Bell 2002: 18). It was anticipated that this would lead to a greater number of successful prosecutions of lawyers for involvement in money laundering, and it seems clear that POCA 2002 provides ample provision for such prosecutions. A prosecutor involved in prosecuting money laundering cases stated that:

> The money laundering [aspect of POCA 2002], I think, is fine. . . . You know, it can always be slightly improved, but I think the legislation, as it is, is very good indeed. I think it's one of the most draconian regimes that we know in the world.
>
> [CPS1]

Interviews with law enforcement personnel working in financial investigation units (FIUs) or otherwise involved in the investigation of organised crime and money laundering echoed some of the reasons for the low number of prosecutions highlighted in the literature, identifying particular and significant challenges associated with the investigation and prosecution of professionals suspected of facilitating money laundering. These challenges include difficulties with proving the guilty knowledge of the professionals and their connections to the criminal proceeds, wariness on the part of the prosecuting authorities when dealing with such cases, and the complexity and specialist nature of money laundering investigations.

Proving the guilty knowledge

A number of interviewees suggested that the primary problem with bringing prosecutions against professionals believed to be involved in facilitating money laundering is proving the "guilty knowledge" of the professional [LE1; LE2; LE5]. They talked about the "high standard" required to demonstrate that the professional "knew or suspected" that the money they handled had come from criminal activity [LE5], and considered that deciding what offence to charge them with was problematic as they "tend to be offences where you've got to prove the knowledge" [LE1]. However, as was highlighted in the previous chapters, securing a conviction for money laundering offences does not require actual knowledge or criminal intent, and under section 330 of POCA 2002 it does not even require actual suspicion for regulated professionals who have failed to disclose money laundering. Only one of the investigators interviewed brought up the possibility of using the section 330 'Failure to Disclose' offence as a means of prosecution with a lower burden of proof, suggesting that their unit was involved in ongoing discussions about pursuing prosecutions using this offence, rather than "trying to prove these guys were involved in money laundering", due to the "lower burden of proof" it required [LE4]. The CPS prosecutor interviewed noted the lack of section 330 prosecutions that he had seen [CPS1].

A number of the interviews with practitioners connected to bodies responsible for investigating organised crime groups suggested that there was a small number of solicitors and other professionals that were known to police because of their connection to criminal groups. Interviewee LE1 suggested that they "probably know most" of the professionals involved in criminality:

> [T]he percentage of people who are involved in this side of life is very, very small. I don't know, it's 3%, 4%, can't really put a figure on it, but it's very low. It always has been very low. And that means we probably know most of them.
>
> [LE1]

Likewise, there was considered to be a "small core group" of legal professionals involved with the organised crime groups in one force's area:

LE2: I would say, if we set up ten money laundering investigations tomorrow, I could name you nine of the ten lawyers that would be involved in the investigations. Pretty much.

RESEARCHER: So it's a small group that are doing it?

LE2: It's a very small core group, maybe three or four firms of solicitors, and maybe even only one solicitor within that firm who deals with that side of it.

This investigator went on to highlight the problem of "proving the guilty knowledge" discussed above, suggesting that, while they knew who this core group of professionals involved with organised crime was, they would not be able to prove this:

> While we can sit as police officers and say "well we know, because they're involved in every organised crime group", proving that individual guilty knowledge on each occasion that they carry out conveyancing [is difficult], because the solicitor will simply argue that "well my job's to carry out the conveyancing".
>
> [LE2]

When asked if anything was being done about individuals like this, in terms of investigation or prosecution, interviewee SA1 responded:

> Probably not. I think if, if anybody could prove out and out dishonesty . . . then they could be indicted along with the criminal. But . . . they can always get away with it by suggesting that they're only doing what they've been instructed to do. And I think that would be the defence. . . . He or she could then just simply say: "I only did what my client told me". . . . But proving that to the standard required is of course difficult, because it would have to be beyond reasonable doubt if you're going to prosecute.
>
> [SA1]

Again, the suggestion that it would not be possible to gain a conviction for a solicitor because they would argue that "my job's to carry out the conveyancing" contrasts with what was seen in the cases, which showed a number of examples of solicitors who had been convicted for carrying out conveyancing for someone buying property with the proceeds of crime. In some of these cases, it was accepted that the solicitor "had not known, or indeed suspected" [SDT – Tidd] that their client was involved in money laundering.

Establishing the connection between professional and proceeds

Difficulties with acquiring the evidence required for successful prosecutions, gaining a clear picture of the criminality involved, and being able to demonstrate the links between the professional and the criminal proceeds were also highlighted as challenges in the investigation and prosecution of professionals suspected of facilitating money laundering [LE1; LE3; LE9]. Professionals such as lawyers are "a step away" [LE3] from the 'dirty' money and aim to "provide plausible deniability" as "part and parcel of their protection against . . . criminal justice threats" [LE1], making them more difficult to convict than those directly involved in criminality:

> Their whole service is made to make it difficult. So clearly it is more difficult to convict a professional than a drugs courier. . . [b]ecause the drugs courier is directly attached physically to the criminal evidence, and in order to actually even identify the evidence as criminal you've got to do quite a bit of work to be able to place the [professional's] activities in the context which makes it criminal.
>
> [LE1]

However, the very nature of the professional's role in many of the cases examined in this research was based on their proximity to the funds; having direct involvement in transactions that involved criminal proceeds passing through their firm's client account or being used as property deposits. There would be no need to link the professional to the predicate criminality, if it was accepted that the funds were criminal proceeds. Of course, these cases appeared to be primarily related to solicitors who had been convicted *following* the conviction of the predicate offender, so the illicit nature of the funds had been established. Trying to bring a prosecution against a professional without this step would be more difficult.

Confidentiality and legal professional privilege

The issues of legal professional privilege (LPP) and client confidentiality were also identified as making evidence gathering problematic [LE1], as access to material held by a lawyer that is subject to legal professional privilege will be limited for law enforcement. As discussed in Chapter 5, the need to ensure that privilege is respected can increase the time and resources required in a criminal investigation, and claims of LPP may cause delays to investigations and impede the gathering of evidence (FATF 2013; Middleton 2008). Even though LPP does not apply to 'documents which themselves form part of a criminal or fraudulent act, or communications which take place in order to obtain advice with the intention of carrying out an offence' (LSAG 2018: 103), complexity in the scope and application of principles of confidentiality and privilege in relation to money laundering, and the potential for misunderstanding, divergent interpretations and false claims, may still create challenges for investigations (see Chapter 5).

A lack of 'victims'

A further challenge arises from there being no 'victims' to make statements or provide evidence against the professional. Unlike in cases of misconduct by professionals *against* their client – such as fraud or misappropriation or mishandling of client funds – the facilitation of money laundering involves professionals acting *for* their client, as interviewee SA2 highlighted:

> Part of the issue is, what you would often do for other offences is – other offences can be against the client, for example if you take a client's money that you're not supposed to – so a client's statement actually goes towards proving the offence. If a solicitor has actively assisted a client in money laundering, then you have a real big difficulty in that you can't approach that client.
>
> [SA2]

Therefore, the client – the predicate offender – is not available to use as a prosecution witness or to provide evidence against the professional, adding to the difficulties of evidence gathering in these cases.

Complexity of the cases

Another issue raised by interviewees from law enforcement was the complexity of money laundering cases, and the specialist knowledge required to fully understand the role played by professionals in such cases. As highlighted earlier in the book, the transactions which act to facilitate money laundering by legal professionals tend to be the 'normal' transactions associated with their specific occupational role. While investigators based in FIUs and the Regional Asset Recovery Teams (RARTs) have a degree of relevant knowledge and financial expertise, and will have received training in this area, there was a clear feeling that they lacked the specialist knowledge to fully understand the processes and transactions involved in the facilitation of money laundering; for example, the details of conveyancing processes, the setting up or management of corporate vehicles, or the use of complex financial transactions. The complexity of such cases means that they are very time-consuming, expensive and resource intensive [LE5]. Investigators related having to resort to seeking expert advice while pursuing such cases, for example to understand a series of conveyancing transactions; a situation that they found frustrating and "expensive, very expensive" [LE4].

Outside of the 'comfort zone'

A prosecutor, who has extensive experience in money laundering cases, suggested that the potential complexities of cases involving facilitation by professionals, and the *perception* that they would be "too difficult to investigate" and to "prove", means that the police are reluctant to make professionals the focus of investigations. He suggested that there was a nervousness to go outside of their "comfort zone" (i.e. the traditional 'serious and organised' crimes and criminals that are the usual targets) and take on complex cases that require knowledge and experience that they might not have. This creates a barrier for the police to even attempt to investigate such cases. He also noted the time- and resource-intensive nature of such investigations (and money laundering investigations in general):

> [A]gain, it's a police thing. . . . I think it's possibly the comfort zone thing. It's . . . more financial and regulatory. And, you know, people are gonna get slightly nervous about investigating solicitors and accountants, because, you know, it requires all kinds of forensic input and legal privilege issues.
>
> . . .
>
> I kind of get a sense that there isn't really the appetite to do it because it seems complex. And also, let's be honest, resources. I mean, they are not easy jobs to do. They're not your run-of-the-mill investigations, looking at compromised professionals. And in an era of decreasing budgets, it's hard enough to get people to look at long-term money laundering investigations, which are very time-intensive and require a lot of resources – resources, you know, depleting on a daily basis. . . . And I think maybe they get put on the back burner. That's the sense I get.
>
> [CPS1]

Reluctance from prosecutors

On the other hand, it was suggested by an investigator in a Regional Asset Recovery Team that there was a reluctance from the Crown Prosecution Service (CPS) to prosecute professionals suspected of being involved in money laundering, claiming that their professional status led to a degree of "wariness" by prosecutors:

> CPS want[s] to be certain. You know, if we're going to actually be accusing professional people of wrongdoing, we need to make sure it's absolutely nailed on. So that's another element to it, I think, that there's a little bit of wariness there.
>
> [LE9]

However, the CPS prosecutor interviewed disagreed, arguing that, rather than there being a lack of desire to prosecute, the blockages occurred earlier on in the process. He suggested that "there are lots of options and opportunities out there to pursue prosecutions", but felt that "there's not a huge amount going on" by the police in regards to this, and indicated that this was partly because of the lack of an "overall strategy" or the appropriate prioritisation to address the issue [CPS1].

A question of priorities?

> I don't think there's been a strategic objective to go after these people. Obviously there are going to be some exceptions . . . but in terms of local police, I mean, not that many things are being investigated, or at least referred to us for consideration and charges. . . . It could be because it's in the

too-difficult-to-do drawer. It could be because they think it's just too, you know, too difficult to investigate, and also too difficult to prove.

[CPS1]

The prosecutor suggested that there has not been "a strategic objective" – or "the appetite" – to pursue professionals who facilitate money laundering. This clearly conflicts with the official rhetoric about the 'growing trend' of professionals becoming involved in money laundering, and the apparent prioritisation of the issue from policy makers, governmental organisations and law enforcement at national and international level, as has been discussed earlier in the book. This rhetoric, and the idea that professionals who facilitate organised crime should be a strategic priority, was reflected in other comments by the prosecutor, who suggested that it was "the big theme" that

going after the suits . . . is the key to it. It's like I said, if we can cut them off at the knees there, then there's nothing they can do with the proceeds of crime.

[CPS1]

We all seem to accept, and we always hear the mantra, that we need to go after the suits and . . . facilitators.

[CPS1]

However, he suggested, the notion of focusing on "the suits" does not seem to translate to the ground-level of policing, even though "it should be a priority":

These are rogue professionals. They are enablers. They are the people who organised crime groups are utilising. And we need to deal with them and convict them, and get confiscation orders even, and take them out of the business.

But . . . there just aren't very many cases that people are talking about [within the RARTs]. So from that I gather that it's not happening that often. I don't know where the breakage is. . . . At what stage is a decision made by the police to investigate, and on what information, what's the minimum amount of information they require to go in and investigate? Doesn't seem to happen that often.

. . .

We're not . . . getting in the reports. And when we get them in, we're not pursuing those people who have breached the regulations. . . . We all accept there's a huge problem. . . . But we're not really managing to get to the stage that we're effectively . . . that they're looking over their shoulders at us.

[CPS1]

The prosecutor's comments raise a number of interesting issues. They suggest a breakdown in communication and processes between the different actors responsible for investigating and prosecuting professionals involved in money laundering, suggesting that within RARTs there is a lack of awareness of the decision-making processes involved when forces decide whether to investigate a professional. In addition, when reports of suspected professionals are received at a regional level, these appear not to be pursued, suggesting the lack of priority afforded to these cases that he was concerned about. A sense of frustration was evident at this point of the interview; it was very clear that the prosecutor felt strongly that this was a problem that was not being dealt with as it should be. While he had sympathy for the difficulties inherent in cases of this kind, he was clearly frustrated that such cases were not being investigated or referred to the regional level and felt that this was primarily down to failures in strategic planning and lack of prioritisation by investigators.

Interviews with law enforcement personnel also highlighted a disconnect between this issue being talked about as a priority at the higher level and the lack of priority at the local level. If a professional came up in an investigation into an organised crime group being run by the force, it was felt that this would not be proactively investigated or referred to the FIU for investigation. The priority would be seizing the criminal product and confiscating proceeds and any assets held by the offenders; the opportunity for further investigation into the financial aspects of the group, and any professionals that were involved in the management of the group's finances, would rarely be taken:

> [T]he focus has been to move on to the next inquiry. If it's drugs, the drugs they've got, you know, they've got the confiscation, so the houses, the assets will be stripped away.
>
> [LE4]

> We very rarely . . . get any referral of an organised crime group involving money laundering. Or of complicit professionals, which has never happened.
>
> [LE4]

The result of this is, firstly, that very few investigations into professionals are initiated. More broadly, however, it means a lack of intelligence being collected in this area and so "the intelligence picture is, well, it's completely devoid of any picture" [LE4]. If this was a greater priority at force level, then more intelligence would be routinely gathered and this would allow someone to have an overview, and be able to see, for example: "hang on that solicitor's appeared here too, and over there" [LE4]. But this is not done, and data are not routinely gathered, and this was a clear source of frustration to investigators in this unit.

The reference made by the CPS prosecutor to "the mantra, that we need to go after the suits and . . . facilitators" [CPS1] was echoed by interviewees involved in organised crime policing, who asserted that there was a focus at senior level on these individuals. For example, a senior member of one of the police forces said:

> I think it's been quite explicit . . . that "gatekeepers" . . . are a priority. That theme remains the same: . . . professionals, gatekeepers are very much individuals they want to take down, because they service a broad range of criminals. Strategically there's every case in the main for targeting these sorts of people.
>
> I'm a firm believer that the way to really tackle organised crime needs to be more orientated around money rather than commodity. Because it is always going to be the case that the type of individual you're likely to be able to prosecute, when your efforts are orientated around the actual process of trafficking, are units that can be easily replaced. You've got to, I think, try and tackle the networks that support them.
>
> [LE1]

Investigators within the FIU of the force agreed with this:

> What I would say is from a policing perspective, in the last three or four years there has been a real awareness in senior management of the Proceeds of Crime Act and the importance of tackling money laundering to disrupt future activity, or with a view to asset confiscation. And sort of coming away from this "it's all about chasing the powder".
>
> [LE2]

These quotes suggest a notable shift in focus for organised crime policing, suggesting a move away from the traditional focus on those involved directly with the criminal commodity ("chasing the powder") to targeting the criminal finances and associated laundering activity, and the gatekeepers who enable it. However, what was evident from the interviews with investigators was that such a shift was not actually happening at the ground level, with the highest priority still being the 'real' criminals involved in the primary criminality. For example, the same investigator suggested that charging professionals with offences related to the assistance they provided to an organised crime group would jeopardise the prosecution of the group itself, which is "principally who we're wanting to charge" [LE2]. The reason for this is that the professional could be used as a witness in the prosecution of the other offenders, and so there is a reluctance "to put them to court for their involvement in the money laundering because they are required as witnesses" [LE2]. Illustrating this, he discussed a specific operation where a "circle of professionals" was reported as being involved with an organised crime group, but prosecution of these professionals "fell on the sword", because they needed to use them as witnesses to "get the principal members of the organised crime group" [LE2].

This view was echoed by investigators in another police force, who described the benefits that solicitors and other professionals could bring to a criminal case as witnesses:

> A lot of solicitors we'll use as witnesses as well, won't we? If we feel that there's not going to be enough evidence to get them charged, because we can never prove their knowledge of the origins of the money. Then we use them as witnesses as well. . . . The main offender is obviously going to be the drug dealer, the armed robber or whatever. . . . So they will be used as witnesses and they will give statements.
>
> [LE4]

Furthermore, professionals can be used in the asset confiscation process. The confiscation of criminals' assets has become a significant priority for law enforcement, so being able to make use of professionals to assist in asset confiscation would provide an incentive for not pursuing prosecutions against these professionals:

> So, we'll use them as a witness, simply because it helps us with the confiscation process, at the end of the day to make sure the lad doesn't keep his house, and he loses the property.
>
> [LE4]

Shifting priorities?

It is important, at this stage, to note that these interviews were carried out during 2013 and 2014. At that point in time, the issue of 'gatekeeper professionals' and 'professional enablers' had been on the (national and international) political agenda for a number of years, and the need to focus on these individuals was being discussed across the policing and regulatory landscape. However, in the years since, the 'problem' of legal and financial professionals, estate agents and trust and company services providers, for example, facilitating money laundering has become even higher profile in the UK and elsewhere.[3] Does this mean, then, that if interviews were carried out now with prosecutors and members of law enforcement at force and regional level, responses would be different? Would

---

3 For example, with high profile international cases such as the 'Panama Papers' and 'Paradise Papers', and investigations into the so-called 'Global Laundromat' and 'Azerbaijani Laundromat' (see Chapter 4). 'Professional enablers' were a key feature of the UK government's 2018 *Serious and Organised Crime Strategy* (Home Office 2018), and the 'facilitators' employed by criminal networks 'to give themselves a veil of legitimacy' featured prominently in the speech given by the Minister for Security and Economic Crime, Ben Wallace, when launching the *Strategy* in November 2018 (www.gov.uk/government/speeches/minister-launches-updated-serious-and-organised-crime-strategy [Accessed 31 July 2019]).

there have been a noticeable shift in priorities, with the focus on 'gatekeepers' seen in official rhetoric being replicated in action at the ground level? Furthermore, would this have translated to greater confidence in making professionals the focus of money laundering investigations? These, and other questions about the current criminal justice response to professionals suspected of involvement in facilitating money laundering, should be considered an important area for future research.

A shared response? The role of regulators in criminal investigations

The range of challenges and complexities associated with investigating and prosecuting professionals suspected of involvement in the facilitation of money laundering, and the suggested lack of prioritisation of these actors in investigations, raises broader questions about priorities in relation to the criminal investigation and prosecution of different actors involved in the organisation of 'organised' and economic crimes, and about who should have responsibility for their control. For example, should the focus of criminal justice agencies be on the professionals or those involved in the primary criminality? Does this depend on the nature and 'level' of the primary criminality – for example, should professionals involved in 'high-end' money laundering, or money laundering related to serious economic crimes such as major frauds and grand corruption, be a greater priority for law enforcement than those involved in the laundering of profits from illicit market-based activities, such as drug trafficking? Should the focus and prioritisation, or nature of the response, differ between local, regional and national/international (i.e. NCA) levels of policing? And, what is the role for *regulators*, as opposed to law enforcement bodies, in responding to professionals suspected of facilitating money laundering?

There was a view from both law enforcement practitioners and members of professional and regulatory bodies that regulators could – and should – play a role in this response, thus alleviating some of the challenges of the criminal justice response and allowing law enforcement to focus on the primary offenders. One of the financial investigators interviewed highlighted that the presence of these regulatory bodies provided "another recourse" for dealing with professionals suspected of involvement in money laundering:

> I mean the solicitor, if they're committing offences or doing anything [wrong], then you know there's a professional body that can look at the solicitor, so there's another recourse to go with that.
>
> [LE3]

This was said in the context of a discussion about the use of a solicitor as a witness against the "target" of an investigation, who the prosecuting authority was "saying 'right, he's the person that we want to get'" [LE3]. In cases such as this, the investigator stated that consideration has to be given to "what the objectives of the case [are] and who has to go for it" [LE3]. His statement indicates that the primary objectives of the criminal justice response should be acting against those involved in the primary criminality, as the professionals involved can be dealt with by the relevant professional or regulatory bodies.

An interviewee from one of the regulatory bodies suggested that the tendency of law enforcement to focus on the "criminals", or the "bigger players" [SA2], and choose not to prosecute professionals in exchange for witness testimony, often resulted in the professional being referred to them for action:

> They will quite frequently bring things to our attention because they won't necessarily take action against the solicitor, because they . . . tend to focus on the criminals, that's clear. We've seen quite a few solicitors who the police would say. . . "well yes, they are definitely involved", but in exchange for witness testimony and things of that nature they're not going to be prosecuted. Because they really want to catch the money launderer rather than those enablers. . . . I think that's quite a common theme to be honest.
>
> [SA2]

Investigators in other FIUs agreed that there was a role for the regulators in dealing with professionals, if there were difficulties with putting together a criminal case. It was suggested that they would "expect the SRA to do something on that" if they were unable to bring criminal charges against a solicitor they suspected had facilitated money laundering [LE7]. They pointed out some of the advantages regulators had in such investigations, drawing attention to the specialist knowledge and experience of the professions and their working practices that regulators held, and their greater access to information:

> They've got the whole picture. They've got the client ledger sheets and everything on the computer, they should be able to access it. . . . And they've got the experience to see where money's being shifted.
>
> [LE5]

The advantages held by regulators in investigating professional misconduct were also highlighted by a member of one of the regulatory bodies, who emphasised their ability to view privileged material unavailable to the police, and thereby circumvent the problem of legal professional privilege that criminal investigators face:

> [O]ne of the advantages . . . is we can do something the police can't, which is we can inspect material which is subject to the client's legal professional privilege. Now obviously we can't use that, we can't disclose it to anyone to the detriment of the client. But that's a very powerful tool which people often overlook. So, you know, if the lawyer's been doing lots of transactions

for the client and the police turn up, and they say "you can't have that, it's privileged", then we can go in and have a look at it. And that's why we've managed to break open a few of these cases over the years.

[SA3]

In a series of publications examining misconduct by legal professionals, Middleton and Levi (Middleton 2005; Middleton and Levi 2004, 2015) have argued that a regulatory response is more likely to be effective than criminal prosecution in cases of lawyer wrongdoing, because it can avoid the considerable challenges faced by criminal justice agencies in the investigation and prosecution of such cases and allows for a broader range of responses. They suggest that a regulatory response can avoid some of the barriers to criminal investigation and prosecution that have been highlighted in this chapter, such as the difficulties of obtaining sufficient evidence and the complex, time- and resource-intensive, and specialist nature of investigations (Middleton 2005; Middleton and Levi 2004, 2015). A key difference between a criminal justice response and a regulatory response is that there is a broad range of sanctions that can be imposed by regulators, including fines, imposing conditions of practice such as supervision or conditional licences, suspension or striking off. As such, they may be able to more accurately target the problem identified and provide a more tailored and appropriate response. These sanctions can be imposed for professional misconduct, and therefore a regulatory response does not require proof of criminal activity. Furthermore, they can be imposed more quickly than criminal justice proceedings would take, and at a lower cost (Middleton and Levi 2015). Therefore, Middleton (2005: 811) argues, 'regulatory enforcement action that seeks to prove facilitative wrongdoing by the professional . . . may be more effective than criminal prosecution in protecting the public'. Relying solely on a criminal justice response can 'leave a gap through which dishonest practitioners who avoid criminal conviction might escape' (Middleton 2005: 812).

A *shared response*, involving both criminal justice and regulatory processes, may be the most effective approach to (suspected) professional involvement in money laundering. This would involve law enforcement and regulators working together when a legal professional was identified during the course of a financial investigation, for example, or potential involvement in money laundering was identified through routine monitoring by the SRA or other anti-money laundering supervisors (identification of non-compliance with the Money Laundering Regulations, such as failures in risk assessment, record-keeping or other required anti-money laundering procedures, could be dealt with through regulatory processes alone). Investigators from regulatory bodies would have the specialist skills, knowledge and understanding that the law enforcement personnel interviewed felt they lacked, which added to the difficulty and complexity of criminal investigations. In addition, regulators would be able to circumvent the problem of legal professional privilege that criminal investigators face, as they are able to view material that is considered privileged that the police would not be able to inspect. A shared response would also enable law enforcement to focus on those involved in the primary criminality, or on cases involving more serious or 'high-level' offending, which may be of particular benefit in times of limited resources. The decision about whether criminal or regulatory enforcement action was the most appropriate would need to be made on a case-by-case basis, taking account of both the nature of the wider predicate criminality and the nature of the facilitation involved. This book has shown the wide variation in the types of action or non-action by legal professionals that could be considered as 'facilitating money laundering', and the different levels of intent or 'knowingness' involved. It may be more appropriate for regulators to deal with what would be considered the less serious cases, with lower levels of intent or a lack of active involvement, with criminal prosecution pursued for those suspected of knowingly providing assistance to individuals or groups involved in serious criminality, for example.

However, a shared response such as this would require close collaboration and a good working relationship between those involved in investigating and prosecuting 'organised' and financial crimes and those involved in supervising legal professionals. Interviews with regulators, prosecutors and members of law enforcement identified problems with the relationship between regulators and criminal justice bodies, including a lack of trust and misunderstandings in the way they work together, which could have implications for the effectiveness of such an approach.

Challenges for a shared response: the relationship between regulators and law enforcement

The following is an extract from an interview with two investigators in a financial intelligence unit, in response to being asked about their dealings with the SRA:

LE4: On occasion we do get them involved – if we're worried about a practice. In fact, if we have any interaction with a practice, we'd engage with them. They tend to, they're the regulation side aren't they, they're not really. . .

LE5: Well, I certainly know from colleagues in [a different team], they're dealing with them as we speak, but I don't think . . . they're not too – I'm trying to think of the right word – impressed. . .

RESEARCHER: With what they do?

LE5: With what the SRA have not done. You know, they've promised what they're going to do and then they're asking us to provide the evidence against the lawyer. You know, they're supposed to be parallel investigations and they're supposed to help us, because they're supposed to be the experts and be able to understand what's been going on within the practice, because we can't see the whole picture. I know certainly from one colleague in there, she's been asked to provide the evidence for them. What's that all about?

LE4: Yeah, they tend to. . .

LE5: Sit back. . .

LE4: Yeah, we'll go with them, but they tend to want to be at arm's length from us, don't want to be seen to be, . . . they'll want to make their own judgment. So if we go in to execute warrants, they'll come with us but then they'll do their own enquiry afterwards. Or they may do it without us, but there's very little interaction beyond that as to what their objectives are and what the outcome is. They seem to go their own way.

This extract reflects a negative view of the actions of the regulatory bodies that was echoed by other interviewees from law enforcement. It only gives one side of the story, and it is impossible to make a judgement about the actual circumstances being discussed, but it clearly demonstrates a tension between the two agencies. It indicates a lack of trust in the SRA and a lack of respect for their role in investigations, and suggests that this might be reciprocated. The final comment in the extract suggests that the police feel that the SRA have a similar lack of trust and so "want to be at arm's length from us" and "go their own way" in investigations. This part of the interview gave the impression that the two bodies were working separately rather than working together – and, in fact, almost working against each other – with a lack of communication and no common objectives. There also appears to be a lack of understanding of each other's responsibilities, with interviewee LE5 remarking on his colleagues being asked to provide evidence to the SRA when it was felt that this should have been the other way round, as "they're supposed to be the experts". Another interviewee echoed these views, suggesting that there were problems with communication from the regulators following a referral:

And I suppose, if it goes nowhere, or you think you can't prove it . . . we would then refer it to the SRA. I'm not sure that we necessarily find out what goes on, or that they're particularly quick in how they do it. I could be doing them a disservice. But my sense is, you know, anecdotally, that people tell me that once it goes to the SRA, they don't really hear what's happened.
[CPS1]

The lack of feedback – this time *from* law enforcement – and problems of communication were also mentioned during the interviews with members of regulatory bodies, although their comments on their working relationship with the police were more positive overall:

The police are, and law enforcement are, getting increasingly better at feeding back to us what's happening in relation to things that we're reporting or what other people are reporting. But obviously they don't want to prejudice any ongoing investigation, so sometimes we can find out absolutely nothing about it until we see it in the newspapers.
[SA2]

We do get information; police will contact us and say they're concerned about something. And will alert us if they're going to arrest a solicitor.
[SA3]

There also seemed to be the feeling from some on the criminal justice side that the disciplinary powers that regulators had, or the sanctions they imposed, were not sufficient. On two occasions the regulators were referred to as "toothless":

> The SRA have massive amounts of intelligence around different solicitors and people doing things they shouldn't be doing. But their sanctions are quite difficult, you know, they can say to somebody: "You can't practise. You can't do this. You've got to, you know, do things like that". But they seem to all get round them. I don't understand it. A bit of a toothless tiger I feel.
>
> [LE9]

In reference to the sanctions that the SRA can impose on "rogue solicitors", interviewee CPS1 said:

> [W]ell, that's really a toothless sanction. There's nothing there. You know, people are not really convinced that there's a sanction there.
>
> [CPS1]

It was suggested that regulators were "cautious in their approach" to imposing sanctions on professionals involved in wrongdoing:

> [T]hey can shut them down can't they, or take over a practice. And it does happen. We do hear these things, but in our experience we haven't really seen that sort of disruption to a practice. They seem very cautious in their approach.
>
> [LE4]

These interviewees did not provide examples of why such sanctions were "toothless" or solicitors who had been able to "get round them". It seemed to be more an impression that the sanctions were not effective, rather than specific experience demonstrating this. This again demonstrated a lack of faith in the role of the regulators, or a misunderstanding of their capabilities and what they are able to do in respect of imposing sanctions – as highlighted earlier, regulators have a range of sanctions available to use, from fines and supervisory arrangements to removal from the roll of solicitors. These quotes suggest that those within the criminal justice system believed that these sanctions were not used effectively, and so emphasise the need for better communication between regulators and criminal justice bodies.

The interview data therefore show a conflict between criminal justice practitioners' views that regulators should play more of a role in the response to professionals suspected of involvement in money laundering, and the lack of trust they have in them to play that role effectively. There also appeared to be a notable lack of communication between law enforcement and regulators, and a misunderstanding of each other's role, objectives and modes of working, which must have a detrimental impact on their ability to work together effectively. This has implications for the provision of an appropriate and effective shared response;

if regulators were to play a greater role in dealing with professionals involved in money laundering and other misconduct as suggested, there would need to be a greater level of trust and more effective communication between all those involved in the response.

Conclusion

As members of the legal profession and part of the regulated sector under the Money Laundering Regulations, lawyers' involvement in the facilitation of money laundering in the UK would be a breach of both their professional standards and the requirements of the Regulations. It is also likely to constitute a criminal offence under POCA 2002. This means that there is a role for both criminal justice bodies (i.e. law enforcement, prosecuting authorities) and regulatory bodies in the response to suspected involvement in money laundering. This response may include investigation by relevant policing and/or regulatory bodies and, if warranted, criminal prosecution and/or disciplinary proceedings (for example, through the SDT). Regulatory, professional and criminal justice bodies also share responsibility for preventing lawyers becoming involved in facilitating money laundering. In line with approaches to white-collar and corporate crime more broadly, prevention is based on the dual goal of *compliance* with Money Laundering Regulations and professional standards and *deterrence*, through the enforcement of criminal law, regulations, professional rules and codes of conduct. A compliance approach requires a willingness to comply, and so will not be effective for those intent on facilitating money laundering; on the other hand, strategies of deterrence assume rational, calculated offending decisions to be deterred by the risk of sanctions, and so are considered most suitable for 'amoral calculators' (see e.g. Croall 2003: 51). This research has shown that lawyers who facilitate money laundering would not fit neatly into either of these categories, and so an approach combining compliance and deterrence is appropriate. In England and Wales, the SRA is responsible for ensuring compliance with the Money Laundering Regulations and with professional standards, but the Law Society also has an important role to play, encouraging compliance through education, training and guidance. In Scotland and Northern Ireland, all these functions are carried out by the Law Society of Scotland and the Law Society of Northern Ireland, respectively. The enforcement of relevant laws, regulations and professional standards falls to the police, prosecuting authorities, regulators and disciplinary tribunals responsible for the investigation, prosecution and sanctioning of those who breach them. In this model, therefore, deterrence is not solely the responsibility of criminal justice bodies and processes, with a range of actors involved in both criminal and regulatory enforcement (see Table 8.1).

As the anti-money laundering supervisor for solicitors in England and Wales (a role delegated from the Law Society, the named supervisory authority under the Money Laundering Regulations), the SRA is responsible for monitoring its members to ensure compliance with anti-money laundering requirements. Therefore, breaches of these requirements will in some instances be identified through their routine monitoring processes (though this is a significant task: the SRA regulates

Table 8.1 Current responses to legal professional involvement in the facilitation of money laundering (examples from England and Wales)

Compliance	Deterrence
Encouraging compliance with: – Money Laundering Regulations – Professional standards **Through:** – Monitoring, risk assessment, information campaigns (e.g. SRA) – Education, guidance, training (e.g. Law Society)	**Enforcement of:** – Criminal law (e.g. POCA 2002) – Regulations (e.g. MLR 2017) – Professional standards, rules and codes of conduct (e.g. SRA Principles, Code of Conduct, Accounts Rules) **Through:** – *Detection* during criminal investigation into predicate offender(s) or offence(s) or routine monitoring by regulatory bodies (e.g. SRA) – *Investigation* by police (local [e.g. force FIUs], regional [e.g. RARTs] and national/international [e.g. NCA]) and/or regulatory bodies (e.g. SRA) – *Prosecution* (criminal or regulatory) by prosecuting authorities (e.g. CPS) and/or regulatory bodies (e.g. SRA) – *Sanctioning* (criminal or regulatory) by criminal courts, disciplinary tribunals (e.g. SDT) and/or regulatory bodies (e.g. SRA)

over 10,000 law firms, and recent anti-money laundering 'thematic reviews' involved engagement with just 252 [in 2014–2015; see SRA 2016], 50 [in 2017; see SRA 2018a] and 59 [in 2018; see SRA 2019a] of these firms). Such breaches can be dealt with through regulatory processes alone. For example, the 2017 review led to six of the 50 firms being taken into the SRA's disciplinary process (SRA 2018a) and following the 2018 review, which focused on trust and company service provision, 26 firms were referred into the disciplinary process (SRA 2019a). With these 26 firms, there was no evidence found of 'actual money laundering or that firms had any intention to be involved in criminal activities'; rather statutory breaches of the Money Laundering Regulations were identified which raised 'significant concerns about some firms' vulnerability to unwittingly assisting money launderers' (SRA 2019a: 3). More serious cases, some involving 'actual money laundering', may also be identified through the SRA's regulatory processes. For example, during the 2014–2019 period, more than 60 cases related to 'potential improper money movements' were taken to the SDT, resulting in more than 40 solicitors being struck off, voluntarily coming off the roll of solicitors, or being suspended from practising (SRA 2019a: 4).

However, because of the relationship with the proceeds-generating primary criminality, many lawyers found to have been involved in the facilitation of money laundering (in the broad sense demonstrated in this book, from complicit involvement to failure to disclose suspicions of money laundering to breaches of the Money Laundering Regulations) will be identified through investigations into the predicate offence(s) or offender(s) by law enforcement. In such cases, who should then take responsibility for investigating and, if appropriate, prosecuting and sanctioning the legal professional? This chapter has discussed the challenges and complexities associated with the criminal investigation and prosecution of legal professionals suspected of facilitating money laundering, including issues of legal professional privilege and client confidentiality; lack of direct victims to provide evidence or act as witnesses; the complexity and time- and resource-intensive nature of money laundering investigations; and the specialist knowledge required to understand the transactions involved and the role that professionals play in such transactions. It has also shown that there may be a lack of strategic focus on the role of legitimate professionals ('the suits') in assisting criminal groups at the ground level of policing, with those involved in the primary criminality (the 'real' criminals) considered a greater priority. Instead, professionals were more likely to be used as witnesses than pursued for prosecution, and it appeared in some instances that little was done about those professionals that were known to be connected to criminal groups.

Both law enforcement practitioners and members of professional and regulatory bodies interviewed expressed the view that regulators had a role to play in responding to professionals suspected of involvement in money laundering, to provide an alternative response to criminal investigation and prosecution. This would involve law enforcement and regulators working together when a legal professional was identified during a criminal investigation or potential participation in money laundering was identified through routine monitoring by professional or regulatory bodies. Such a shared response would utilise the specialist skills, knowledge and understanding of regulatory investigators and their ability to circumvent issues of legal professional privilege, and enable law enforcement to focus on those involved in the primary criminality, or on cases involving more serious offending.

A shared response to the complex and multi-layered issue of legal professional involvement in the facilitation of money laundering would require effective communication and collaboration between regulators, police and prosecuting authorities. This chapter highlighted problems in the relationship between law enforcement and the SRA, including a lack of communication, respect and trust, and a misunderstanding of each other's roles, objectives and modes of working, that had a detrimental impact on their ability to work together effectively and so would have implications for the provision of a shared response. With the progression of the anti-money laundering agenda since the fieldwork for this book was conducted, and the increasing focus on dealing with 'professional enablers' who facilitate money laundering, further research is required to establish the current state of the relationship between law enforcement and regulators in the UK and if it is fit to meet the government's stated aim of a cooperative approach to disrupting 'complicit professionals' through 'criminal, civil, or, in collaboration with the SRA, regulatory means' (HM Treasury/Home Office 2015: 43).

9 Understanding and controlling the facilitation of money laundering

A research and policy agenda

Introduction

This concluding chapter draws together the key findings and arguments of the book, develops an agenda for future research and analysis, and discusses potential strategies for controlling the facilitation of money laundering. The book has shown that the facilitation of money laundering by legal professionals is not a homogenous phenomenon; it is complex and multi-faceted, comprising a variety of actions, purposes, actors and relationships. This variation needs to be recognised in both criminological analysis and policy development. This chapter begins by outlining the many ways in which the nature of the facilitation of money laundering can vary, and how this is reflected in official discourse and legislative frameworks. It then focuses on the decisions that can lead to legal professionals' involvement in money laundering: a decision to assist the predicate offender in laundering their criminal proceeds, or decisions they make as part of their routine occupational role which result in such involvement. These decisions will be shaped by their multi-level situational contexts, and the following section of the chapter develops a framework for further analysis and empirical investigation which identifies the micro-, meso- and macro-level contexts that may influence lawyers' involvement in facilitating money laundering and raises questions about their nature, how they interact with each other, and how they influence individual action and decision-making. The final part of the chapter suggests potential strategies for controlling the facilitation of money laundering. Variation in the nature of legal professionals' involvement in money laundering, and the challenges and limitations inherent in individual strategies, mean that a combination of approaches is required. This should focus on fostering compliance with Money Laundering Regulations and professional standards, rules and codes of conduct; deterring misconduct through effective and proportionate detection, investigation, prosecution and sanctioning, and increasing awareness amongst the legal profession of the likely implications of misconduct; inhibiting structural factors that create opportunities for legal professionals to facilitate money laundering or make them vulnerable to being exploited for money laundering purposes; and influencing decisions taken by legal professionals when providing services or conducting transactions that could act to facilitate money laundering.

Heterogeneity in the facilitation of money laundering

Within official discourse, individuals who (can) facilitate money laundering by or on behalf of others by means of their legitimate occupational position are characterised as 'gatekeepers' or 'professional enablers' (see Chapter 1). While understandable in the policy context – to draw attention to a particular issue and provide an easily recognisable term of reference – the use of singular concepts such as these acts to conflate a range of actors, actions and relations in a way that is unhelpful for the purposes of analysis or policy development. It suggests a homogeneity that does not reflect the complex and multi-faceted nature of the 'facilitation of money laundering'; as this book has shown, there is variation in:

- the actions (or non-action) for which professionals can be considered to have facilitated money laundering, and for which they can be convicted of a money laundering offence;
- the nature, purpose and complexity of the transactions or processes involved;
- the nature and form of the criminal proceeds;
- the relationship between the professional and the predicate offender;
- the benefit received by the professional for their role in the laundering; and
- the degree of complicity, knowledge and intent involved.

Chapter 4 showed the multiplicity of ways that legal professionals can be considered to have facilitated money laundering, and for which they can be convicted of a money laundering offence in the UK. This reflects the broad and inclusive construction of the 'facilitation of money laundering' in official discourse and legislative frameworks. For example, national government, law enforcement and regulatory documents discuss variously: the role of professionals in assisting organised crime groups to invest in property or high-value goods or set up front businesses, integrating illicit funds into UK and global banking systems, or concealing the proceeds of corruption and income on which no tax has been paid behind corporate structures and in off-shore jurisdictions; the risk of exploitation of professionals or abuse of professional services by those with criminal proceeds to launder; and compliance (or lack thereof) with Money Laundering Regulations and the Proceeds of Crime Act (e.g. Home Office 2013, 2018; HM Treasury/Home Office 2015, 2017; NCA 2015, 2018; SRA 2018a). The UK Crown Prosecution Service (CPS 2018) refers to professionals who 'in the course of their work facilitate money laundering by or on behalf of other persons' in relation to the offence contained in section 328 of POCA 2002. The section 328 offence includes a number of qualifiers which expand the scope of such facilitation, stating that a person commits an offence if they *enter into or become concerned in* an arrangement which they *know or suspect* facilitates (*by whatever means*) the *acquisition, retention, use or control* of criminal property *by or on behalf of* another person (POCA 2002, s.328[1]; emphases added). Not only does 'acquisition, retention, use or control' cover a range of activities related to the proceeds of crime, but the definition of 'criminal property'[1] and the requirement that the offender 'knows or suspects' the facilitative nature of the 'arrangement' introduce the ambiguous and subjective concept of 'suspicion' (see Chapters 2 and 7). The concept of 'criminal property' is also broad in scope, encompassing all forms of criminal conduct and using the vague concept of 'benefit' (see Kebbell 2017). Furthermore, the failure to disclose offence in section 330 of POCA 2002 means that regulated professionals can be considered to have facilitated money laundering on the basis of actions they did not take, not just actions they took.

The processes by which the proceeds of crimes for profit are used, moved or concealed, and the role that professionals play in these processes, will depend on the nature of the proceeds and the objectives of the person(s) who generated them. For example, the management of cash proceeds will have different requirements to the management of funds in electronic form, and the scale of the illicit funds may affect the approach taken and the need for a professional to be involved. If criminal proceeds are being used to buy property, there will inevitably be a role for a legal professional to conduct the conveyancing; if the objective of the predicate offender(s) is to create distance between themselves and the funds, the role for a legal professional would be essentially different. Furthermore, the complexity of these processes and related transactions (and thus the roles that a professional might play in them) will vary. For example, they could involve the creation of complex financial transactions to move funds around and conceal their illicit origin, including the use of off-shore tax havens or the formation, administration or management of companies or trusts, or involve straightforward transfers of funds into – and subsequent disbursements out of – a solicitor's firm's client account. They may involve the purchase or sale of one or a small number of local residential properties, or more complex high-value real estate transactions using shell companies to conceal beneficial ownership.

Chapter 5 highlighted the various forms of relationship that can exist between the professional and the predicate offender and the different ways and extents that professionals financially benefit from involvement in money laundering. For example, beyond a solicitor-client relationship, other dynamics – such as personal or family connections or the presence of a 'broker' – may be involved. This could influence the actions of the professionals and the decisions they take; for example, a broker in the relationship can enhance trust in the client's legitimacy, and family relations may create pressure to act in a certain way. In relation to financial benefit, while some professionals receive direct financial gain, others acquire little or no apparent benefit, or simply the normal fee for the transaction they conducted. Finally, as shown in Chapter 6, the involvement of legal professionals in the facilitation of money laundering may not always be the result of an active, knowing

---

1 Criminal property is defined as property that 'constitutes a person's benefit from criminal conduct or it represents such a benefit (in whole or part or whether directly or indirectly), and the alleged offender knows or suspects that it constitutes or represents such benefit' (POCA 2002, s.340).

choice to assist the predicate offender. Undoubtedly, there are lawyers who are fully complicit, active participants in laundering, who know that they are facilitating transactions involving criminal proceeds and intend to do so. However, in many instances the lawyer's role will occur on the 'borders of knowingness', without clear intent or a deliberate choice to offend (see Chapters 6 and 7).

The situational contexts of decision-making

The facilitation of money laundering by legal professionals involves decision-making: there must either be a decision to facilitate money laundering, or a decision to proceed with a certain transaction, provide a certain service, agree to act for a certain client, or not make a disclosure under the Money Laundering Regulations, for example. The decision *to facilitate money laundering* refers to an active, knowing choice to assist the predicate offender in the laundering of their criminal proceeds, and so represents a decision to commit an offence. This may be motivated by (personal or organisational) financial benefit or competitive advantage, and involve taking advantage of opportunities created by occupational, organisational or other factors (see Chapter 5). However, lawyers can become involved in the facilitation of money laundering without making an active decision to do so, through the decisions they make as part of their routine occupational role. These would be decisions about particular clients, transactions, services or funds, such as decisions to: proceed with a transaction requested by a client; act as conveyancer in a property purchase or sale; provide legal or financial advice or assistance to an individual or business (or a friend or family member); or move funds through their firm's client account. They could also include the decision *not to* ask certain questions or request further information, or report a suspicion of money laundering to the firm's Money Laundering Reporting Officer (MLRO) or relevant authorities. Chapter 6 discussed the various points of decision-making for the solicitors in some of the cases analysed in this research and the particular circumstances leading up to and surrounding these points, at which choices were made which led – in some way – to the facilitation of money laundering.

The individual actions and decision-making of legal professionals will be influenced by the multi-layered social context in which they are 'situated' (Vaughan 2007: 7; also, Vaughan 2002; Suchman 2007). Therefore, decisions that legal professionals make about particular clients, transactions, services or funds, as part of their routine occupational role, that act to facilitate money laundering will be shaped by and emerge from a range of micro-, meso- and macro-level factors, including: the nature of their occupational role and organisational setting; the nature and dynamics of their relationships with other actors involved; and the wider legislative, policy and regulatory environment. Understanding legal professionals' involvement in the facilitation of money laundering as situated action stresses the links between the choices they make and the contexts in which they are made, and sees the behaviours and activities that act to facilitate money laundering as being produced by the interaction between individual, organisation and environment (Vaughan 2002, 2007).

Towards an analytical framework

This section develops a framework to further examine this interaction and guide future analysis of the role of legal professionals in the facilitation of money laundering. It aims to (1) draw attention to the various situational contexts that may shape lawyers' involvement in facilitating money laundering, (2) consider how these contexts could interact with each other and shape individual action and decision-making, and (3) identify questions and gaps for further research and analysis. The framework is based on Vaughan's theory of organisational misconduct (Vaughan 1983: 54–104; see also Vaughan 1992, 2002), which was designed to explain violations of laws and regulations by individuals in organisational roles, and was introduced in Chapter 3. The theory highlighted the relationship between individual action and three aspects of the organisational context and wider environment:

1   The **competitive environment**, which includes competition from other organisations and the scarcity of resources, which generate pressures upon organisations to violate the law or regulatory norms in order to achieve certain goals.
2   The **regulatory environment**, which relates to the relationship between regulators and those they regulate. The structure of this relationship may mitigate the effectiveness of the regulators in controlling and deterring violations, contributing to individual decisions to violate.
3   **Organisational characteristics**, which provide opportunities to violate. Such characteristics include structures, processes and transactions.

(Adapted from Vaughan 1983, 2002)

Vaughan's model is supported by subsequent research and theoretical development in the field of white-collar crime and organisational misconduct highlighting the need to consider how organisational characteristics (e.g. culture, strategy and structure) interact with the wider industry, culture and the regulatory environment to produce white-collar crime, and how these factors influence opportunities and individual decision-making (see Huisman 2016). It thus provides a broad 'scaffolding' (Vaughan 2002: 125) for analysing a range of organisational misconduct. The findings developed through the course of this book allow for the creation of a more specific framework for analysing the facilitation of money laundering by legal professionals.

The framework is set out in Figure 9.1. It shows the various micro-, meso- and macro-level factors that could influence the individual actions and decision-making of legal professionals, and so lead to their involvement in money laundering. Unlike Vaughan's model, it includes factors at the micro-level: the individual characteristics of actors involved and the relationships between them. The framework suggests that analytical focus and empirical investigation should be directed towards the range of situational contexts identified, to fully understand their nature, how they interact with each other, how they influence individual

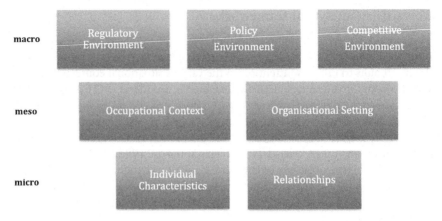

| macro | Regulatory Environment | Policy Environment | Competitive Environment |

| meso | Occupational Context | Organisational Setting |

| micro | Individual Characteristics | Relationships |

Figure 9.1 Framework for analysing the facilitation of money laundering

action and decision-making, and thus how they shape the facilitation of money laundering.

Regulatory environment

The regulatory environment for legal professionals in the UK in relation to money laundering consists of the complex and constantly evolving mix of professional and regulatory bodies, law enforcement organisations, prosecuting authorities, disciplinary tribunals, regulations and criminal law discussed in Chapter 8.[2] Its aim is to prevent legal professionals from becoming involved in facilitating money laundering, by ensuring compliance with relevant anti-money laundering frameworks and with professional standards more broadly; investigating and prosecuting those suspected of such involvement, through criminal justice and/ or regulatory mechanisms; and sanctioning those who are found to have committed criminal and/or regulatory offences. The regulatory environment for legal professionals in the UK is shaped by regional (i.e. EU Money Laundering Directives) and global (i.e. FATF Recommendations) standards, but has UK-specific dynamics (and, also, varies between countries of the UK). Of course, lawyers and law firms do not always conduct business in a single jurisdiction, and so the regulatory environment for a particular firm, legal professional or even transaction may incorporate the various (and sometimes very different) regulatory systems and processes of multiple jurisdictions (see e.g. Levi 2018).

---

2 This conceptualisation of 'regulatory environment' assumes a broad meaning of regulation as 'any process or set of processes by which norms are established, the behaviour of those subject to the norms monitored or fed back into the regime, and for which there are mechanisms for holding the behaviour of regulated actors within the acceptable limits of the regime (whether by enforcement action or by some other mechanism)' (Scott 2001: 331). It therefore includes both regulatory and police/criminal justice mechanisms and frameworks.

The actions and decision-making of legal professionals will be shaped by the nature of their regulatory environment, and the relationship between regulatory actors and those being regulated. For example, the regulatory environment should have a positive impact, encouraging compliance with anti-money laundering regulations and procedures and fostering decisions about clients, funds or transactions that do not facilitate money laundering. Any failures or limitations in the regulatory environment, however, will mitigate its effectiveness and may shape decision-making in a negative way. For example, difficulties in detection, investigation or prosecution of those suspected of facilitating money laundering may limit deterrence efforts; poor guidance or support from professional and regulatory bodies may affect individuals' or firms' ability to comply; and an overly close or interdependent relationship between regulators and regulatees may compromise regulatory effectiveness (e.g. 'regulatory capture'). Chapter 8 began to question the current framework for regulating legal professionals in relation to money laundering in the UK, highlighting some of the challenges involved in the criminal investigation and prosecution of lawyers suspected of facilitating money laundering and in the relationship between professional regulators and law enforcement organisations. Further research and analysis should:

- aim for a greater understanding of the various elements that make up different regulatory environments, and how these elements intersect and interact with each other and the professionals within their purview;
- compare regulatory environments in different jurisdictions and consider what the regulatory environment looks like for law firms, lawyers and transactions that cross more than one jurisdiction;
- examine the role of more recent additions to the regulatory environment, such as the civil society actors who play an increasing role in highlighting areas of concern or potential misconduct (e.g. Global Witness, Transparency International);
- question the purpose and priorities of the actors within the regulatory environment, and whether there are competing or conflicting priorities between (or within) actors; and
- try to understand how the nature of the regulatory environment(s) shapes the decision-making of those within.

Policy environment

The regulatory environment in which legal professionals operate is shaped by their designation as 'gatekeepers' to the financial system and potential 'professional enablers' of money laundering, and is intrinsically connected to the global anti-money laundering regime. The global anti-money laundering regime comprises a range of legislative and policy frameworks, standards and institutions and is founded on the perception of money laundering as a significant crime problem, driver of serious criminality, and threat to the integrity of the global financial system (see Chapter 2). The threat from 'dirty' money has created a policy environment which positions the prevention of money laundering as a high priority, and we should try to understand the implications of this for those it impacts. In other words, how does the emphasis on preventing money laundering, and the policies and practices that result from this, influence the actions and decision-making of legal professionals, how they carry out their legitimate occupational role, and the way they are regulated (and policed)? Consideration should also be given to the way in which the policy environment has shaped how the facilitation of money laundering is constructed: how and why particular acts or omissions by professionals are characterised as 'wrongful' or 'bad'; who makes (and who should make) these characterisations and why; and to what extent these characterisations are (or should be) linked to the harmfulness of the acts or omissions.

Competitive environment

Vaughan's framework highlighted the 'competitive environment' as a key factor to explain violations of laws and regulations by those in organisational roles. She suggested that competition for economic success, power and resources generates pressures to achieve certain goals, creating the 'structural impetus' for misconduct (Vaughan 2002: 126). Law enforcement and regulatory actors interviewed during this research identified the 'competitive advantage' gained by lawyers who help others to launder the proceeds of their crimes, and the pressures generated by financial difficulties or business uncertainty which may lead to involvement in money laundering. The nature of the legal services market in the UK has changed notably in recent years, with a range of innovations intended to increase competition, variety and flexibility within the market (including the introduction of Alternative Business Structures and the rise of online provision and 'freelance' solicitors; see Chapter 5). The 2017 UK *National Risk Assessment of Money Laundering and Terrorist Financing* suggests that this may lead to opportunities for accessing legal services without engaging a firm supervised for anti-money laundering purposes (HM Treasury/Home Office 2017: 52). One manifestation of the increasingly competitive nature of the legal services market, which was highlighted as a concern by some of the solicitors interviewed, is the emergence of a business model which uses large teams of non-lawyers (supervised by a qualified lawyer) to process a high turnover of conveyancing files (described as 'conveyancing factories' or 'conveyancing farms'; see Chapter 5). Developments such as this, which increase workload and decrease oversight, could have significant implications for the decisions taken by those involved in real estate transactions, which are known to present a money laundering risk. There is, therefore, a need for a greater understanding of the market for legal services provision, the nature of this market and how it is changing, and the impact that this has on the decision-making of those operating within the market. Possible questions for analysis include:

- Is there a culture of competition within legal services provision?
- If so, how does such a culture manifest, and is this changing?

- How do legal professionals experience competition, or pressures to achieve certain goals or financial success?
- Are these experienced differently – and does the extent of a culture of competition differ – in different types or sizes of legal practice?
- How does the nature of the legal services market influence the decision-making of legal professionals in relation to transactions that could act to facilitate money laundering?

Occupational context

At the meso-level of analysis, Vaughan (2002: 127) refers to the opportunities present in an organisation's 'structure, processes and transaction systems' that enable members of the organisation 'to act on structural pressures and violate laws, rules, and regulations in order to meet organization goals'. She conceives of the organisational setting broadly, however, to include not just formal organisations but also social groups (Vaughan 2002). In the framework presented here, the meso-level focuses both on legal professionals' direct organisational setting (i.e. the firm or practice they are based in; discussed below) and the legal profession as a whole. Chapter 5 showed how the structures, processes and transactions of the legal profession can provide opportunities to facilitate money laundering, and also make those within the profession vulnerable to coming into contact with illegally derived funds. Transactions involving criminal proceeds are essentially the same as the legitimate transactions that legal professionals carry out as part of their normal occupational role, and the nature of this role provides legitimate and specialised 'access' to functions and processes that can facilitate money laundering. This allows transactions with illicit funds to be 'hidden' amongst legitimate transactions (or allows the illicit nature of the funds to be hidden *from* the legal professional). Furthermore, principles of confidentiality and legal professional privilege may shield interactions between lawyers and their clients from external scrutiny, and so enable the facilitation of money laundering or decrease the likelihood of its detection. Some occupational features will apply to a range of 'professional enablers', but others, such as legal professional privilege, will be specific to certain professions. Therefore, analysis of the role of any legitimate occupational or professional actor in the facilitation of money laundering should ask:

1   What are the characteristics of the profession or occupational role, and how are these implicated in individual action and decision-making? For the legal profession, these characteristics include, inter alia: its routine business activities, services and processes, such as conveyancing, the provision of financial advice, and trust and company service provision; the role of confidentiality and legal professional privilege; the nature of client (or trust) accounts; the transactions carried out or facilitated as a function of the occupational role; and the professional status, skills and experience of those within the profession.

2   Where are the relevant points of decision-making within the structures, processes and transactions of the profession and what shapes the choices made

at these points? For example, for legal professionals, these may include the points at which a client is taken on, a transaction is progressed or service is initiated, customer due diligence processes are undertaken, or certain 'red flags' are raised.

Organisational setting

There is an extensive body of literature on the ways that organisational characteristics and dynamics can shape misconduct within and by organisations (see Chapters 3 and 5). The nature of the organisational setting will influence individual actions and decision-making, with organisational culture, structure and strategy playing a role in the behaviour of those within (e.g. Gross 1980; Punch 2008, 2011; Campbell and Göritz 2014; Huisman 2016; Tomlinson and Pozzuto 2016). This book has considered – to a limited extent – how this applies to the involvement of legal professionals in the facilitation of money laundering, with Chapter 5 discussing how the organisational setting(s) in which lawyers are situated may provide opportunities to assist others in laundering, and create vulnerabilities for individuals and organisations that provide legal services. There is considerable scope for furthering our understanding of how the characteristics of the various types of organisation in which legal professionals work can influence their decision-making, and make it more or less likely for them to become involved in facilitating laundering. This should involve examination of:

1   The different types of organisations that provide legal services (e.g. large international City firms, small 'high street' practices, sole practitioners, and new or emerging forms of provider such as Alternative Business Structures and 'conveyancing factories') and their nature, form and structure; that is:

    •   what kind of business they do, the nature of their clients and the extent (local or global) of their reach;
    •   their size and complexity, i.e. number of employees (lawyers and others), level of turnover, management levels and sub-divisions, centralised or decentralised structures;
    •   how authority, accountability, roles, responsibilities, information flows and decision-making processes are structured or allocated;
    •   the organisation of compliance processes and management;
    •   the amount of anti-money laundering training and guidance provided;
    •   the extent and nature of internal oversight processes and procedures, in general and in relation to particular (e.g. 'high-risk') activities or transactions;
    •   the degree of external oversight exposed to, e.g. from the Solicitors Regulation Authority;
    •   the level of autonomy of legal professionals in different positions within the organisation, and in different types of organisation.

2   Whether and how the structure, culture and strategy of different forms of legal practice influence:

- the types of decision that lawyers (or other employees) have to take in relation to their clients, the transactions they are involved in and the services they provide;
- the processes by which these decisions are made, and the factors or considerations which shape them;
- compliance with anti-money laundering requirements and the effectiveness of internal oversight processes and procedures.

Relationships

As well as the organisational setting, occupational context and wider regulatory, policy and competitive environments, the choices made by legal professionals will also be shaped by individual-level factors, such as the characteristics of actors involved and the relationships between them. There is at least one social relationship inherent to the facilitation of money laundering: that between the facilitator (e.g. legal professional) and generator of the criminal proceeds (the primary, or predicate, offender[s]). Chapter 5 identified a number of different forms this relationship might take, including the solicitor-client relationship which will be present in all cases and provides access to certain services and a superficial appearance of legitimacy to actions and transactions. There may also be a personal or family dynamic, or some form of broker to the relationship. This could create pressure to act in a certain way, affect the potential financial benefit to the professional, or introduce a further element of trust to the relationship. Therefore, the nature of the relationship between the professional and the predicate offender will influence the actions of the professionals and the choices they make. Further analysis of this relationship and its effects on decision-making would be welcome, although there would be challenges with finding data that would allow this. For example, greater understanding of the ways in which the relationship forms and is maintained would be of considerable benefit: How and why do the different actors come into contact? Do they belong to 'pre-existing networks of relationships' (Edwards and Levi 2008: 363), do they come together for a single event, or does that event represent the beginning of a longer-term relationship? Who initiates the relationship? What role do brokers play? How important is trust in the relationship and how is this established?

Other relationships worth considering include those between legal professionals and actors within the regulatory environment, discussed above, and relationships between different members of law firms. As highlighted in Chapter 3, the notion of an 'isolated decision-maker' is not appropriate for those who work in organisations, because of the inevitable interactions with others within the organisational setting, in which 'the preferences and subjective assessments of the interacting parties are shared and become part of each individual's decision-making gestalt' (Benson, Van Slyke and Cullen 2016: 8).

Individual characteristics

Individual action and decision-making will not only be shaped by external factors. The rationality of choices which lead to involvement in the facilitation of money laundering will be bounded by the perceptions, emotions and biases of those making them, the information they possess and how they process it, and their personal attributes (e.g. Simon 1957, 1996; Nee and Meenaghan 2006; Van Gelder 2013, 2017; see Chapter 3). Characteristics such as age, gender, professional history and socio-economic situation, as well as individual cognitive frames and personalities, will interact with the situational factors discussed above to shape individual action. Information on individual characteristics was limited in the data collected in this research, and it is unlikely that there would be sufficient data on cases of professional involvement in money laundering for robust quantitative analysis of trends in personal characteristics. However, future research and analysis in this area should take account of the potential role of personal characteristics and how these might affect decision-making, and consider the way that individual factors interact with other micro-, meso- and macro-level contexts.

Controlling the facilitation of money laundering

The variation in the nature of legal professionals' involvement in the facilitation of money laundering, as discussed in the first part of this chapter, means that there cannot be a single approach to controlling it. Cooperative strategies to aid or encourage compliance with the Money Laundering Regulations and professional standards are an important element. (This makes the assumption that the Money Laundering Regulations *should* be complied with; the nature and appropriateness of such regulations, and how they are constructed, on what foundations and by whom, should always be questioned). On the basis that compliance with the Regulations and with the professional standards, rules and codes of conduct set out by professional and regulatory bodies (see Chapter 8) is the desired outcome, those responsible for ensuring compliance should do what they can to help individuals and firms that want to comply to do so. This includes providing adequate and up-to-date education, training and guidance on the detail of the Money Laundering Regulations and legal professionals' obligations in relation to these. The Solicitors Regulation Authority (SRA) and Law Societies in the UK strive to do this and there is considerable information available to legal professionals to understand their obligations in relation to the Regulations. There may be variation in the *capacity* of lawyers in different types of firms to comply with the Regulations; for example, large firms will have greater resources to invest in training and compliance programmes while sole practitioners and small practices may find it more difficult to keep up with the (ever-changing) guidance provided and lack the resources to enable staff to access training sessions.

Professional standards for the legal profession are focused more broadly than the prevention of money laundering, but involvement in money laundering would be a clear breach of these standards and current (*SRA Handbook*, SRA 2017) and upcoming (*SRA Standards and Regulations*, SRA 2019d) frameworks for professional conduct for solicitors in England and Wales, for example, include specific rules and principles that involvement in laundering or a breach of the Money Laundering Regulations would contravene (see Chapter 8). The SRA adopts an 'outcomes-focused' approach to regulation, which aims to avoid strict rules and 'encourage practitioners to use their professional judgement . . . to decide how to achieve the required outcomes' (Rees 2013: 12). Its forthcoming *SRA Standards and Regulations* intend to remove some of the prescriptive rules in the current framework to 'allow solicitors greater freedom to use their professional judgement in considering how they meet the standards' (SRA 2019c). However, while much of the framework is based on high-level principles, such as upholding the rule of law and acting with integrity, there are rules-based elements, such as the Accounts Rules which aim to keep client money safe and ensure client accounts are used only for appropriate purposes (SRA 2017, 2019d). Specific rules that address behaviours that might facilitate money laundering should be made as clear, straightforward and easy to apply in day-to-day practice as possible.

As well as providing the means for compliance, in the form of clear rules and adequate guidance, there is also the need to foster the desire to comply. Research on compliance in a range of business sectors identifies three main types of motivation for compliance with regulations: economic (material), social and normative (see e.g. Winter and May 2001; Kagan, Gunningham and Thornton 2011; Nielsen and Parker 2008; Parker and Nielsen 2011). Awareness of the professional – and therefore financial – consequences of a failure to comply with the Money Laundering Regulations or professional standards would encourage economic motivations for compliance. Social motivations, based on a commitment to earning the approval and respect of others, would be engendered by the association of a failure to comply with a sense of 'social opprobrium' or disapproval by peers, regulators and the public (Parker and Nielsen 2011: 11). This might be easier to achieve with those in a high-status professional position such as lawyers, for whom honesty, integrity, and upholding the rule of law and the proper administration of justice are key principles (SRA 2019d). Strategies directed at economic and social motivations might include publicising incidences of non-compliance through professional bodies and industry publications, for example, to highlight professional and financial consequences and signal disapproval (though care should be taken with the public shaming of individuals, especially as it is possible to breach rules and regulations without intent, as this book has shown).

Normative motivations relate to a commitment to obey regulations out of 'a sense of moral agreement with the specific regulation or a generalized sense of moral duty to comply with the regulation' (Parker and Nielsen 2011: 11; see Winter and May 2001: 677–678). They require a belief that the regulation is just, and trust in the legitimacy of the regulatory process (Parker and Nielsen 2011; see also Tyler 2006, 2009). Belief in the justness of the Money Laundering Regulations will be aided by a view of money laundering as morally wrong; it is likely that most legal professionals will hold this view, in line with public perceptions and political rhetoric about the harmfulness and threat from 'dirty' money. However, there may be less consensus about the legitimacy and fairness of the Regulations themselves and the requirement for legal professionals to comply with them. The inclusion of the legal profession in the 'gatekeeper' requirements of the anti-money laundering regime has been controversial from the outset (see e.g. Xanthaki 2001; Shepherd 2009; Mitsilegas and Vavoula 2016; Tilahun 2020). Concerns have been raised about the implications of reporting obligations under the Money Laundering Regulations for the principle of lawyer-client confidentiality, and the potential for conflict between duty to a client and the duty to report suspicious activity (e.g. Helgesson and Mörth 2018, 2019). Tilahun (2020) suggests that there is an 'unarticulated institutional consciousness' within the legal profession that sees the gatekeeping role as a threat to the position of lawyers as public interest actors and to the self-governance of the profession. Lawyers in the UK have described their anti-money laundering obligations 'as a threat to their independence' (Helgesson and Mörth 2019: 266), and suggested that the structure of related legal frameworks has created a discredited, weakened and cumbersome regime (Kebbell 2017).

Involvement of the profession in developing and amending aspects of the anti-money laundering framework which affect its members will improve its perceived legitimacy; this can be done through consultation processes such as the recent Law Commission review of the Suspicious Activity Reporting scheme (Law Commission 2019). Tilahun (2020) suggests that 'across-the-board' regulatory regimes overlook factors and concerns specific to individual sectors; full acceptance of the regulatory framework by the legal profession would require it to take into account the culture and nuances of the profession. Trust in the legitimacy of the *regulatory process* will be influenced by the relationship between legal professionals and their regulators. The separation of representative and regulatory functions which occurred when the SRA was established in England and Wales, in a move away from a model of self-regulation (see Chapter 8), may have had a negative effect on this relationship. Where the professional body has retained responsibility for regulation (e.g. in Scotland and Northern Ireland) there may be greater trust in the regulatory process (this requires empirical testing). Where the functions are separate, the professional body would need to support the regulatory body, but this support would need to be earned.

Cooperative strategies to promote compliance with Money Laundering Regulations and professional standards will only be of use with legal professionals who want to comply. For those who make an active decision *to facilitate money laundering*, as characterised earlier in the chapter, such strategies will have less effect and a focus on deterrence may be more useful. Current methods to try and deter involvement in money laundering are focused on the enforcement of criminal law, regulations and professional standards, by criminal justice and regulatory bodies and processes, and were summarised in Chapter 8, Table 8.1. Deterrence research and theory supports the certainty of punishment, rather than its severity or celerity (i.e. swiftness), as being the most important component of the deterrence process. This has been shown in work on both individual offending (see Nagin 2013 for an overview) and corporate offending (e.g. Braithwaite and Makkai 1991; Makkai and Braithwaite 1994; Cohen 2000; Simpson et al. 2014). The certainty of punishment is 'the product of a series of conditional probabilities – the probability of apprehension given commission of a crime, the probability of prosecution given apprehension, the probability of conviction given prosecution, and the probability of sanction given conviction' (Nagin 2013: 201). Therefore, effective deterrence of those intending to facilitate money laundering would require a strong likelihood that their actions would be detected and that they would be successfully prosecuted and sanctioned. More accurately, it is the *perception* that apprehension, prosecution, conviction and sanction would be likely that would create the deterrent effect. Deterrence strategies would need to focus on effective detection of legal professional participation in money laundering and, where appropriate, successful prosecution of those involved, *and* increase perceptions amongst the profession of the likely implications of misconduct. This could be achieved through awareness campaigns to publicise regulatory action and subsequent sanctions, akin to those suggested for activating economic and social motivations for compliance.

The detection of legal professional involvement in money laundering is most likely to occur during a criminal investigation into the primary offender(s) or offence(s) or through routine monitoring or investigation by professional or regulatory bodies. In 'high-end' money laundering, involving the proceeds of corruption, major frauds or tax evasion, the role of professionals may be identified by whistleblowers (such as in the Panama Papers case), investigative journalists or civil society organisations, such as Transparency International. There are considerable challenges for the detection, investigation and prosecution of 'professional enablers', which have been discussed through the course of this book. The essential similarity of transactions involving criminal proceeds to the 'normal' transactions that legal professionals conduct as a part of their routine occupational role, and the actions and behaviours that they entail, means that they can be hidden amongst legitimate business activity. Structures and processes of law firms and the legal profession as a whole, such as a lack of internal oversight over particular activities or transactions, the ability to act autonomously in certain positions or types of practice, and principles of confidentiality and legal professional privilege, may hinder the detection and investigation of potential misconduct. *External* oversight by professional and regulatory bodies can only go so far (clearly external actors cannot monitor all financial transactions and related activities within all practices), and will be limited by disparities between the size of the task (the SRA regulates more than 10,000 law firms across England and Wales, for example) and time and resource levels. Criminal investigation and prosecution – following the identification of lawyers suspected of assisting criminal groups, by those involved in the policing of serious and organised crime, for example – face challenges related to gathering the evidence required to make a case and the complex and specialist nature of such investigations. Investigation and prosecution through regulatory, rather than criminal justice, mechanisms would overcome some of these challenges, due to the specialist knowledge, greater understanding of the working practices of the profession, and access to material and investigatory processes of professional and regulatory bodies. Furthermore, regulators have a broad range of sanctions available so may be able to more accurately target the problem identified and provide a more tailored and appropriate response, and regulatory sanctions can be imposed more quickly than criminal justice proceedings would take, and at a lower cost (Middleton and Levi 2015; see Chapter 8).

Enforcement action should be appropriate and proportional, as well as aiming for effective deterrence. A number of the solicitors analysed in this research, who received a criminal conviction for their role in facilitating money laundering, were judged to have not been actively or knowingly engaged in the laundering. (This is possible because of the wide scope of anti-money laundering legislation in the UK, which allows for conviction without criminal intent or actual knowledge that laundering was taking place; see Chapter 7.) On the other hand, law enforcement practitioners interviewed suggested that there were solicitors who were involved with every organised crime group within their force area and that a core group of law firms would be likely to feature in most money laundering investigations. These professionals are not targeted by law enforcement in many cases, however, because of a greater focus on the primary offenders (see Chapter 8). Many of the transactions involved in the cases analysed were not complex transactions and there was little indication of 'high-end' money laundering or the use of corporate vehicles or off-shore bank accounts. None of the cases related to the laundering of proceeds of corporate offending such as bribery, and only one involved the proceeds of political corruption (see Chapter 4).

In certain cases, criminal prosecution and robust sanctions are appropriate; for example, cases where lawyers (or firms) have participated in 'high-end' money laundering, involving the proceeds of serious economic crimes such as corruption or tax evasion, or provide services for multiple individuals or groups engaged in criminal activity. However, for those whose role in facilitating money laundering is less active or intentional, or is considered to be unwitting or based on poor judgement, a regulatory response would be both more practicable and proportionate. Regulatory action should not be the answer in all cases as it does not provide the same moral condemnation or signal the gravity of the offending in the same was as criminal prosecution and sanctions (Croall 2003). Therefore, a shared and cooperative response to the suspected facilitation of money laundering is suggested, involving law enforcement and regulators working together when a legal professional is identified during the course of a financial investigation, for example, or potential involvement in money laundering is identified through the course of routine monitoring by the professional or regulatory bodies. An effective shared response would require, firstly, greater prioritisation of suspected 'professional enablers' in criminal and financial investigations at the 'ground level' of policing, not just in high-level rhetoric, and, secondly, effective communication and collaboration between regulators, police and prosecuting authorities.

Another approach to preventing the facilitation of money laundering would be to focus on structures, rather than on individuals and their motivations to comply or offend. This book has discussed a range of structural factors that create opportunities for legal professionals to facilitate money laundering, or make them vulnerable to being exploited for laundering purposes. Strategies to prevent such structural opportunities/vulnerabilities do not need to worry about levels of intent to facilitate money laundering, willingness to comply with rules and regulations or susceptibility to deterrence, and developing such strategies does not require knowledge about *why* professionals become involved in money laundering, just *how* they do so. For example, conveyancing processes, the use of client accounts, and trust and company service provision have all been identified as points of opportunity/vulnerability. A lack of internal oversight of these particular activities or transactions will increase their capacity to be misused. These are fundamental elements of lawyers' legitimate occupational role, so cannot be eliminated, but attempts can be made to reduce their susceptibility to exploitation for money laundering. For example, no single lawyer within a firm should have 'sole operational control' of the client account as one of the solicitors in this research was found to have (Chapter 5). Having someone within the firm who is not a lawyer and would not use the client account be responsible for monitoring the account and funds that pass through it would be one way of increasing oversight. The rule in the SRA's Account Rules that stipulates '[p]ayments into, and transfers or withdrawals from, a client account must be in respect of instructions relating to an underlying transaction (and the funds arising therefrom) or to a service forming part of your normal regulated activities' (SRA 2017, section 14.5) addresses the potential for client accounts to be misused, but the SRA cannot monitor all client accounts within individual law firms to check for adherence to the rule. The role of oversight *within* firms is therefore critical.[3]

The role of conveyancing in the facilitation of money laundering is due to the use of criminal proceeds to buy property, which requires the involvement of a solicitor or licensed conveyancer. There are a number of measures aimed at preventing this, including requirements to check the identities of purchasers and the source of funds being used to make the purchase. Decreased oversight of conveyancing processes, such as in the kinds of large-scale 'conveyancing factories' highlighted in Chapter 5, and which may be a consequence of the move towards greater flexibility in the legal services market discussed in the same chapter, may reduce the effectiveness of such requirements. There are a number of steps in the

---

3 There is growing discussion about the prospect of law firms externalising client account functions by using 'third-party managed accounts' (TPMAs) instead of holding client money themselves (see SRA 2019e; Legal Futures 2019). This raises some interesting questions. Would the use of TPMAs provide an additional layer of oversight of transactions, or remove oversight from the firm and those within who have obligations under the Money Laundering Regulations? Who would be responsible for ensuring adherence to the SRA rule on underlying transactions?

process of purchasing property and a range of actors involved, including banks and estate agents, and so preventing the purchase of property using criminal proceeds requires a more holistic approach than focusing solely on legal professionals' role in the process. The use of 'special purpose vehicles' (i.e. companies) to purchase high-value property is of particular concern in relation to 'high-end' money laundering (NCA 2018). Measures to increase transparency in relation to the beneficial ownership of various forms of corporate vehicles represent a structural approach to preventing money laundering. Further analysis of the structures, processes and transactions of the legal profession and its wider environment will help identify opportunities/vulnerabilities for money laundering within the profession and factors (e.g. increasing competition in the legal services market) which shape them. Alongside this should be research looking at the processes by which the proceeds of crime for profit are managed more broadly, to identify the points in these processes where measures to inhibit opportunities/ vulnerabilities could be directed.

This chapter has stressed the importance of thinking about the decisions taken by legal professionals which lead to their involvement in the facilitation of money laundering. It was argued earlier in the chapter that, while some legal professionals who become involved in laundering will have made a decision *to facilitate money laundering*, others will have become involved through a decision or decisions made as part of their routine occupational role. The final suggested strategy for controlling the facilitation of money laundering, therefore, would involve identifying the various points of decision-making for lawyers when conducting financial and commercial transactions in different organisational and regulatory contexts. Once identified, consideration could be given as to how to ensure that the 'correct' choices were made at these points. (This raises further questions about what the 'correct' decisions are and who gets to decide that.) Table 9.1 provides a summary of the potential strategies for controlling the facilitation of money laundering discussed in this chapter, focused on encouraging compliance with Money Laundering Regulations and professional standards, deterring misconduct, inhibiting opportunity/vulnerability structures, and influencing the decisions taken by legal professionals when providing services or conducting transactions that could act to facilitate money laundering.

A combination of approaches is required due to the variation in the nature of legal professional involvement in money laundering and the challenges or limitations inherent in individual strategies. For example, difficulties in detection, investigation and prosecution and the unsuitability of deterrence approaches for those who do not make an active choice to facilitate laundering mean that, on its own, the enforcement of criminal laws and regulations would be insufficient. On the other hand, methods to assist lawyers wishing to comply would be ineffective for those seeking to launder others' criminal proceeds. The identification of structural opportunities or vulnerabilities for money laundering allows the development of measures which do not need to take into account the reasons for, or levels of intent or knowingness in, legal professionals' involvement in

Table 9.1 Strategies for controlling the facilitation of money laundering

1. *Promoting compliance*

   Measures to enhance the means and desire to comply with Money Laundering Regulations and professional standards, rules and codes of conduct, such as:
   - Adequate and up-to-date education, training and guidance on the detail of the Money Laundering Regulations and legal professionals' obligations in relation to these.
   - Clear and easy-to-apply rules that specifically address behaviours that might facilitate money laundering within the professional standards framework.
   - Availability of training and guidance on the Money Laundering Regulations and professional standards framework which takes account of the capacities of different types/sizes of law firm to access it.
   - Highlighting the professional and financial consequences of non-compliance.
   - Reinforcing the professional and ethical principles of the legal profession.
   - Ensuring that the Money Laundering Regulations and professional standards, rules and codes of conduct are fair and reasonable, and that the profession perceives and accepts them as fair and reasonable. For example:
     - include the profession in development of the anti-money laundering/regulatory framework
     - ensure that the anti-money laundering/regulatory framework takes account of the specific culture, perceptions and requirements of the profession
     - consider proportionality and competing priorities in development of the anti-money laundering/regulatory framework.
   - Enhance the legitimacy of, and trust in, the regulatory process, through a cooperative relationship between members of the profession and those responsible for their regulation and anti-money laundering supervision.
   - Ensure meaningful and appropriate enforcement of laws, rules and regulations (see below).
   - Ensure awareness within the profession that laws, rules and regulations would be meaningfully and appropriately enforced.

2. *Enforcing laws, rules and regulations*

   Meaningful and appropriate enforcement of criminal law, regulations, and professional standards, rules and codes of conduct to:
   (i)   deter active, knowing involvement in the facilitation of money laundering
   (ii) signal seriousness of misconduct
   (iii) enhance perceptions of regulatory and criminal justice processes as effective and proportionate

   Achieved through:
   - Increased detection.
     - Paying attention to potential role of lawyers in all relevant criminal/financial investigations
     - Increasing routine monitoring by regulatory/supervisory bodies
     - Considering role of whistleblowers, investigative journalists and civil society organisations in identifying role of lawyers in 'high-end' money laundering.

(*Continued*)

Table 9.1 (Continued)

- Effective investigation.
  - Collaboration and cooperation between regulators, police and prosecuting authorities
  - Use of investigators with relevant skills
  - Management by appropriate level/function of policing (e.g. force, regional or national/international; focus on organised or economic crimes) or regulators (e.g. experience in/knowledge of anti-money laundering).
- Successful and appropriate prosecution.
  - Case-by-case decision on whether to pursue criminal or regulatory prosecution, based on specific circumstances of the case
  - Collaboration and cooperation between regulators, police and prosecuting authorities
  - Understanding of relevant legislation, regulations, and processes and transactions of the legal profession.
- Appropriate sanctioning.
  - Use of whole range of available (criminal or regulatory) sanctions, targeted at specific case.

3. *Reducing opportunities/vulnerabilities*

   Measures to inhibit structural factors that provide opportunities for legal professionals to facilitate money laundering or make them vulnerable to being exploited for laundering purposes, such as:

   - Greater oversight of client account transactions, conveyancing processes etc. within firms.
   - Less autonomy for legal professionals involved in conducting transactions or providing services which could facilitate money laundering.
   - Coordinated and supported approach to checking identity and source of funds in property purchases (i.e. involving all actors in the sale/purchase process and with the guidance needed to do this effectively).
   - Increased transparency and other measures to inhibit the use of corporate structures to conceal the identities of individuals involved in property purchases or the movement of illicit funds.

   Further research and analysis is required to understand the full range of opportunities/vulnerabilities for money laundering by or through the legal profession and develop strategies for reducing them. This should include examination of (i) the structures, processes and transactions of the profession and its wider environment and (ii) the processes by which illicit finance is managed more broadly.

4. *Influencing decision-making*

   Map the points of decision-making for legal professionals, in relation to their clients, the transactions they are involved in and the services they provide, in different organisational and regulatory contexts.

   Understand the factors that shape choices made at these points.

   Develop strategies for influencing the choices made at these points to reduce the likelihood that they will lead to the facilitation of money laundering.

money laundering. How this involvement is produced by the decisions made as part of legal professionals' routine occupational role, rather than decisions about whether to offend or not or to comply or not, creates the potential to shape these decisions to prevent them from leading to the facilitation of money laundering.

Further research and analysis on current and potential strategies for controlling the facilitation of money laundering is needed. The anti-money laundering agenda is consistently fast-moving, with regular updates to EU Money Laundering Directives and UK Money Laundering Regulations, increasing government rhetoric on the threats from money laundering and its facilitators, and the ever-evolving regulatory and policing landscape. As highlighted in Chapter 8, up-to-date analysis of the policing of 'professional enablers' and their prioritisation at local, regional and national levels would be of benefit. Research on the current nature of the regulatory environment and relationships between police, prosecuting authorities and regulators would also be beneficial. Greater understanding of the opportunities/vulnerabilities for money laundering within the legal profession and across the whole process(es) of managing criminal proceeds or other forms of illicit finance is required, and of the points of decision-making for legal professionals when providing services or conducting transactions that could act to facilitate money laundering. Finally, as preventing the facilitation of money laundering by lawyers becomes increasingly high-profile and high-priority, four questions seem particularly important: How do we do this most effectively? How do we do this proportionately? To what extent can we do this and what is adequate or acceptable? How do we balance this objective with the other roles and responsibilities of the profession and those that regulate it?

Appendix
Convictions, disciplinary proceedings and sanctions

This table provides detail about the solicitors' criminal convictions and the sentences received, whether they appeared in front of the Solicitors Disciplinary Tribunal (or Scottish Solicitors' Discipline Tribunal) and, if so, the disciplinary sanction(s) they received.

Table A.1 Convictions, disciplinary proceedings and sanctions

Case No.	Name	Date of Conviction	Offence convicted for (incl. relevant legislation)	Sentence	Disciplinary Action Taken?	Disciplinary Sanction[a]
1	Jonathan Duff	01/07/2002	**Drug Trafficking Act 1994 s.52(1):** Failure to disclose knowledge or suspicion of money laundering (2 counts)	6 months' imprisonment	Solicitors Disciplinary Tribunal: 20/05/2003	Struck off the roll of solicitors
2	Paul Winter Morris	12/03/2003	**Criminal Justice Act 1988 s.93(a):** Assisting another to retain or control benefit of criminal conduct (3 counts)	5 years' imprisonment	Solicitors Disciplinary Tribunal: 24/02/2004	Struck off the roll of solicitors
3	Andrew Young	09/09/2004	**Criminal Justice Act 1988 s.93(a):** Assisting another to retain or control benefit of criminal conduct (2 counts)	27 months' imprisonment	No record	
4	Peter Obidi	08/10/2004	**Criminal Justice Act 1988 s.93(a):** Assisting another to retain or control benefit of criminal conduct	6 months' imprisonment	Solicitors Disciplinary Tribunal: 08/11/2005	Struck off the roll of solicitors (charge included other offences of conduct unbefitting a solicitor)
5	Brian Dougan	22/05/2006	**Criminal Justice Act 1988 s.93(c):** Concealing or disguising the proceeds of criminal conduct	3 months' imprisonment	No record	
6	Philip Griffiths	19/06/2006	**POCA 2002 s.330:** Failure to disclose: regulated sector	6 months' imprisonment	Solicitors Disciplinary Tribunal: 24/07/2007	Struck off the roll of solicitors

(*Continued*)

Table A.1 (Continued)

Case No.	Name	Date of Conviction	Offence convicted for (incl. relevant legislation)	Sentence	Disciplinary Action Taken?	Disciplinary Sanction[a]
7	Gerard Hyde	02/03/2007	**Criminal Justice Act 1988 s.93(c):** Concealing or disguising the proceeds of criminal conduct	42 months' imprisonment	Solicitors Disciplinary Tribunal: 09/12/2008	Struck off the roll of solicitors
8	Jonathan Krestin	19/11/2008	**POCA 2002 s.328:** Entering into or becoming concerned in an arrangement facilitating the acquisition, retention, use or control of criminal property (1 count)	Fine of £5,000	Solicitors Disciplinary Tribunal: 27/10/2010	Severe reprimand
9	Mohammed Jahangir Farid	02/04/2009	**POCA 2002 s.328:** Entering into or becoming concerned in an arrangement facilitating the acquisition, retention, use or control of criminal property	4 years' imprisonment	Solicitors Disciplinary Tribunal: 17/02/2011	Prohibited from being employed or remunerated in connection with his practice as a solicitor, by a solicitor/recognised body
10	Rachel Taylor	22/05/2009	**POCA 2002 s.327:** Concealing, disguising, converting, transferring or removing criminal property from England and Wales, Scotland or Northern Ireland (1 count)	39 weeks' imprisonment, suspended for 18 months 200 hours community work Fine of £5,015	Solicitors Disciplinary Tribunal: 22/09/2010	Suspended for 12 months

	Name	Date	Charges	Sentence		Outcome
11	Anthony Blok	30/06/2009	**POCA 2002 s. 327** (1 count), **s.328** (1 count), **s.330** (1 count) Perverting the course of justice (1 count) Perjury (1 count)	4 years' imprisonment	Solicitors Disciplinary Tribunal: 01/12/2010	Prohibited from having name restored to roll of solicitors (removed name himself in 2009)
12	Aminat Afolabi	14/07/2009	**POCA 2002 s.328:** Entering into or becoming concerned in an arrangement facilitating the acquisition, retention, use or control of criminal property (1 count) **POCA 2002 s.329:** Acquiring, using or having possession of criminal property (1 count)	18 months' imprisonment	Solicitors Disciplinary Tribunal: 12/01/2012	Struck off the roll of solicitors
13	Shadab Khan	30/09/2009	**POCA 2002 s.328:** Entering into or becoming concerned in an arrangement facilitating the acquisition, retention, use or control of criminal property (1 count) **POCA 2002 s.330:** Failure to disclose: regulated sector (2 counts)	4 years' imprisonment	Solicitors Disciplinary Tribunal: 15/12/2011	Struck off the roll of solicitors
14	Martin Wilcock	22/09/2010	**POCA 2002 s.330:** Failure to disclose: regulated sector (1 count)	£2,515 fine	Solicitors Disciplinary Tribunal: 30/05/2012	Suspended for 3 months

(Continued)

Table A.1 (Continued)

Case No.	Name	Date of Conviction	Offence convicted for (incl. relevant legislation)	Sentence	Disciplinary Action Taken?	Disciplinary Sanction
15	Bhadresh Gohil	22/11/2010 and 06/12/2010	Number of offences under **POCA 2002 s.327** and **s.328** Conspiracy to defraud Conspiracy to make false instruments	£10 years' imprisonment	Solicitors Disciplinary Tribunal: 08/10/2012	Struck off the roll of solicitors
16	James Thorburn-Muirhead	19/02/2011	**POCA 2002 s.330:** Failure to disclose: regulated sector (1 count) Theft and false accounting (4 counts)	16 months' imprisonment	Solicitors Disciplinary Tribunal: 09/12/2011	Struck off the roll of solicitors
17	Nicholas Heywood	12/12/2011	**POCA 2002 s.327:** Concealing, disguising, converting, transferring or removing criminal property from England and Wales, Scotland or Northern Ireland (1 count) **POCA 2002 s.342:** Prejudicing a money laundering investigation (2 counts)	12 months' imprisonment	Solicitors Disciplinary Tribunal: 16/10/2012	Struck off the roll of solicitors
18	Andrew Tidd	06/02/2012	**POCA 2002 s.330:** Failure to disclose: regulated sector (5 counts)	4 months' imprisonment, suspended for 12 months	Solicitors Disciplinary Tribunal: 17/12/2013	Fine £2,500 (reduced from £5,000 due to financial circumstances)

| 19 | Richard Housley | 29/01/2013 | **POCA 2002 s.328:** Entering into or becoming concerned in an arrangement facilitating the acquisition, retention, use or control of criminal property (1 count) **POCA 2002 s.330:** Failure to disclose: regulated sector (1 count) Income tax fraud | 4 years' imprisonment | Scottish Solicitors' Discipline Tribunal: 26/06/2015 | Struck off the roll of solicitors |
| 20 | Andrew Wormstone | 07/02/2013 | **POCA 2002 s.328:** Entering into or becoming concerned in an arrangement facilitating the acquisition, retention, use or control of criminal property (1 count) | 30 months' imprisonment | Solicitors Disciplinary Tribunal: 24/10/2013 | Struck off the roll of solicitors |

[a]: In addition to these sanctions, all were made to pay costs

Bibliography

Alalehto, T. (2003) 'Economic Crime: Does Personality Matter?' *International Journal of Offender Therapy and Comparative Criminology*, 47(3): 335–355.

Albanese, J. (2000) 'The Causes of Organized Crime: Do Criminals Organize Around Opportunities for Crime or Do Criminal Opportunities Create New Offenders?' *Journal of Contemporary Criminal Justice*, 16(4): 409–423.

Alexander, K. (2001) 'The International Anti-Money-Laundering Regime: The Role of the Financial Action Task Force', *Journal of Money Laundering Control*, 4(3): 231–248.

Alexander, L. and Furzan, K.K. (2009) *Crime and Culpability: A Theory of Criminal Law*. Cambridge, UK: Cambridge University Press.

Alldridge, P. (2008) 'Money Laundering and Globalization', *Journal of Law and Society*, 35(4): 437–463.

Alldridge, P. (2016) *What Went Wrong with Money Laundering Law?* London: Palgrave Macmillan.

Anand, V., Ashforth, B. and Joshi, M. (2004) 'Business as Usual: The Acceptance and Perpetuation of Corruption in Organizations', *Academy of Management Executives*, 18: 39–53.

Ayres, I. and Braithwaite, J. (1992) *Responsive Regulation: Transcending the Deregulation Debate*. New York: Oxford University Press.

Babiak, P. and Hare, R. (2007) *Snakes in Suits: When Psychopaths Go to Work*. New York: Harper Collins.

Badar, M.E. (2013) *The Concept of Mens Rea in International Criminal Law: The Case for a Unified Approach*. London: Bloomsbury Publishing.

Bell, R. (2002) 'The Prosecution of Lawyers for Money Laundering Offences', *Journal of Money Laundering Control*, 6(1): 17–26.

Bello, A. and Harvey, J. (2017) 'From a Risk-based to an Uncertainty-based Approach to Anti-money Laundering Compliance', *Security Journal*, 30(1): 24–38.

Benson, K. (2018) 'Money Laundering, Anti-Money Laundering and the Legal Profession', in C. King, C. Walker and J. Gurulé (eds.) *The Palgrave Handbook of Criminal and Terrorism Financing Law*. London: Palgrave MacMillan.

Benson, M. (1985) 'Denying the Guilty Mind: Accounting for Involvement in a White-Collar Crime', *Criminology*, 23(4): 583–607.

Benson, M., Madensen, T. and Eck, J. (2009) 'White-Collar Crime from an Opportunity Perspective', in S. Simpson and D. Weisburd (eds.) *The Criminology of White-Collar Crime*. New York: Springer, pp. 175–193.

Benson, M. and Manchak, S. (2014) 'The Psychology of White-Collar Crime', in *Oxford Handbooks Online in Criminology and Criminal Justice*. New York: Oxford University Press.

Benson, M. and Moore, E. (1992) 'Are White-Collar and Common Offenders the Same? An Empirical and Theoretical Critique of a Recently Proposed General Theory of Crime', *Journal of Research in Crime and Delinquency*, 29(3): 251–272.

Benson, M. and Simpson, S. (2015) *Understanding White-Collar Crime: An Opportunity Perspective* (2nd ed.). Abingdon: Routledge.

Benson, M. and Simpson, S. (2018) *Understanding White-Collar Crime: An Opportunity Perspective* (3rd ed.). Abingdon: Routledge.

Benson, M., Van Slyke, S. and Cullen, T. (2016) 'Core Themes in the Study of White-Collar Crime', in S. Van Slyke, M. Benson and F. Cullen (eds.) *The Oxford Handbook of White-Collar Crime*. Oxford: Oxford University Press, pp. 1–24.

Bergström, M. (2018) 'The Global AML Regime and the EU AML Directives: Prevention and Control', in C. King, C. Walker and J. Gurulé (eds.) *The Palgrave Handbook of Criminal and Terrorism Financing Law*. London: Palgrave Macmillan, pp. 33–56.

Blickle, G., Schlegel, A., Fassbender, P. and Klein, U. (2006) 'Some Personality Correlates of Business White-Collar Crime', *Applied Psychology*, 55(2): 220–233.

Blum, J., Levi, M., Naylor, R. and Williams, P. (1998) *Financial Havens, Banking Secrecy and Money Laundering*. Vienna: United Nations.

Bonger, W. and Horton, H. (1916) *Criminality and Economic Conditions*. Boston: Little, Brown and Company.

Braithwaite, J. (1985) 'White Collar Crime', *Annual Review of Sociology*, 11: 1–25.

Braithwaite, J. (2002) *Restorative Justice and Responsive Regulation*. Oxford: Oxford University Press.

Braithwaite, J. and Geis, G. (1982) 'On Theory and Action for Corporate Crime Control', *Crime and Delinquency*, 28(2): 292–314.

Braithwaite, J. and Makkai, T. (1991) 'Testing an Expected Utility Model of Corporate Deterrence', *Law & Society Review*, 25: 7–39.

Brantingham, P. and Brantingham, P. (1993) 'Environment, Routine, and Situation: Toward a Pattern Theory of Crime', in R. Clarke and M. Felson (eds.) *Routine Activity and Rational Choice*. New Brunswick: Transaction Publishers.

Brantingham, P. and Brantingham, P. (2011) 'Crime Pattern Theory', in R. Wortley and L. Mazerolle (eds.) *Environmental Criminology and Crime Analysis* (2nd ed.). Abingdon: Willan Publishing.

Braun, V. and Clarke, V. (2006) 'Using Thematic Analysis in Psychology', *Qualitative Research in Psychology*, 3(2): 77–101.

Campbell, J. and Göritz, A. (2014) 'Culture Corrupts! A Qualitative Study of Organizational Culture in Corrupt Organizations', *Journal of Business Ethics*, 120: 291–311.

Center for Global Development (2015) *Unintended Consequences of Anti-Money Laundering Policies for Poor Countries. A CGD Working Group Report*. Washington, DC: Center for Global Development.

Charlow, R. (1992) 'Willful Ignorance and Criminal Culpability', *Texas Law Review*, 70(6): 1351–1429.

Chevrier, E. (2004) 'The French Government's Will to Fight Organized Crime and Clean Up the Legal Professions: The Awkward Compromise Between Professional

Secrecy and Mandatory Reporting', *Crime, Law and Social Change*, 42(2–3): 189–200.

Clementi, D. (2004) *Review of the Regulatory Framework for Legal Services in England and Wales: Final Report*, December. Available at: https://webarchive.nationalarchives.gov.uk/+/www.legal-services-review.org.uk/content/report/index.htm [Accessed 31 July 2019].

Clinard, M. and Meier, R. (2011) *Sociology of Deviant Behavior* (14th ed.). Belmont, CA: Wadsworth.

Clinard, M. and Quinney, R. (1973) *Criminal Behavior Systems: A Typology*. New York: Holt, Rinehart and Winston.

Clinard, M. and Yeager, P. (1980) *Corporate Crime*. New York: Free Press.

Cohen, L. and Felson, M. (1979) 'Social Change and Crime Rate Trends: A Routine Activity Approach', *American Sociological Review*, 44(4): 588–608.

Cohen, M.A. (2000) 'Empirical Research on the Deterrent Effect of Environmental Monitoring and Enforcement', *The Environmental Law Reporter*, 30(4): 10245–10252.

Coleman, J. (1995) 'Motivation and Opportunity: Understanding the Causes of White Collar Crime', in G. Geis, R. Meier and L. Salinger (eds.) *White Collar Crime* (3rd ed.). New York: Free Press, pp. 360–381.

Cornish, D. (1994) 'The Procedural Analysis of Offending and Its Relevance for Situational Prevention', in R.V. Clarke (ed.) *Crime Prevention Studies, vol. 3*. Monsey, NY: Criminal Justice Press, pp. 152–196.

Cornish, D. and Clarke, R. (1986) *The Reasoning Criminal*. New York: Springer-Verlag.

Cornish, D. and Clarke, R. (2002) 'Analyzing Organized Crimes', in A. Piquero and S. Tibbetts (eds.) *Rational Choice and Criminal Behavior: Recent Research and Future Challenges*. New York: Routledge, pp. 41–64.

Cornish, D. and Clarke, R. (eds.) (2014) *The Reasoning Criminal: Rational Choice Perspectives on Offending*. New Brunswick, NJ: Transaction Books.

CPS (2018) *Crown Prosecution Service Legal Guidance: Proceeds of Crime Act 2002 Part 7 – Money Laundering Offences*. Available at: www.cps.gov.uk/legal-guidance/proceeds-crime-act-2002-part-7-money-laundering-offences [Accessed 29 July 2019].

Crawford, A. (2007) 'Crime Prevention and Community Safety', in M. Maguire, R. Morgan and R. Reiner (eds.) *Oxford Handbook of Criminology* (4th ed.). Oxford: Oxford University Press, pp. 866–909.

Croall, H. (2001) *Understanding White Collar Crime*. Buckingham: Open University Press.

Croall, H. (2003) 'Combating Financial Crime: Regulatory Versus Crime Control Approaches', *Journal of Financial Crime*, 11(1): 45–55.

Cummings, L. and Stepnowsky, P. (2011) 'My Brother's Keeper: An Empirical Study of Attorney Facilitation of Money Laundering Through Commercial Transactions', *Journal of the Professional Lawyer* (1): 1–36.

Dalton, D. and Kesner, I. (1988) 'On the Dynamics of Corporate Size and Illegal Activity: An Empirical Assessment', *Journal of Business Ethics*, 7: 861–870.

Di Nicola, A. and Zoffi, P. (2004) 'Italian Lawyers and Criminal Clients. Risks and Countermeasures', *Crime, Law and Social Change*, 42(2–3): 201–225.

Dodge, M. (2009) *Women and White-Collar Crime*. Upper Saddle River, NJ: Prentice Hall.

Dodge, M. (2016) 'Gender Constructions', in S. Van Slyke, M. Benson and F. Cullen (eds.) *The Oxford Handbook of White-Collar Crime*. Oxford: Oxford University Press, pp. 200–213.

Does de Willebois, van der E., Halter, E., Harrison, R., Park, J.W. and Sharman, J.C. (2011) *The Puppet Masters: How the Corrupt Use Legal Structures to Hide Stolen Assets and What to Do About It*. Washington, DC: The International Bank for Reconstruction and Development/The World Bank.

Eck, J. (1994) *Drug Markets and Drug Places: A Case-Control Study of the Spatial Structure of Illicit Drug Dealing*. PhD Dissertation: University of Maryland, Baltimore.

Edwards, A. and Levi, M. (2008) 'Researching the Organization of Serious Crimes', *Criminology and Criminal Justice*, 8(4): 363–388.

Elliott, R. (2010) 'Examining the Relationship Between Personality Characteristics and Unethical Behaviors Resulting in Economic Crime', *Ethical Human Psychology and Psychiatry*, 12: 269–276.

Europol (2013) *EU Serious and Organised Crime Threat Assessment: SOCTA 2013*. The Hague: Europol.

FATF (2003) *FATF 40 Recommendations*. Paris: Financial Action Task Force.

FATF (2008) *Risk-Based Approach: Guidance for Legal Professionals*. Paris: Financial Action Task Force.

FATF (2010) *Global Money Laundering & Terrorist Financing Threat Assessment*. Paris: Financial Action Task Force.

FATF (2013) *Money Laundering and Terrorist Financing Vulnerabilities of Legal Professionals*. Paris: Financial Action Task Force.

FATF (2016) *Anti-Money Laundering and Counter-Terrorist Financing Measures: Canada – Mutual Evaluation Report*, September 2016. Paris: Financial Action Task Force.

FATF (2019a) *What Is Money Laundering?* Available at: www.fatf-gafi.org/faq/moneylaundering/ [Accessed 29 July 2019].

FATF (2019b) *Who We Are?* Available at: www.fatf-gafi.org/about/ [Accessed 29 July 2019].

FCA (2019) *Office for Professional Body Anti-Money Laundering Supervision*. Available at: www.fca.org.uk/opbas [Accessed 31 July 2019].

Felson, M. (1986) 'Routine Activities, Social Controls, Rational Decisions, and Criminal Outcomes', in D. Cornish and R. Clarke (eds.) *The Reasoning Criminal: Rational Choice Perspectives on Offending*. New York: Springer-Verlag, pp. 119–128.

Finckenauer, J. (2005) 'Problems of Definition: What Is Organized Crime?' *Trends in Organized Crime*, 8(3): 63–83.

Flick, U., Garms-Homolova, V., Herrmann, W., Kuck, J. and Rohnsch, G. (2012) '"I Can't Prescribe Something Just Because Someone Asks for It . . .": Using Mixed Methods in the Framework of Triangulation', *Journal of Mixed Methods Research*, 6(2): 97–110.

Fortson, R. (2010) 'Money Laundering Offences Under POCA 2002', in W. Blair and R. Brent (eds.) *Banks and Financial Crime – The International Law of Tainted Money*. Oxford: Oxford University Press, pp. 155–202.

Friedrichs, D. (1996) *Trusted Criminals: White Collar Crime in Contemporary Society*. Belmont, CA: Wandsworth.

Friedrichs, D. and Schwartz, M. (2008) 'Low Self-Control and High Organizational Control: The Paradoxes of White-Collar Crime', in E. Goode (ed.) *Out of Control: Assessing the General Theory of Crime*. Stanford, CA: Stanford University Press, pp. 145–159.

Gallant, M. (2005) *Money Laundering and the Proceeds of Crime: Economic Crime and Civil Remedies*. Cheltenham, UK: Edward Elgar.

Gallant, M. (2013) 'Lawyers and Money Laundering Regulation: Testing the Limits of Secrecy in Canada', *3rd Global Conference on Transparency Research, Paris*, October 2013. Available at: https://papers.ssrn.com/sol3/papers.cfm?abstract_id=2336219 [Accessed 29 July 2019].

Geis, G. (2000) 'On the Absence of Self-Control as the Basis for a General Theory of Crime: A Critique', *Theoretical Criminology*, 4(1): 35–53.

Gelemerova, L. (2009) 'On the Frontline Against Money-Laundering: The Regulatory Minefield', *Crime, Law and Social Change*, 52(1): 33–55.

Gelemerova, L. (2011) *The Anti-Money Laundering System in the Context of Globalisation: A Panopticon Built on Quicksand?* Nijmegen: Wolf Legal Publishers.

Gentzik, D. (2000) 'Laundering and Lawyers – The Payment of Legal Fees and Money-laundering Offences in Germany and the UK', *Journal of Money Laundering Control*, 4(1): 76–88.

Gilmore, W. (2004) *Dirty Money: The Evolution of Money Laundering Countermeasures* (3rd ed.). Strasbourg: Council of Europe.

Gilmore, W. and Mitsilegas, V. (2007) 'The EU Legislative Framework Against Money Laundering and Terrorist Finance: A Critical Analysis in Light of Evolving Global Standards', *International and Comparative Law Quarterly*, 56: 119–141.

Global Witness (2015a) *Mystery on Baker Street: Brutal Kazakh Official Linked to £147M London Property Empire*. London: Global Witness. Available at: www.globalwitness.org/en/campaigns/corruption-and-money-laundering/mystery-baker-street/ [Accessed 12 April 2018].

Global Witness (2015b) *Blood Red Carpet*. London: Global Witness. Available at: www.globalwitness.org/en/reports/surrey-mansion-used-hide-suspect-funds/ [Accessed 12 April 2018].

Goldstraw-White, J. (2012) *White-Collar Crime: Accounts of Offending Behaviour*. Basingstoke: Palgrave Macmillan.

Goodey, J. (2008) 'Human Trafficking: Sketchy Data and Policy Responses', *Criminology and Criminal Justice*, 8(4): 421–442.

Gottfredson, M. and Hirschi, T. (1990) *A General Theory of Crime*. Stanford, CA: Stanford University Press.

Grabosky, P. (2013) 'Beyond *Responsive Regulation*: The Expanding Role of Non-State Actors in the Regulatory Process', *Regulation and Governance*, 7: 114–123.

Gross, E. (1980) 'Organization Structure and Organizational Crime', in G. Geis and E. Stotland (eds.) *White-Collar Crime: Theory and Research*. Los Angeles, CA: Sage, pp. 52–70.

Gruppo, A. (2003) *Synthetic Drugs Trafficking in Three European Cities: Major Trends and the Involvement of Organised Crime, Final Report*. Turin: Gipiangrafica.

Gurulé, J. (1995) 'The Money Laundering Control Act of 1986: Creating a New Federal Offense or Merely Affording Federal Prosecutors an Alternative Means of Punishing Specified Unlawful Activity?' *American Criminal Law Review*, 32: 823–854.

Hagan, F. (1983) 'The Organized Crime Continuum: A Further Specification of a New Conceptual Model', *Criminal Justice Review*, 8(2): 52–57.

Hagan, F. (2006) '"Organized Crime" and "Organized Crime": Indeterminate Problems of Definition', *Trends in Organized Crime*, 9(4): 127–137.

Harvey, J. (2008) 'Just How Effective Is Money Laundering Legislation?' *Security Journal*, 21(3): 189–211.

Heffernan, M. (2011) *Willful Blindness: Why We Ignore the Obvious at Our Peril*. London: Simon and Schuster UK Ltd.

Helgesson, K.S. and Mörth, U. (2016) 'Involuntary Public Policy-Making by For-Profit Professionals: European Lawyers on Anti-Money Laundering and Terrorism Financing', *Journal of Common Market Studies*, 54(5): 1216–1232.

Helgesson, K.S. and Mörth, U. (2018) 'Client Privilege, Compliance and the Rule of Law: Swedish Lawyers and Money Laundering Prevention', *Crime, Law and Social Change*, 69: 227–248.

Helgesson, K.S. and Mörth, U. (2019) 'Instruments of Securitization and Resisting Subjects: For-Profit Professionals in the Finance-Security Nexus', *Security Dialogue*, 50(3): 257–274.

Hirschi, T. and Gottfredson, M. (1989) 'The Significance of White-Collar Crime for a General Theory of Crime', *Criminology*, 27(2): 359–371.

HM Treasury/Home Office (2015) *UK National Risk Assessment of Money Laundering and Terrorist Financing 2015*. London: HM Treasury/Home Office.

HM Treasury/Home Office (2017) *National Risk Assessment of Money Laundering and Terrorist Financing 2017*. London: HM Treasury/Home Office.

Home Office (2013) *Serious and Organised Crime Strategy*, October 2013. London: Home Office.

Home Office (2018) *Serious and Organised Crime Strategy*, November 2018. London: Home Office.

Home Office/HM Treasury (2016) *Action Plan for Anti-Money Laundering and Counter Terrorist Finance*. London: Home Office/HM Treasury.

Huisman, W. (2016) 'Criminogenic Organizational Properties and Dynamics', in S. Van Slyke, M. Benson and F. Cullen (eds.) *The Oxford Handbook of White-Collar Crime*. Oxford: Oxford University Press, pp. 435–462.

Huisman, W. (2017) 'Offender Decision-Making in Corporate and White-Collar Crime', in W. Bernasco, J-L. van Gelder and H. Elffers (eds.) *The Oxford Handbook of Offender Decision Making*. Oxford: Oxford University Press, pp. 684–722.

Huisman, W. and Vande Walle, G. (2010) 'The Criminology of Corruption', in G. De Graaf, P. von Maravic and P. Wagenaar (eds.) *The Good Cause: Theoretical Perspectives on Corruption*. Leverkusen: Barbara Budrich Publishing, pp. 115–145.

Huisman, W. and van Erp, J. (2013) 'Opportunities for Environmental Crime', *British Journal of Criminology*, 53(6): 1178–1200.

IBA (2011) *International Principles on Conduct for the Legal Profession*. London: International Bar Association.

IBA (2014) *A Lawyer's Guide to Detecting and Preventing Money Laundering*. International Bar Association, American Bar Association and the Council of Bars and Law Societies of Europe. London: International Bar Association.

IMF (2018) *IMF and the Fight Against Money Laundering and the Financing of Terrorism*. International Monetary Fund Factsheet. Washington, DC: IMF Communications Department. Available at: www.imf.org/en/About/Factsheets/

Sheets/2016/08/01/16/31/Fight-Against-Money-Laundering-the-Financing-of-Terrorism [Accessed 29 July 2019].

IRN Research (2019) *UK Legal Services Market 2019: Market Trends Report*, February. London: IRN Research.

Kagan, R., Gunningham, N. and Thornton, D. (2011) 'Fear, Duty, and Regulatory Compliance: Lessons from Three Research Projects', in C. Parker and V.L. Nielsen (eds.) *Explaining Compliance: Business Responses to Regulation*. Cheltenham: Edward Elgar, pp. 37–58.

Karstedt, S. (2016) 'Middle-Class Crime: Moral Economies Between Crime in the Streets and Crime in the Suites', in S. Van Slyke, M. Benson and F. Cullen (eds.) *The Oxford Handbook of White-Collar Crime*. Oxford: Oxford University Press, pp. 168–199.

Kebbell, S. (2017) ' "Everybody's Looking at Nothing" – The Legal Profession and the Disproportionate Burden of the Proceeds of Crime Act 2002', *Criminal Law Review*, 10: 741–753.

Kirby, D. (2008) 'The European Union's Gatekeeper Initiative: The European Union Enlists Lawyers in the Fight Against Money Laundering and Terrorist Financing', *Hofstra Law Review*, 37(1): 261–311.

Kostakos, P. and Antonopoulos, G. (2010) 'The "good", the "bad" and the "Charlie": The Business of Cocaine Smuggling in Greece', *Global Crime*, 11(1): 34–57.

Kramer, R. (1982) 'Corporate Crime: An Organizational Perspective', in P. Wickman and T. Dailey (eds.) *White-Collar and Economic Crime: Multidisciplinary and Cross-National Perspectives*. Lexington, VA: Lexington Books.

Kupatadze, A. (2008) 'Organized Crime Before and After the Tulip Revolution: The Changing Dynamics of Upperworld-Underworld Networks', *Central Asian Survey*, 27(3–4): 279–299.

Langdon-Down, G. (2018) 'New Model Armies', *Law Gazette*, 26 March 2018. Available at: www.lawgazette.co.uk/features/new-model-armies/5065393.article [Accessed 29 July 2019].

Lankhorst, F. and Nelen, H. (2004) 'Professional Services and Organised Crime in the Netherlands', *Crime, Law and Social Change*, 42(2–3): 163–188.

Law Commission (2018) *Anti-Money Laundering: The SARs Regime, Consultation Paper No.236*, July 2018. Available at: www.lawcom.gov.uk/document/anti-money-laundering-the-sars-regime/ [Accessed 25 August 2019].

Law Commission (2019) *Anti-Money Laundering: The SARs Regime – Report*, June 2019. Available at: www.lawcom.gov.uk/document/anti-money-laundering-the-sars-regime-2/ [Accessed 25 August 2019].

Law Society Scotland (2017) *The New ML Regulations: What They Mean to You and Your Practice*. Presentation by the Law Society Scotland, AML Roadshow. Edinburgh: Law Society Scotland.

Layder, D. (1998) *Sociological Practice: Linking Theory and Social Research*. London: Sage.

Legal Futures (2019) *Big Law Firm "Will Ditch Client Account by End of Year"*, 20 August 2019. Available at: www.legalfutures.co.uk/latest-news/big-law-firm-will-ditch-client-account-by-end-of-year/ [Accessed 8 September 2019].

Legal Services Board (2017) *Evaluation: ABS and Investment in Legal Services 2011/12–2016/17: An Analysis of Investment in Legal Services Since the Introduction of ABS Licensing*. London: Legal Services Board.

Levi, M. (2002) 'Money Laundering and Its Regulation', *Annals of the American Academy of Political and Social Science*, 582: 181–194.

Levi, M. (2007) 'Pecunia Non Olet? The Control of Money-laundering Revisited', in F. Bovenkerk and M. Levi (eds.) *The Organized Crime Community: Essays in Honor of Alan A. Block*. New York: Springer, pp. 161–182.

Levi, M. (2008a) 'Organized Fraud and Organizing Frauds: Unpacking Research on Networks and Organization', *Criminology and Criminal Justice*, 8(4): 389–419.

Levi, M. (2008b) *The Phantom Capitalists: The Organization and Control of Long-Firm Fraud* (2nd ed.). Aldershot: Ashgate.

Levi, M. (2010) 'Combating the Financing of Terrorism: A History and Assessment of the Control of Threat Finance', *British Journal of Criminology*, 50(4): 650–669.

Levi, M. (2012) 'The Organization of Serious Crimes for Gain', in M. Maguire, R. Morgan and R. Reiner (eds.) *The Oxford Handbook of Criminology* (5th ed.). Oxford: Oxford University Press, pp. 595–622.

Levi, M. (2014) 'Money Laundering', in L. Paoli (ed.) *The Oxford Handbook of Organized Crime*. Oxford: Oxford University Press, pp. 419–443.

Levi, M. (2015) 'Money for Crime and Money from Crime: Financing Crime and Laundering Crime Proceeds', *European Journal on Criminal Policy and Research*, 21(2): 275–297.

Levi, M. (2018) 'White-Collar Crime, Organised Crime and the Regulation of "Enablers"', *PACCS Research Blog*. Available at: www.paccsresearch.org.uk/blog/white-collar-crime-organised-crime-mike-levi/ [Accessed 2 September 2019].

Levi, M. and Lord, N. (2017) 'White-Collar and Corporate Crime', in A. Liebling, S. Maruna and L. McAra (eds.) *The Oxford Handbook of Criminology* (6th ed.). Oxford: Oxford University Press, pp. 722–743.

Levi, M. and Maguire, M. (2004) 'Reducing and Preventing Organised Crime: An Evidence Based Approach', *Crime, Law and Social Change*, 41: 397–469.

Levi, M., Nelen, H. and Lankhorst, F. (2004) 'Lawyers as Crime Facilitators in Europe: An Introduction and Overview', *Crime, Law and Social Change*, 42(2–3): 117–121.

Levi, M. and Reuter, P. (2009) 'Money Laundering', in M. Tonry (ed.) *The Oxford Handbook of Crime and Public Policy*. Oxford: Oxford University Press, pp. 356–380.

Linstead, S., Maréchal, G. and Griffin, R. (2014) 'Theorizing and Researching the Dark Side of Organization', *Organization Studies*, 35(2): 165–188.

Listwan, S., Piquero, N.L. and Van Voorhis, P. (2010) 'Recidivism Among a White-Collar Sample: Does Personality Matter?' *Australian and New Zealand Journal of Criminology*, 43: 156–174.

Lord, N. and Doig, A. (2014) 'Transnational Corporate Corruption', in G. Bruinsma and D. Weisburd (eds.) *Encyclopedia of Criminology and Criminal Justice*. New York: Springer, pp. 5289–5302.

Lord, N., Flores Elizondo, C. and Spencer, J. (2017) 'The Dynamics of Food Fraud: The Interactions Between Criminal Opportunity and Market (Dys)Functionality in Legitimate Business', *Criminology & Criminal Justice*, 17(5): 605–623.

Lord, N. and Levi, M. (2016) 'Organising the Finances for and the Finances from Transnational Corporate Bribery', *European Journal of Criminology*, 14(3): 365–389.

Lord, N., Spencer, J., Bellotti, E. and Benson, K. (2017) 'A Script Analysis of the Distribution of Counterfeit Alcohol Across Two European Jurisdictions', *Trends in Organized Crime*, 20: 252–272.

Lord, N., van Wingerde, K. and Campbell, L. (2018) 'Organising the Monies of Corporate Financial Crimes via Organisational Structures: Ostensible Legitimacy, Effective Anonymity, and Third-Party Facilitation', *Administrative Sciences*, 8(2): 17.

Loughrey, J. (2011) *Corporate Lawyers and Corporate Governance*. Cambridge: Cambridge University Press.

LSAG (2018) *Anti-Money Laundering: Guidance for the Legal Sector*, March 2018. Legal Sector Affinity Group. Available at: www.lawsociety.org.uk/policy-campaigns/articles/anti-money-laundering-guidance/ [Accessed 29 July 2019].

Lyman, M. and Potter, G. (2000) *Organized Crime* (2nd ed.). New York: Prentice-Hall.

Madensen, T. (2016) 'Opportunities for Crime', in S. Van Slyke, M. Benson and F. Cullen (eds.) *The Oxford Handbook of White-Collar Crime*. Oxford: Oxford University Press, pp. 382–408.

Makkai, T. and Braithwaite, J. (1994) 'The Dialectics of Corporate Deterrence', *Journal of Research in Crime and Delinquency*, 31(4): 347–373.

Maltz, M. (1976) 'On Defining Organized Crime: The Development of a Definition and Typology', *Crime and Delinquency*, 22(3): 338–346.

Maruna, S. and Copes, H. (2005) 'What Have We Learned from Five Decades of Neutralization Research?' *Crime and Justice: A Review of Research*, 32: 221–320.

Mascini, P. (2016) 'Comparing Assumptions Underlying Regulatory Inspection Strategies: Implications for Oversight Policy', in S. Van Slyke, M. Benson and F. Cullen (eds.) *The Oxford Handbook of White-Collar Crime*. Oxford: Oxford University Press, pp. 521–539.

Merriam-Webster (ed.) (2011) *Merriam-Webster's Dictionary of Law* (2nd ed.). Springfield, MA: Merriam Webster.

Middleton, D. (2004) *Solicitors, High-Yield Investment Fraud and Money Laundering: A Case Study of How the Regulatory Framework and Norms of Professional Responsibility Address the Conduct of Solicitors who Facilitate Wrongdoing*. Unpublished thesis: University of Birmingham, UK.

Middleton, D. (2005) 'The Legal and Regulatory Response to Solicitors Involved in Serious Fraud: Is Regulatory Action More Effective Than Criminal Prosecution?' *British Journal of Criminology*, 45: 810–836.

Middleton, D. (2008) 'Lawyers and Client Accounts: Sand Through a Colander', *Journal of Money Laundering Control*, 11(1): 34–46.

Middleton, D. and Levi, M. (2004) 'The Role of Solicitors in Facilitating "Organized Crime": Situational Crime Opportunities and Their Regulation', *Crime, Law and Social Change*, 42(2–3): 123–161.

Middleton, D. and Levi, M. (2015) 'Let Sleeping Lawyers Lie: Organized Crime, Lawyers and the Regulation of Legal Services', *British Journal of Criminology*, 55(4): 647–668.

Mitsilegas, V. (2006) 'Countering the Chameleon Threat of Dirty Money: "Hard" and "Soft" Law in the Emergence of a Global Regime Against Money Laundering and Terrorist Financing', in A. Edwards and P. Gill (eds.) *Transnational Organised Crime: Perspectives on Global Security*. Oxon: Routledge, pp. 195–211.

Mitsilegas, V. and Vavoula, N. (2016) 'The Evolving EU Anti-Money Laundering Regime: Challenges for Fundamental Rights and Rule of Law', *Maastricht Journal of European and Comparative Law*, 23(2): 261–293.

Morselli, C. (2009) *Inside Criminal Networks*. New York: Springer.

Morselli, C. and Giguere, C. (2006) 'Legitimate Strengths in Criminal Networks', *Crime, Law and Social Change*, 45: 185–200.

Moscow Communiqué (1999) *Ministerial Conference of the G-8 Countries on Combating Transnational Organized Crime (Moscow, October 19th–20th 1999) Communiqué*. Available at: www.justice.gov/sites/default/files/ag/legacy/2004/06/09/99MoscowCommunique.pdf [Accessed 10 September 2019].

Murray, K. (2013) 'A Square Go: Tackling Organised Crime Where It Doesn't Want to Be Tackled', *Journal of Money Laundering Control*, 16(2): 99–108.

Murray, K. (2015) 'Walking the Walk: Practical Measures to Undermine the Business of Organised Crime', *Journal of Financial Crime*, 22(2): 199–207.

Nagin, D. (2013) 'Deterrence in the Twenty-First Century', *Crime and Justice*, 42: 199–263.

Nance, M. (2018) 'The Regime That FATF Built: An Introduction to the Financial Action Task Force', *Crime, Law and Social Change*, 69: 109–129.

Naylor, R.T. (2004) *Wages of Crime: Black Markets, Illicit Finance, and the Underworld Economy*. Ithaca: Cornell University Press.

NCA (2014) *National Strategic Assessment of Serious and Organised Crime 2014*. London: National Crime Agency.

NCA (2015) *National Strategic Assessment of Serious and Organised Crime 2015*. London: National Crime Agency.

NCA (2016) *National Strategic Assessment of Serious and Organised Crime 2016*. London: National Crime Agency.

NCA (2017) *National Strategic Assessment of Serious and Organised Crime 2017*. London: National Crime Agency.

NCA (2018) *National Strategic Assessment of Serious and Organised Crime 2018*. London: National Crime Agency.

NCA (2019) *National Strategic Assessment of Serious and Organised Crime* 2019. London: National Crime Agency.

Nee, C. and Meenaghan, A. (2006) 'Expert Decision Making in Burglars', *British Journal of Criminology*, 46(5): 935–949.

Nelen, H. and Lankhorst, F. (2008) 'Facilitating Organized Crime: The Role of Lawyers and Notaries', in D. Siegel and H. Nelen (eds.) *Organized Crime: Culture, Markets and Policies*. New York: Springer, pp. 127–142.

Nelken, D. (2012) 'White-collar and Corporate Crime', in R. Reiner, M. Maguire and R. Morgan (eds.) *The Oxford Handbook of Criminology* (5th ed.). Oxford: Oxford University Press, pp. 623–659.

Nielsen, V.L. and Parker, C. (2008) 'To What Extent Do Third Parties Influence Business Compliance?' *Journal of Law and Society*, 35: 309–340.

OECD (2001) *Behind the Corporate Veil: Using Corporate Entities for Illicit Purposes*. Paris: Organisation for Economic Co-Operation and Development.

OPBAS (2019) *Anti-Money Laundering Supervision by the Legal and Accountancy Professional Body Supervisors: Themes from the 2018 OBPAS Anti-money Laundering Supervisory Assessments*, March 2019. London: OPBAS/FCA. Available at: www.fca.org.uk/publication/opbas/themes-2018-opbas-anti-money-laundering-supervisory-assessments.pdf [Accessed 31 July 2019].

Palmer, D. (2013) *Normal Organizational Wrongdoing: A Critical Analysis of Theories of Misconduct in and By Organizations*. Oxford: Oxford University Press.

Palmer, D., Smith-Crowe, K. and Greenwood, R. (eds.) (2016) *Organizational Wrongdoing: Key Perspectives and New Directions*. Cambridge: Cambridge University Press.

Paoli, L. (2002) 'The Paradoxes of Organized Crime', *Crime, Law and Social Change*, 37(1): 51–97.

Paoli, L. and Vander Beken, T. (2014) 'Organized Crime: A Contested Concept', in L. Paoli (ed.) *The Oxford Handbook of Organized Crime*. Oxford: Oxford University Press, pp. 13–31.

Parker, C. (2013) 'Twenty Years of Responsive Regulation: An Appreciation and Appraisal', *Regulation and Governance*, 7: 2–13.

Parker, C. and Nielsen, V.L. (2011) 'Introduction', in C. Parker and V.L. Nielsen (eds.) *Explaining Compliance: Business Responses to Regulation*. Cheltenham: Edward Elgar, pp. 1–36.

Passas, N. (2002) 'Cross-border Crime and the Interface Between Legal and Illegal Actors', in P. van Duyne, K. von Lampe and N. Passas (eds.) *Upperworld and Underworld in Cross-Border Crime*. Nijmegen: Wolf Legal Publishers, pp. 11–41.

Paternoster, R. and Simpson, S. (1993) 'A Rational Choice Theory of Corporate Crime', in R. Clarke and M. Felson (eds.) *Routine Activity and Rational Choice: Advances in Criminological Theory*. New Brunswick, NJ: Transaction Books, pp. 37–58.

Paternoster, R. and Simpson, S. (1996) 'Sanction Threats and Appeals to Morality: Testing a Rational Choice Model of Corporate Crime', *Law and Society Review*, 30(3): 549–584.

Payne, B. (2012) *White-Collar Crime: The Essentials*. Thousand Oaks, CA: Sage.

Pearce, F. (1976) *Crimes of the Powerful*. London: Pluto.

Pearce, F. and Tombs, S. (1998) *Toxic Capitalism: Corporate Crime and the Chemical Industry*. Aldershot: Ashgate.

Piquero, N.L. (2012) 'The Only Thing We Have to Fear Is Fear Itself: Investigating the Relationship Between Fear of Falling and White-Collar Crime', *Crime and Delinquency*, 58(3): 362–379.

Piquero, N.L., Exum, M.L. and Simpson, S. (2005) 'Integrating the Desire-for-control and Rational Choice in a Corporate Crime Context', *Justice Quarterly*, 22(2): 252–280.

Piquero, N.L., Schoepfer, A. and Langton, L. (2008) 'Completely Out of Control or the Desire to be in Control? How Low Self-Control and the Desire for Control Relate to Corporate Offending', *Crime and Delinquency*, 56(4): 627–647.

Piquero, N.L., Tibbetts, S. and Blankenship, M. (2005) 'Examining the Role of Differential Association and Techniques of Neutralization in Explaining Corporate Crime', *Deviant Behavior*, 26: 159–188.

Pontell, H. and Geis, G. (2007) 'Preface', in H. Pontell and G. Geis (eds.) *International Handbook of White-Collar and Corporate Crime*. New York: Springer.

President's Commission on Organized Crime (1984) *The Cash Connection: Organized Crime, Financial Institutions, and Money Laundering*. Insterim Report to the President and the Attorney General, October 1984. Washington, DC.

Punch, M. (1996) *Dirty Business: Exploring Corporate Misconduct: Analysis and Cases*. London: Sage.

Punch, M. (2008) 'The Organization Did It: Individuals, Corporations and Crime', in J. Minkes and L. Minkes (eds.) *Corporate and White-Collar Crime*. London: Sage, pp. 102–121.

Punch, M. (2011) 'The Organizational Component in Corporate Crime', in J. Gobert and A. Pascal (eds.) *European Developments in Corporate Criminal Liability.* Oxon: Routledge, pp. 101–113.

Ramachandran, V., Collin, M. and Juden, M. (2018) 'De-risking: An Unintended Negative Consequence of AML/CFT Regulation', in King, C., Walker, C and Gurulé, J. (eds.) *The Palgrave Handbook of Criminal and Terrorism Financing Law.* London: Palgrave Macmillan, pp. 237–272.

Rees, V. (2013) *Transforming Regulation and Governance in the Public Interest.* Prepared for Council of the Nova Scotia Barristers' Society, October 15, 2013. Available at: https://nsbs.org/sites/default/files/cms/news/2013-10-30trans-formingregulation.pdf [Accessed 31 July 2019].

Savona, E., Riccardi, M. and Berlusconi, G. (eds.) (2016) *Organised Crime in European Businesses.* Abingdon, UK: Routledge.

Schein, E. (1992) *Organizational Culture and Leadership.* San Francisco: Jossey-Bass.

Schneider, S. (2005) 'Testing the Limits of Solicitor-Client Privilege: Lawyers, Money Laundering and Suspicious Transaction Reporting', *Journal of Money Laundering Control,* 9(1): 27–47.

Schrager, L. and Short, J. (1978) 'Towards a Sociology of Organisational Crime', *Social Problems,* 25(4): 407–419.

Scott, C. (2001) 'Analysing Regulatory Space: Fragmented Resources and Institutional Design', *Public Law* (Summer): 329–353.

SDT (2019) *About Us.* Available at: www.solicitorstribunal.org.uk/about-us [Accessed 31 July 2019].

Shapiro, S. (1990) 'Collaring the Crime Not the Criminal: Liberating the Concept of White-Collar Crime', *American Sociological Review,* 55(1): 346–369.

Shepherd, K. (2009) 'Guardians at the Gate: The Gatekeeper Initiative and the Risk-Based Approach for Transactional Lawyers', *Real Property, Trust & Estate Law Journal,* 43: 607–670.

Shover, N. and Hochstetler, A. (2006) *Choosing White-Collar Crime.* New York: Cambridge University Press.

Shover, N., Hochstetler, A. and Alalehto, T. (2013) 'Choosing White-Collar Crime', in F. Cullen and P. Wilcox (eds.) *The Oxford Handbook of Criminological Theory.* Oxford: Oxford University Press, pp. 475–493.

Sikka, P. (2008) 'Enterprise Culture and Accountancy Firms: New Masters of the Universe', *Accounting, Auditing and Accountability Journal,* 21(2): 268–295.

Simon, H. (1957) *Administrative Behaviour.* New York: Palgrave MacMillan.

Simon, H. (1996) *An Empirically Based Microeconomics.* Cambridge: Cambridge University Press.

Simpson, S. (1986) 'The Decomposition of Antitrust: Testing a Multi-Level, Longitudinal Model of Profit-Squeeze', *American Sociological Review,* 51: 859–875.

Simpson, S. and Piquero, N.L. (2002) 'Low Self-Control, Organizational Theory and Corporate Crime', *Law and Society Review,* 36(3): 509–548.

Simpson, S., Piquero, N.L and Paternoster, R. (2002) 'Rationality and Corporate Offending Decisions', in A. Piquero and S. Tibbetts (eds.) *Rational Choice and Criminal Behavior: Recent Research and Future Challenges.* New York: Routledge.

Simpson, S. and Rorie, M. (2011) 'Motivating Compliance: Economic and Material Motives for Compliance', in C. Parker and V. Lehmann Nielsen (eds.) *Explaining Compliance: Business Response to Regulation*: Cheltenham, UK: Edward Elgar Publishers, pp. 59–77.

Simpson, S., Rorie, M., Alper, M. and Schell-Busey, N. (2014) *Corporate Crime Deterrence: A Systematic Review*. Campbell Systematic Review. Oslo: The Campbell Collaboration.

Sinha, G. (2020) 'Risk-Based Approach: Is It the Answer to Effective Anti-Money Laundering Compliance?' in K. Benson, C. King and C. Walker (eds.) *Assets, Crimes and the State: Innovations in 21st Century Legal Responses*. Abingdon: Routledge.

Slapper, G. and Tombs, S. (1999) *Corporate Crime*. Harlow: Longman.

Soudijn, M. (2012) 'Removing Excuses in Money Laundering', *Trends in Organized Crime*, 15(2–3): 146–163.

Soudijn, M. (2014) 'Using Strangers for Money: A Discussion on Money-Launderers in Organized Crime', *Trends in Organized Crime*, 17(3): 199–217.

Spencer, J. (2007) 'The Illicit Movement of People Across Borders: The UK as a Destination Country and the Disorganisation of Criminal Activity', in P. van Duyne, A. Maljevic, M. van Dijck, K. von Lampe and J. Harvey (eds.) *Crime Business and Crime Money in Europe: The Dirty Money of Illegal Enterprise*. Nijmegen: Wolf Legal Publishers, pp. 115–134.

SRA (2014) *Cleaning Up: Law Firms and the Risk of Money Laundering*, November. Birmingham, UK: Solicitors Regulation Authority.

SRA (2016) *Research and Analysis: The Changing Legal Services Market*. Birmingham, UK: Solicitors Regulation Authority.

SRA (2017) *SRA Handbook (Version 19)*. Available at: www.sra.org.uk/handbook [Accessed 6 September 2019].

SRA (2018a) *Preventing Money Laundering and Financing of Terrorism: A Thematic Review*, March. Birmingham: Solicitors Regulation Authority.

SRA (2018b) *SRA Risk Assessment on Anti-Money Laundering and Terrorist Financing*, March. Available at: www.sra.org.uk/sra/how-we-work/reports/aml-risk-assessment.page# [Accessed 29 July 2019].

SRA (2019a) *A Thematic Review of Trust and Company Service Providers*, May. Birmingham: Solicitors Regulation Authority.

SRA (2019b) *What We Do*. Available at: www.sra.org.uk/sra/how-we-work/what-we-do.page [Accessed 31 July 2019].

SRA (2019c) *SRA Confirms November Launch for New Regulatory Model*, Press Release 20 March. Available at: www.sra.org.uk/sra/news/press/standards-regulations-start-date-2019.page [Accessed 31 July 2019].

SRA (2019d) *SRA Standards and Regulations*, Updated 20 March. Available at: www.sra.org.uk/globalassets/documents/sra/standards-regulations.pdf?version=4a1aba [Accessed 6 September 2019].

SRA (2019e) *Changing How you Handle Client Money?* News Release, 28 February. Available at: www.sra.org.uk/sra/news/sra-update-71-tpma/ [Accessed 8 September 2019].

Stadler, W. and Benson, M. (2012) 'Revisiting the Guilty Mind: The Neutralization of White-Collar Crime', *Criminal Justice Review*, 37(4): 494–511.

Suchman, L. (1987) *Plans and Situated Actions: The Problem of Human-Machine Communication*. New York: Cambridge University Press.

Suchman, L. (2007) *Human-Machine Reconfigurations: Plans and Situated Actions* (2nd ed.). New York: Cambridge University Press.

Sutherland, E. (1940) 'White-Collar Criminality', *American Sociological Review*, 5(1): 1–12.

Sutherland, E. (1945) 'Is "White-Collar Crime" Crime?' *American Sociological Review*, 10(2): 132–139.

Sutherland, E. (1947) *Principles of Criminology* (4th ed.). Chicago: University of Chicago Press.

Sutherland, E. (1949) *White Collar Crime*. New York: Dryden.

Sykes, G. and Matza, D. (1957) 'Techniques of Neutralization: A Theory of Delinquency', *American Sociological Review*, 22: 664–670.

Terry, L. (2010) 'An Introduction to the Financial Action Task Force and Its 2008 Lawyer Guidance', *Journal of the Professional Lawyer*, 3–68.

Thanki, B., Carpenter, C., Cutress, J., Goodall, P., King, H., Loveridge, R., Oppenheimer, T., Yeo, N. and Phelps, R. (2018) *The Law of Privilege*. Oxford: Oxford University Press.

Tilahun, N. (2020) 'Legal Professionals as Dirty Money Gatekeepers: The Institutional Problem', in K. Benson, C. King and C. Walker (eds.) *Assets, Crimes and the State: Innovations in 21st Century Legal Responses*. Abingdon: Routledge.

Tomlinson, E. and Pozzuto, A. (2016) 'Criminal Decision Making in Organizational Contexts', in S. Van Slyke, M. Benson and F. Cullen (eds.) *The Oxford Handbook of White-Collar Crime*. Oxford: Oxford University Press, pp. 367–381.

Transparency International (2016) *London Property: A Top Destination for Money Launderers*. London: Transparency International/Thomson Reuters. Available at: www.transparency.org.uk/publications/london-property-tr-ti-uk/#.Ws8YMi_Myi4 [Accessed 12 April 2018].

Transparency International (2017) *Hiding in Plain Sight: How UK Companies Are Used to Launder Corrupt Wealth*. London: Transparency International.

Tsingou, E. (2010) 'Global Financial Governance and the Developing Anti-Money Laundering Regime: What Lessons for International Political Economy', *International Politics*, 47(6): 617–637.

Tusikov, N. (2008) 'Mortgage Fraud and Organized Crime in Canada: Strategic Intelligence Brief', *Trends in Organized Crime*, 11(3): 301–308.

Tyler, T. (2006) *Why People Obey the Law*. Princeton: Princeton University Press.

Tyler, T. (2009) 'Self-Regulatory Approaches to White-Collar Crime: The Importance of Legitimacy and Procedural Justice', in S. Simpson and D. Weisburd (eds.) *The Criminology of White-Collar Crime*. New York: Springer, pp. 195–216.

Unger, B. and Ferwerda, J. (2011) *Money Laundering in the Real Estate Sector: Suspicions Properties*. Cheltenham, UK: Edward Elgar.

UNODC (2019) *Introduction to Money-Laundering*. Available at: www.unodc.org/unodc/en/money-laundering/introduction.html [Accessed 29 July 2019].

US Department of the Treasury (2019) *Money Laundering*. Available at: https://home.treasury.gov/policy-issues/terrorism-and-illicit-finance/money-laundering [Accessed 29 July 2019].

Van de Bunt, H. (2010) 'Walls of Secrecy and Silence: The Madoff Case and Cartels in the Construction Industry', *Criminology and Public Policy*, 9(3): 435–453.

Van Duyne, P. (2003) 'Money Laundering Policy: Fears and Facts', in P. van Duyne, K. von Lampe and J. Newell (eds.) *Criminal Finances and Organizing Crime in Europe*. Nijmegen, Netherlands: Wolf Legal Publishers, pp. 72–109.

Van Duyne, P. (2004) 'The Creation of a Threat Image: Media, Policy Making and Organised Crime', in P. van Duyne, M. Jager, K. von Lampe and J. Newell (eds.) *Threats and Phantoms of Organised Crime, Corruption and Terrorism*. Nijmegen: Wolf Legal Publishers, pp. 21–50.

Van Duyne, P. and Di Miranda, H. (1999) 'The Emperor's Clothes of Disclosure: Hot Money and Suspect Disclosures', *Crime, Law and Social Change*, 31(3): 245–271.

Van Duyne, P., Harvey, J. and Gelemerova, L. (2016) 'The Monty Python Flying Circus of Money Laundering and the Question of Proportionality', in G. Antonopoulos (ed.) *Illegal Entrepreneurship, Organized Crime and Social Control: Essays in Honor of Professor Dick Hobbs*. Cham, Switzerland: Springer International, pp. 161–188.

Van Duyne, P., Harvey, J. and Gelemerova, L. (2018) *The Critical Handbook of Money Laundering: Policy, Analysis and Myths*. London: Palgrave Macmillan.

Van Duyne, P. and Levi, M. (2005) *Drugs and Money: Managing the Drug Trade and Crime-Money in Europe*. Abingdon, UK: Routledge.

Van Gelder, J. (2013) 'Beyond Rational Choice: The Hot/Cool Perspective of Criminal Decision-Making', *Psychology, Crime and Law*, 19(9): 745–763.

Van Gelder, J. (2017) 'Dual-Process Models of Criminal Decision Making', in W. Bernasco, J-L. van Gelder and H. Elffers (eds.) *The Oxford Handbook of Offender Decision Making*. Oxford: Oxford University Press, pp. 166–180.

Van Gestel, B. (2010) 'Mortgage Fraud and Facilitating Circumstances', in K. Bullock, R. Clarke, V. Ronald and N. Tilley (eds.) *Situational Prevention of Organised Crime*. Cullompton, UK: Willan, pp. 111–129.

Varese, F. (2010) 'General Introduction: What Is Organized Crime?' in F. Varese (ed.) *Organized Crime: Critical Concepts in Criminology*. London: Routledge, pp. 1–33.

Vaughan, D. (1983) *Controlling Unlawful Organizational Behavior*. Chicago: University of Chicago Press.

Vaughan, D. (1992) 'The Macro-Micro Connection in "White-Collar Crime" Theory', in K. Schlegel and D. Weisburd (eds.) *White-Collar Crime Reconsidered*. Boston: Northeastern University Press, pp. 124–147.

Vaughan, D. (1996) *The Challenger Launch Decision: Risky Technology, Culture, and Deviance at NASA*. Chicago: University of Chicago Press.

Vaughan, D. (1998) 'Rational Choice, Situated Action, and the Social Control of Organizations', *Law and Society Review*, 32(1): 23–61.

Vaughan, D. (1999) 'The Dark Side of Organizations: Mistake, Misconduct and Disaster', *Annual Review of Sociology*, 25: 271–305.

Vaughan, D. (2002) 'Criminology and the Sociology of Organisations', *Crime, Law and Social Change*, 37(2): 117–136.

Vaughan, D. (2007) 'Beyond Macro- and Micro-Levels of Analysis, Organizations, and the Cultural Fix', in H. Pontell and G. Geis (eds.) *International Handbook of White-Collar and Corporate Crime*. New York: Springer, pp. 3–24.

Verhage, A. (2009) 'Between the Hammer and the Anvil? The Anti-Money Laundering-Complex and Its Interactions with the Compliance Industry', *Crime, Law and Social Change*, 52: 9–32.

Verhage, A. (2011) *The Anti Money Laundering Complex and the Compliance Industry*. Abingdon: Routledge.

Von Lampe, K. (2015) *Organized Crime: Analyzing Illegal Activities, Criminal Structures, and Extra-Legal Governance*. New York: Sage.

WEF (2012) *Organized Crime Enablers: A Report for the Global Agenda on Organized Crime*. Geneva: World Economic Forum.

Weisburd, D., Wheeler, S., Waring, E. and Bode, N. (1991) *Crimes of the Middle Classes: White Collar Offenders in the Federal Courts*. New Haven/London: Yale University Press.

Winter, S. and May, P. (2001) 'Motivation for Compliance with Environmental Regulations', *Journal of Policy Analysis and Management*, 20: 675–698.

Wittig, T. (2011) *Understanding Terrorist Finance*. London: Palgrave Macmillan.

Wright Mills, C. (1940) 'Situated Actions and Vocabularies of Motive', *American Sociological Review*, 5: 904–913.

Xanthaki, H. (2001) 'Lawyers' Duties Under the Draft EU Money Laundering Directive: Is Confidentiality a Thing of the Past?' *Journal of Money Laundering Control*, 5(2): 103–114.

Zaitch, D. (2003) 'Recent Trends in Cocaine Trafficking in the Netherlands and Spain', in D. Siegel, H. van de Bunt and D. Zaitch (eds.) *Global Organized Crime: Trends and Developments*. Dordrecht: Kluwer Academic Publishers, pp. 7–18.

Zona, F., Minoja, M. and Coda, V. (2012) 'Antecedents of Corporate Scandals: CEOs' Personal Traits, Stakeholders' Cohesion, Managerial Fraud and Imbalanced Corporate Strategy', *Journal of Business Ethics*, 17: 1595–1603.

Index

Note: Page numbers in *italics* refer to figures. Page numbers in **bold** refer to tables. Page numbers followed by 'n' refer to notes.

Printed in the United States
by Baker & Taylor Publisher Services